Models of Psychopathology

D1474261

Lisa M. Hooper • Luciano L'Abate
Laura G. Sweeney • Giovanna Gianesini
Peter J. Jankowski

Models of Psychopathology

Generational Processes and Relational Roles

 Springer

Lisa M. Hooper
Department of Educational Studies
  in Psychology
Research Methodology, and Counseling
The University of Alabama
Tuscaloosa, AL, USA

Laura G. Sweeney
Nova Southeastern University
Ft. Lauderdale, Florida, USA

Peter J. Jankowski
Department of Psychology
Bethel University
St Paul, MN, USA

Luciano L'Abate
Department of Psychology
Georgia State University
Atlanta, GA, USA

Giovanna Gianesini
Department of Applied Psychology
University of Padova
Padova, Italy

ISBN 978-1-4614-8080-8   ISBN 978-1-4614-8081-5 (eBook)
DOI 10.1007/978-1-4614-8081-5
Springer New York Heidelberg Dordrecht London

Library of Congress Control Number: 2013948917

Printed on acid-free paper

Springer is part of Springer Science+Business Media (www.springer.com)

Foreword

There is little doubt that families matter for their members' physical as well as mental health. They do so because families are a primary source of care—an essential element in intergenerational and intragenerational relationships. The way parents care for their children and make sure that their needs are being met is of crucial importance for their security, health, and development. Similarly, care provided to the older generation is of key significance when physical abilities decrease and self-reliant modes of life become difficult if not impossible. Last but not least, partners and siblings typically expect and rely on mutual support and solidarity. No man (nor woman) is an island as John Donne asserted almost 400 years ago. Yet, families matter because patterns of close relationships may go wrong. They may go wrong despite close ties keeping their members trapped in unhealthy relationships. And there are many ways to go wrong. This is the topic of the present book.

The authors' main interest is to describe and explain how roles and relational processes are linked to psychopathology. Viewing intimate relationships and the family in particular as a likely pathogenic context has a considerable tradition in clinical psychology, developmental psychopathology, and foremost in approaches based on family systems theory. Many studies have shown how unhealthy patterns of relationships may undermine the individual potential for development and increase the risk for physical and mental illness. Given such evidence, a major question relates to the adequate theoretical framing and suitable models that may guide a deeper understanding of relevant processes.

Lisa M. Hooper, Luciano L'Abate, Laura G. Sweeney, Giovanni Gianesini, and Peter J. Jankowski refer to the deadly drama triangle (DT) as a key concept foregrounding four manipulative roles which may be played out reactively, repetitively, and simultaneously by individuals involved in intimate relationships: the role of victim, persecutor, and rescuer. As emphasized by the authors and spelled out in more detail throughout the chapters, the conceptual frame provided by deadly DT allows analyzing dysfunctional roles and unhealthy patterns in close relationships within and beyond families. At the same time, despite its advantages deadly DT lacks a more differentiated theoretical framing. The authors offer such a framing.

As argued in the first and second chapter, relational competence theory (RCT) provides the concepts and tools for expanding the deadly DT model and developing it into a theory. Relevant links between single components of RCT and the deadly DT model are spelled out in Chap. 2.

This joint conceptual–theoretical framing is used to provide a better understanding of four selected often maladaptive phenomena in relational contexts which have been pointed out as conducive to psychopathology: *Parentification* involves a role reversal in parent–child relations which puts the child in the demanding role of a responsible adult and increases the risk for children to serve not only as rescuer of the weak parent in need but also as his or her victim and/or even persecutor. *Parental alienation* is often seen in the context of divorce and typically involves antagonism between both parents which renders one or both as victim of the other's efforts as persecutor. Most notably, the parent who tries to get the child involved in an alliance against the other parent sees himself or herself as "rescuer" of the child. In the case of *bullying*, the persecutor has often experienced being a victim in previous relationships, pointing to the salience of previous experiences in the socialization process. Furthermore, roles as bully (persecutor) and victim may even switch in the context of parallel relationships. Finally, the Stockholm syndrome highlights role change at its extreme when victims take sides with their persecutor and seek to assume the role of his or her rescuer or act as persecutor of those who go against their own persecutor.

The book offers an integrated perspective of these phenomena—a perspective which has figured prominently in the work of Luciano L'Abate, an outstanding scholar in the international field of family psychology. Relevant research evidence as well as case examples is used to illustrate and discuss how the shared theoretical concepts and models may be used to better understand the phenomena considered. For those who are not familiar with the deadly DT and RCT, this perspective is likely to broaden their theoretical view and conceptual understanding of maladaptive patterns in close relationships. For experts of the deadly DT and RCT, the rich description of parentification, parental alienation, bullying, and Stockholm syndrome may provide new insight into these highly relevant dysfunctional patterns. No matter whether the reader's interest focuses on clinical work or research in the field of close relationships, the book will be a stimulating source.

München   Sabine Walper

Preface

Generational Processes and Relational Roles, comprises eight chapters, four of which focus on commonly discussed or clinically evidenced twenty-first-century phenomena that *may* be related to psychopathology: (a) parentification, (b) parental alienating behavior, (c) bullying, and (d) Stockholm syndrome. More specifically, as illustrated in these four models (see Chaps. 3–6), this book focuses on the impact of roles and relational processes that may engender pathology or problematic ways of functioning both intrapersonally and interpersonally. Multiple foci and etiologies may be tentatively considered in the context of psychopathology. However, our specific focus is on relational aspects of human behavior and interaction patterns and processes that may engender a range of outcomes from "normal" to "abnormal." Toward this end, the four select models in this book can be placed within a borderline area between what is known as normal or functional and what is considered pathological and disordered (e.g., Axis II personality disorders). This area includes what the *Diagnostic and Statistical Manual of Mental Disorders* (4th ed., text rev.; *DSM-IV-TR*; American Psychiatric Association [APA], 2000) classifies as Cluster B and Cluster C externalizing and internalizing personality disorders, respectively, as well as most apparently normal relationships. However, many apparently normal or functional relationships on closer observation may contain the seeds or underpinnings for possible psychopathology or impaired relational functioning (Cusinato & L'Abate, 2012; Hooper, 2011; Hooper, DeCoster, White, & Voltz, 2011; L'Abate, Cusinato, Maino, Colesso, & Scilletta, 2010).

Using relational competence theory (RCT) and the deadly drama triangle (DT; Karpman, 1968, 2009; L'Abate, 2009a) as theoretical and conceptual foundations, Chap. 1 lays the groundwork for this book. In addition, Chap. 1 describes the similarities and differences among these four selected models—that is, parentification, parental alienating behavior, bullying, and Stockholm syndrome—as evidenced by the clinical, theoretical, and empirical literature. Chapter 2 provides overviews of RCT and the deadly DT and conceptually links the deadly DT to other relevant theoretical models associated with RCT. Chapter 3 introduces the construct of parentification and explores how this construct can lead to a range of roles, relational, and generational outcomes, including psychopathology. Chapter 4 examines an often controversial topic, parental alienation behavior (or commonly described as parental alienation *syndrome*), and puts forward preliminary evidence for the relational and generational aspects of parental alienating behavior and its possible outcomes. Chapter 5 discusses the relational and generational aspects and potential pathological outcomes of bullying, and Chap. 6 describes how Stockholm syndrome and its aftereffects can be better understood and informed by RCT. For each of these four models, Chaps. 3–6 describe different degrees and types of psychopathology and discuss the extent to which these processes and phenomena (e.g., Stockholm syndrome) are or can be normative. Chapters 7 and 8 proffer information and conclusions on providing care for individuals and their family members with a history related to the four models presented in this book. In addition, final comments consider implications of these models for the empirical study and classification of psychopathology. Finally, Appendices A, B, C, D, E, and F include workbooks that are derived from the theoretical frameworks that undergird this book (i.e., the deadly DT and RCT) and published measures that assess for parentification (Hooper, 2009), parental alienating behavior (Hartson & Payne, 2006), bullying (see Rigby, 1997; Rigby & Slee, 1993, 1995a, 1995b), and Stockholm syndrome (Graham et al., 1995). These workbooks can be administered as written, interactive practice exercises in health promotion and mental health prevention, as well as adjuncts with brief psychotherapy.

Tuscaloosa, AL, USA   Lisa M. Hooper
Atlanta, GA, USA   Luciano L'Abate
Florida, USA   Laura G. Sweeney
Padova, Italy   Giovanna Gianesini
St Paul, MN, USA   Peter J. Jankowski

References

American Psychiatric Association. (2000). *Diagnostic and statistical manual of mental health disorders* (4th ed., text rev.). Washington, DC: Author.

Cusinato, M., & L'Abate, L. (2012). *Advances in relational competence theory: With special attention to alexithymia*. New York: Nova Science.

Graham, D. L. R., Rawlings, E. I., Ihms, K., Latimer, D., Foliano, J., Thompson, A., et al. (1995). A scale for identifying "Stockholm syndrome" reactions in young dating women: Factor structure, reliability, and validity. *Violence and Victims, 10*, 3–22.

Hartson, J., & Payne, B. (2006). *Creating effective parenting plans: A developmental approach for lawyers and divorce professionals*. Chicago, IL: American Bar Association.

Hooper, L. M. (2009). *Parentification inventory*. Available from L. M. Hooper, Department of Educational Studies in Psychology, Research Methodology, and Counseling, The University of Alabama, Tuscaloosa, AL 35487.

Hooper, L. M. (2012). Parentification. In R. J. R. Levesque (Ed.), *Encyclopedia of adolescence* (Vol. 4, pp. 2023–2031). New York: Springer.

Hooper, L. M., DeCoster, J., White, N., & Voltz, M. L. (2011). Characterizing the magnitude of the relation between self-reported childhood parentification and adult psychopathology: A meta-analysis. *Journal of Clinical Psychology, 67*, 1028–1043. doi: 10.1002/jclp.20807

Karpman, S. B. (1968). Fairy tales and script drama analysis. *Transactional Analysis Bulletin, 7,* 39–43.

Karpman, S. B. (2009). Sex games people play: Intimacy blocks, games, and scripts. *Transactional Analysis Journal, 39,* 103–116.

L'Abate, L. (2009a). The drama triangle: An attempt to resurrect a neglected pathogenic model in family therapy theory and practice. *The American Journal of Family Therapy, 37,* 1–11.

L'Abate, L., Cusinato, M., Maino, E., Colesso, W., & Scilletta, C. (2010). *Relational competence theory: Research and applications.* New York: Springer-Science.

Rigby, K. (1997). *The Peer Relations Assessment Questionnaires (PRAQ).* Point Lonsdale, VIC: The Professional Reading Guide.

Rigby, K., & Slee, P.T. (1993). Dimensions of interpersonal relation among Australian children and implications for psychological well-being. *Journal of Social Psychology, 133,* 33–42.

Rigby, K., & Slee, P.T. (1995a). Manual for the Peer Relations Questionnaire (PRQ). Underdale: University of South Australia.

Rigby, K., & Slee, P.T. (1995b). The Peer Relations Questionnaire. Underdale: University of South Australia.

Contents

Chapter 1
Introduction

Psychopathology in its simplest terms means mental illness: when people are distressed, in pain, and unable to function positively and productively at home or work or in both settings. Typically, psychopathology includes what are known as Axis I and Axis II mental disorders as delineated in the *Diagnostic and Statistical Manual of Mental Disorders* (4th ed., text rev.; *DSM–IV–TR*; American Psychiatric Association [APA], 2000). A mental disorder is defined in the *DSM-IV-TR* as a "clinically significant behavioral or psychological syndrome or pattern that occurs in an individual and that is associated with present distress (i.e., painful symptoms, impairment in one or more areas of functioning, and increased risk of suffering) and the syndrome or pattern must not be an expectable and culturally sanctioned response to a particular event" (p. xxxi). Although the etiology of these diverse disorders is complex and remains unclear for many, if not most, disorders described in the *DSM-IV-TR*, much of the discourse among researchers, scholars, and practitioners centers on how pathology, psychological distress, and mental health disorders are evidenced *within* a person. For example, the disorders in the *DSM-IV-TR* are typically considered as deriving from a range of problems and systems: biology, genes, personality, and vulnerabilities within the person. Just as establishing the etiology of mental health disorders can be complex and difficult, the same can be said for differentiating between "normal" and "abnormal" behaviors, signs, and symptoms.

Clarifying what constitutes psychopathology therefore includes establishing what is and is not normal. Toward this end, there has long been some debate on what constitutes normal and abnormal behaviors (Brown & Barlow, 2005). The *DSM-IV-TR* attempts to provide some description of how distinct signs, symptoms, and behaviors cluster to represent abnormality related to a specific clinical diagnosis, such as major depressive disorder. However, even with these carefully delineated categories defined in the *DSM-IV-TR*, diagnosing these disorders still lacks exactness. Describing the range of disorders presented in the *DSM-IV-TR* is beyond the scope of this book; comprehensive and extensive reviews of the *DSM-IV-TR* can be found elsewhere in the literature base (Brown & Barlow, 2005; Widiger & Samuel, 2005).

L.M. Hooper et al., *Models of Psychopathology: Generational Processes and Relational Roles*, DOI 10.1007/978-1-4614-8081-5_1,
© Springer Science+Business Media New York 2014

Although important, the etiology or origin of psychopathology, as outlined in the vast literature on psychopathology, is also not the focus of this book.

The focus of the current book, *Models of Psychopathology: Generational Processes and Relational Roles*, and thus this introductory chapter defines concepts that are fundamental to the four selected models and that constitute and perhaps explain how certain relational models may be pathogenic—that is, how they may produce equal or more severe levels of psychopathology. First, we clarify why we use the term *model* rather than terms such as *paradigm* or *theory*—often mistakenly used as synonymous terms (L'Abate, 2009b). Then, we indicate commonalities that exist among the models of psychopathology that we examine as being related to the basic deadly drama triangle (DT; Karpman, 1968, 2009; L'Abate, 2009a). We also describe the differences that may exist among the models. Finally, we compare and contrast the basic construct of *role*, which is essential to all four models and originates from the deadly DT.

What Is a Model?

A *model* is a visual or verbal summary of a larger structure that (a) derives from an overarching theory and (b) is defined by underlying dimensions that can be empirically validated. As a concrete example, a model of an airplane is a much smaller replica of the larger real plane according to a scale of 1 to a 1,000. In more abstract terms, a model attempts to reduce a complex notion to its simplest, most concrete format.

How is a model different from a paradigm and a theory? A *paradigm* is a particular set of values describing how individuals perceive reality, as evidenced by numerous existing paradigms, such as behaviorism, empiricism, existentialism, or reductionism. A *theory* is a conceptual framework that lends itself to empirical validation through its models. A theory, therefore, underlies a paradigm, with or without conceptual or empirical links between the two. For instance, information processing has been put forward as the reigning paradigm for this century (L'Abate & Sweeney, 2011). By now information processing is universally present in our lives and allows individuals to connect with others all over the world. Underneath this paradigm lie a variety of information processing theories. However, below whatever information theory one may choose, there is the elementary pragmatic model, which has various dimensions that have been evaluated empirically (De Giacomo, Mich, Santamaria, Sweeney, & De Giacomo, 2012; L'Abate, 2009c, 2012).

A conceptual paradigm relevant to the four models considered in this book is Kantor's interbehaviorism (Colesso, 2012; Fryling & Hayes, 2012) to the extent that behavior emerges from interactions and transactions between individuals and not in a vacuum devoid of human relationships, as many personality psychologists have proposed (Cusinato & L'Abate, 2012; L'Abate, Cusinato, Maino, Colesso, & Scilletta, 2010). With regard to theory, and as previously mentioned, the four models considered in this book—parentification, parental alienating behavior, bullying, and Stockholm syndrome—will be viewed as possible extensions of the deadly DT.

Each model has its own dimensions, or more specifically *roles*, that derive or overlap directly with the deadly DT model as well as similarities that are noteworthy. The extent to which each of the four selected models can be empirically and conceptually linked with the deadly DT is explored in Chaps. 3–6.

Commonalities Among the Four Models

In addition to considerable media attention given to the four models presented in this book, empirical studies and conceptual research regarding the four models share some noteworthy similarities that allow and encourage their consideration together under one cover. At least four fundamental commonalities are found among these models of psychopathology: (a) relational, (b) reactive, (c) dynamic, and (d) below or outside the level of awareness and trust. A fifth commonality among some of the models is generational. Although a generational aspect is relevant to some of the selected models included in this book, it has less applicability—if any—to our fourth model, Stockholm syndrome. The potential for short- and long-term psychological individual- and system-level distress derived from and related to these models appears to be clear. Consequently, these pathogenic processes will continue and propagate unless appropriate interventions ameliorate or reduce their (often but not always) pernicious effects.

Relational

Because most intergenerational and generational processes occur within intimate relationships—those that are close, committed, interdependent, and lasting—using the term *relational* is in some ways redundant and implicit in all human relationships. What is made relevant in the four models explored in this book is the search for a classification of intimate relationships rather than of personalities (Cusinato & L'Abate, 2012; L'Abate, 2009a).

Reactive

As explained in Chap. 2, many supposedly functional relationships, as well as most externalizing and internalizing relationships, are reactive in nature. Reactions occur immediately with little or no thought to control, delay, or postpone their expression (L'Abate, 2008). Consequently, reactions may consist of a sudden, unexpected attack, rebuttal, or criticism, either verbal or nonverbal. Often, someone responds to another person without regard to the context, to the short- and long-term consequences of what one says or does, or to any need to control or attempt to control what one says or does.

Dynamic

Dynamic processes are difficult to observe, given that their very nature is quick and changing and depends on an outsider seeing them. Relational dynamics depend on the fact that each individual in the transaction may engage in different roles, depending on how one observes what is going on. Parentification, parental alienating behavior, bullying, and Stockholm syndrome emerge from existing psychopathology, as shown by the deadly DT (Karpman, 1968, 2009; L'Abate, 2009a), which will be described and illustrated in detail in the remaining chapters of this book. They are dynamic, relational, and in some cases (e.g., parentification and parental alienating behavior) but not all cases (e.g., Stockholm syndrome) basic to the generational continuation and propagation of pathological processes from one generation to another. In addition, the importance of roles cannot be overstated, particularly in trying to understand these four phenomena, because all players involved in certain transactions fluctuate continuously and contemporaneously from one role to another, in one way or another.

Below or Outside the Level of Awareness and Trust

One major characteristic of most dysfunctional conditions is inadequate or absent awareness of one's dysfunctionality. Awareness, of course, may vary a great deal from one individual to another and even within the individual, depending on the specific issue of which one is or is not aware, such as hurt feelings (De Giacomo, L'Abate, Pennebaker, & Rumbaugh, 2010; L'Abate, 2011). Awareness may be completely buried in the unconscious and may be difficult to retrieve unless one employs deep hypnosis, psychotherapy, or other methods that allow it to emerge (Bargh, 2007; Hassin, Uleman, & Bargh, 2005). Or awareness may be semipresent and emerge under specific, salient conditions, such as traumas or special events. It may be available to consciousness but may not be expressed, verbally or nonverbally, by whatever limiting individual and contextual conditions may be present at the time, such as taboos about speaking of hurt feelings. Finally, awareness may be consciously available and cease being unconscious when expressed to a trusted individual.

In sum, awareness and trust—are very important to understanding functional and dysfunctional interactions, behaviors, and symptomatology. The processes, roles, and transactions related to these four models—parentification, parental alienating behavior, bullying, and Stockholm syndrome—occur below the level of awareness.

Generational

A comprehensive summary of the generational nature of psychopathology, including representative evidence, was put forward by L'Abate, who reviewed intergenerational bases of psychopathology in detail (see L'Abate 2005, 2011). Since then, research on the generational antecedents of psychopathology has proliferated to such a degree that only few selected and representative references are included here.

Straus and Yodanis (1996) argued that accumulated evidence suggests that corporal punishment is associated with the subsequent aggression of children. Results from Straus and Yodanis' study indicated that this aggression may manifest later in life as physical assaults on spouses. For example, using data from 4,401 couples who participated in the National Family Violence Survey, Straus and Yodanis (1996) reported on this link. Their theoretical model specified three processes: (a) social learning, (b) depression, and (c) truncated development of nonviolent conflict resolution skills. Logistic regression was used to estimate separate models for men and women. Findings were consistent with the theoretical model and allowed these researchers to conclude that because corporal punishment of adolescents occurs in over half of US families, eliminating this practice could reduce some psychological and social processes that increase the likelihood of future physical violence in domestic relationships and perhaps other types of violence, such as emotional, sexual, and verbal abuse.

Other studies have examined the implications of psychopathology, distress, and symptoms emerging across generations. Coleman, Ganong, and Cable (1997) examined perceptions of women's intergenerational family obligations after divorce and remarriage in 190 women and 93 men who responded to a four-paragraph vignette about two women—either a mother and her daughter or a mother and her daughter-in-law—with either the older or younger woman needing the other's help. Conditions in the vignette were systematically varied; in all four vignette variations, the younger woman divorces and remarries. After each vignette was read, participants answered forced-choice and open-ended questions about what they thought the characters in the vignette should do. Based on their responses, the participants believed that family members are obliged to help other family members in times of need, although these obligations are conditional. Participants reported a stronger obligation to help their adult children and a weaker obligation to help elderly mothers and mothers-in-law. In addition, the self-reported obligation toward biological family members was stronger than an obligation toward in-laws. Finally, perceived obligations toward step-grandchildren were considerably weaker than obligations toward biological grandchildren.

Aquilino (1999) explored patterns of agreement and disagreement on the quality of interpersonal relationships in a sample of parents and their young adult children. Data on parent–child closeness, contact, control, and conflict were taken from parent and child interviews in the Longitudinal National Survey of Families and Households. Parents gave more positive reports than did their adult children on six of eight relationship indicators for which parent and child answered identical questions. Parents were especially likely to report higher levels of closeness. Three patterns of dyadic agreement were identified: high agreement (54 %); parent more positive than child (25 %); and child more positive then parent (21 %). Despite these differences in perspective, regression models predicting intergenerational closeness and conflict were nearly invariant across the parent and child data.

Myers (1999) examined how an individual's earlier experiences of residential mobility in his or her family of origin are associated with the experiences of residential mobility in adulthood. Two family-of-origin models were tested. The *socialization model* argues that children learn from their parents' mobility behaviors and then replicate these behaviors in adulthood. The *status-inheritance model* argues that parent–adult child similarity in mobility behaviors results when parents and adult children share characteristics associated with mobility. Myers found that those who move more often as children and adolescents also move more often as adults and are more likely to move in response to several life course transitions.

In another study, Reisig and Fees (2007) investigated older adults' perceptions of well-being following participation in an intergenerational program. Specifically, these researchers examined the relationship between age, years of volunteer service, and sense of well-being among older adults ($n = 46$; 55–100 years of age). Reisig and Fees found that older adults perceived a heightened sense of well-being as a result of intergenerational interactions with youth. Older adults reported that successful aging includes staying active, not worrying about one's problems, feeling young, and keeping up with the children and community. Adults between the ages of 74 and 85 reported experiencing significantly greater satisfaction and enjoyment than their older counterparts reported, particularly in anticipation of working with youth and positive self-perception.

In a more recent study, Busby, Walker, and Holman (2011) explored the association between childhood trauma and perception of self and partner. Their primary interest was to evaluate whether childhood trauma is associated with selection effects of romantic partners, perceptual effects of partners, or reciprocal negativity with partners. Using a large sample of more than 5,400 couples who completed the Relationship Evaluation of the Individual, Family, Cultural, and Couple Contexts (RELATE; Busby, Holman, & Taniguchi, 2001), a 271-item questionnaire was designed to evaluate the relationship between romantically linked partners (i.e., dating, engaged, or married). In addition to assessing the couples' experience, the RELATE inventory measures the contexts in which the couple's system is or has been embedded, such as culture and family of origin. Scale scores of the RELATE inventory were evaluated in previous psychometric studies (see Busby, Crane, Larson, & Christensen, 1995; Busby et al., 2001). In the recent study, Busby and colleagues (2011) divided couples into three groups: (a) those in which neither partner had experienced childhood physical abuse, (b) couples where one of the individuals the woman or the man had experienced abuse, and (c) couples where both partners had experienced abuse. The results indicated that childhood trauma is more likely to be associated with perception effects than with selection effects. Individuals who had been traumatized rated both themselves and their partners as more neurotic and conflictual, even when controlling for overall levels of relationship satisfaction. However, partners of traumatized persons did not consider themselves more neurotic or conflictual than partners in relationships where neither partner was abused.

The representative evidence briefly reviewed here includes examples of both functional and dysfunctional, and generational and intergenerational, sources of normative as well as nonnormative origins. Although other commonalities (i.e., relational, reactive, and dynamic) among the four presented models of psychopathology have less empirical research on which to base our assertions, they are nonetheless important and foundational.

As previously mentioned, three of the four models addressed in this book have generational underpinnings, although Stockholm syndrome is an exception. Thus, there are some differences among the four models that must be considered.

Divergences Among Models

While Stockholm syndrome shares much conceptually with the other models presented in Chaps. 3–6, the model of Stockholm syndrome differs from the others in three ways. First, it may be that many relational processes upon closer inspection reveal pathological functioning; however, it might also be stated that many relational processes that appear pathological may upon closer observation be functional. Stockholm syndrome appears to reflect the latter in that the performance of so-called dysfunctional roles is deemed adaptive. In fact, survival appears to depend upon the victim's shifting roles from victim to rescuer and aligning with the perpetrator against outside would-be rescuers. Second, Stockholm syndrome in its historical connotation diverges from the definition of relational as between intimates in close, committed, and lasting relationships. Stockholm syndrome as an outcome of hostage–captor relating is often initiated by a stranger forcing a relationship upon victims for a limited period of time. While Stockholm syndrome does suggest the development of a sense of intimacy between victim and perpetrator, the persistence of such connection beyond the hostage condition generally does not occur. Stockholm syndrome has also been applied to other situations of traumatic entrapment, for example, child maltreatment and domestic violence, and in this broader meaning of relational Stockholm syndrome does fit the definition of relational as intimates in close, committed, and lasting relationship. Third, the notion of generational antecedents has limited application to the dynamics of Stockholm syndrome. There may be links to intergenerational violence for perpetrators of traumatic entrapment, but from the perspective of the victim it is difficult to see intergenerational ties to the response to entrapment, other than in a general developmental–contextual understanding of human functioning in which both victim and perpetrator enact roles in part based upon their individual developmental histories.

Types and Function of Various Roles in Psychopathology

All four models described in this book require a consideration of roles. A *role* is traditionally defined as a part or character performed by an actor in a drama—hence, a part taken or assumed by anyone. The *APA Dictionary of Psychology* defines *role taking* as the adoption of the role or viewpoint of another person (VandenBos, 2007). The same dictionary defines *role reversal* as a technique used for therapeutic and educational purposes, in which an individual exchanges roles with another individual in order to experience alternate cognitive styles (e.g., problem solving), feelings, and behavioral approaches. In psychodrama the protagonist exchanges roles with an auxiliary in acting out a significant interpersonal situation. *Role shift* happens in any two-person relationship and refers to one partner's adoption of the characteristic behavior of the other.

Two major sources of information about roles include Carter (1987), who examined sex roles and sex typing, as well as Hoopes and Harper (1987), who explored roles learned in families. Hoopes and Harper hypothesized many different roles experienced in families according to the birth order of siblings. Because their work was undergirded by two doctoral dissertations, it is important to evaluate the translatability of their original hypotheses based on additional empirical results and with more current research. Rabin (1987) described Carter's contribution well, with relevant focus on gender-role ascription in the conventional family (pp. 195–197) and gender roles in relationship to division of labor and gender identity (p. 197). For example, Rabin stated:

> Females have been uniformly socialized to take responsibility for the home, be supportive of her husband, and be nurturant to the children. These roles are "ascribed" in that they are gender-based cultural expectations for behavior. Why should gender-role ascription have developed such a powerful cultural factor? There is a certain functional advantage to this strategy. Assigning the expressive and communal domain to women and the instrumental and agentic functions to men ensures that each family will have a range of survival capacities. (p. 195)

> [However] sex role ascription oriented society capable of identifying individual differences in genetically based aptitudes for specific acquired skills... Complementarity no longer assures survival because the family unit is no longer the economic unit and each member of the family must be competent in multiple roles and capacities... The hierarchical power of the conventional family, divided into expressive and instrumental gender roles, was supposed to improve marital satisfaction because it would improve family functional efficiency... However, the hierarchical gender-role ascribed family system produced an unhealthy psychological outcome: wives living as economical parasites and husbands existing as emotional parasites. (p. 196)

Two role topics are particularly relevant for the four models examined in this book: role assumption and role ascription.

Role Assumption

In *role assumption*, individuals voluntarily or involuntarily—liking or disliking it— assume a role. For instance, actors assume, or take on, whatever roles they like to play and receive payment for playing them. Parents assume whatever role is required in the family; indeed, the family is the context for learning the roles of provider, homemaker, student, and worker (Hoopes & Harper, 1987). An important construct related to role assumption, as described by Hoopes and Harper, is the *alliance*: between parents, between one parent and one child, and among siblings. We return to this important construct in Chap. 2.

Role Ascription

Role ascription, in contrast, refers to assigning or ascribing a given role to someone, whether that person likes it or not. For example, in Zimbardo's (2007) famous prison experiment at Stanford University, students were randomly assigned roles of either inmate or guard. The experiment had unexpected consequences, as the students reached such abusive extremes while playing their parts that the experiment had to be discontinued. More recently, when Zimbardo was called by defense lawyers to testify for guards accused of committing atrocious acts against Iraq prisoners at Abu Dhabi, his testimony and evidence were later discounted. When found guilty, the guards involved were punished according to military rules of conduct.

Dimensions of Roles

At least four overlapping dimensions are relevant to the function of roles inside and outside the family: (a) role flexibility versus role rigidity, (b) fixed or permanent roles versus temporary roles, (c) explicit versus implicit roles, and (d) active versus passive roles. Each dimension deserves an explanation.

Role Flexibility Versus Role Rigidity

This dimension covers how malleable one is when playing a particular part. For instance, one parent may assume responsibility for performing certain house chores, but in cases of sickness, the other partner may take over responsibility for the same chores. However, one's role, such as provider for the family, may be so rigidly adhered to that no one else can assume that role in the family. Nonetheless, even the rigid and fixed role may require some flexibility in times of crisis or illness. If the father has assumed the role of provider but is laid off, the mother in the family may have to take over and try to find a job to support the economic function of the family.

Fixed or Permanent Roles Versus Temporary Roles

Some roles, especially in work settings, may be fixed, with little possibility of change. In family systems, some roles such as parentification can be fixed or temporary. The length and type of role has been conjectured to relate to a range of negative and positive outcomes, including maintaining pathological family structures (see Hooper, 2012a, 2012b).

Explicit Versus Implicit Roles

In the family, most roles are explicit. In business, most organizations and companies have and require job descriptions to ensure that no changes can occur without explicit acceptance by those who have been hired for a specific function. In certain situations, we accept that some people have to play certain parts without any explanation or expectations. For instance, if a patient is admitted to a hospital, he or she is implicitly expected to play the role of a patient and follow whatever rules or regulations govern a patient's stay.

Active Versus Passive Roles

The active/passive dimension is especially visible in sports, where players engage in active roles while fans view the action and cheer when their team wins. Within this context, certain players follow predetermined roles (such as quarterback, pitcher, or goalie), and for the sake of team organizations they generally cannot deviate from their assigned roles. Other examples can be found in family systems and other relational contexts described in Chaps. 3–6.

Conclusion

Psychopathology, distress, and mental disorders can emerge and grow from an apparently normative matrix of relationships along many degrees and dimensions of functionality and types of dysfunctionality (Kaslow, 1996). All four models discussed in this book—parentification, parental alienating behavior, bullying, and Stockholm syndrome—have relational and role dimensions. Functional relationships are also fundamental to an understanding of processes that seem neither normal nor abnormal. Whether roles are learned from the family of origin or from some other source or context, roles are the cornerstones of the models included in this book.

This book, *Models of Psychopathology: Generational Processes and Relational Roles*, constitutes a comprehensive conversation about the influence of relationships one has and of the roles one adopts with regard to psychopathology. Some constructs on which the models are based are supported by more empirical research than others, so our literature reviews amass and summarize the clinical, conceptual, and empirical research base. This book presents these four models through a lens of RCT and the deadly DT. This approach affords scholars, researchers, and practitioners an alternate or additional way of making meaning of and drawing preliminary clinical conclusions about psychopathology. Finally, because some of the models have more empirical support than others, the proposed models require further testing, validating, and possibly expanding going forward.

References

American Psychiatric Association. (2000). *Diagnostic and statistical manual of mental health disorders* (4th ed., text rev.). Washington, DC: Author.

Aquilino, W. S. (1999). Two views of one relationship: Comparing parents' and young adult children's reports of the quality of intergenerational relations. *Journal of Marriage and the Family, 61*, 858–870.

Bargh, J. A. (Ed.). (2007). *Social psychology and the unconscious: The automaticity of higher mental processes.* New York: Psychology Press.

Brown, T. A., & Barlow, D. H. (2005). Dimensional versus categorical classification of mental disorders in the fifth edition of the Diagnostic and statistical manual of mental health disorders and beyond: Comment on special section. *Journal of Abnormal Psychology, 114*, 551–556.

Busby, D. M., Crane, D. R., Larson, J., & Christensen, C. (1995). A revision of the dyadic adjustment scale for use with distressed and nondistressed couples: Construct hierarchy and multidimensional scales. *Journal of Marital and Family Therapy, 21*, 289–308.

Busby, D. M., Holman, T. B., & Taniguchi, N. (2001). RELATE: Relationship evaluation of the individual, family, cultural, and couple contexts. *Family Relations, 50*, 308–316.

Busby, D. M., Walker, E. C., & Holman, T. B. (2011). The association of childhood trauma with perceptions of self and the partner in adult romantic relationships. *Personal Relationships, 18*, 547–561.

Carter, D. B. (Ed.). (1987). *Current conceptions of sex roles and sex typing: Theory and research.* New York: Praeger.

Coleman, M., Ganong, L., & Cable, S. M. (1997). Beliefs about women's intergenerational family obligations to provide support before and after divorce and remarriage. *Journal of Marriage and the Family, 59*, 165–176.

Colesso, W. (2012). Produced and spontaneous emergent interactionism. In L. L'Abate (Ed.), *Paradigms in theory construction.* New York: Springer-Science.

Cusinato, M., & L'Abate, L. (2012). *Advances in relational competence theory: With special attention to alexithymia.* New York: Nova Science.

De Giacomo, P., L'Abate, L., Pennebaker, J. W., & Rumbaugh, D. (2010). Amplifications and applications of Pennebaker's analogic to digital model in health promotion, prevention, and psychotherapy. *Clinical Psychology and Psychotherapy, 17*, 355–362.

De Giacomo, P., Mich, L., Santamaria, C., Sweeney, L. G., & De Giacomo, A. (2012). Information processing. In L. L'Abate (Ed.), *Paradigms in theory construction* (pp. 341–363). New York: Springer-Science.

Fryling, M. J., & Hayes, L. J. (2012). Interbehaviorism. In L. L'Abate (Ed.), *Paradigms in theory construction* (pp. 187–205). New York: Springer-Science.

Hassin, R. R., Uleman, J. S., & Bargh, J. A. (Eds.). (2005). *The new unconscious.* New York: Oxford University Press.

Hooper, L. M. (2012a). Parentification. In R. J. R. Levesque (Ed.), *Encyclopedia of adolescence* (Vol. 4, pp. 2023–2031). New York: Springer.

Hooper, L. M. (2012b). Parentification. In K. Keith (Ed.), *Encyclopedia of cross cultural psychology.* New York: Springer.

Hoopes, M. H., & Harper, J. M. (1987). *Birth order roles and sibling patterns in individual and family therapy.* Rockwell, MD: Aspen.

Karpman, S. B. (1968). Fairy tales and script drama analysis. *Transactional Analysis Bulletin, 7*, 39–43.

Karpman, S. B. (2009). Sex games people play: Intimacy blocks, games, and scripts. *Transactional Analysis Journal, 39*, 103–116.

Kaslow, F. W. (1996). History, rationale, and philosophic overview of issues and assumptions. In F. W. Kaslow (Ed.), *Handbook of relational diagnosis and dysfunctional family patterns* (pp. 3–18). New York: Wiley.

L'Abate, L. (2005). *Personality in intimate relationships: Socialization and psychopathology.* New York: Springer-Science.

L'Abate, L. (2008). Applications of relational competence theory to prevention and psychotherapy. In K. Jordan (Ed.), *The quick theory reference guide: A resource for expert and novice mental health professionals* (pp. 475–492). New York: Nova Science.

L'Abate, L. (2009a). The drama triangle: An attempt to resurrect a neglected pathogenic model in family therapy theory and practice. *The American Journal of Family Therapy, 37,* 1–11.

L'Abate, L. (2009b). In search of a relational theory. *American Psychologist, 64,* 776–788.

L'Abate, L. (2009c). Paradigms, theories, and models: Two hierarchical frameworks. In L. L'Abate, P. De Giacomo, M. Capitelli, & S. Longo (Eds.), *Science, mind and creativity: The Bari symposium* (pp. 107–122). New York: Nova Science.

L'Abate, L. (2011). *Hurt feelings: Theory, research, and applications in intimate relationships.* New York: Cambridge University Press.

L'Abate, L. (Ed.). (2012). *Paradigms in theory construction.* New York: Springer-Science.

L'Abate, L., Cusinato, M., Maino, E., Colesso, W., & Scilletta, C. (2010). *Relational competence theory: Research and applications.* New York: Springer-Science.

L'Abate, L., & Sweeney, L. G. (2011). Distance writing as the preferred medium of help and healing in the 21st century. In L. L'Abate & G. S. Sweeney (Eds.), *Research on writing approaches in mental health* (pp. 131–134). Bingley: Emerald Group.

Myers, S. M. (1999). Residential mobility as a way of life: Evidence of intergenerational similarities. *Journal of Marriage and the Family, 61,* 871–880.

Rabin, J. S. (1987). Two-paycheck families: Psychological responses to social change. In B. D. Carter (Ed.), *Current conceptions of sex roles and sex typing: Theory and research* (pp. 193–210). New York: Praeger.

Reisig, C. N., & Fees, B. S. (2007). Older adults' perceptions of well-being after intergenerational experiences with youth. *Journal of Intergenerational Relationships, 4,* 6–22.

Straus, M. A., & Yodanis, C. L. (1996). Corporal punishment in adolescence and physical assaults on spouses in later life: What accounts for the link? *Journal of Marriage and the Family, 58,* 825–841.

VandenBos, G. R. (Ed.). (2007). *APA dictionary of psychology.* Washington, DC: American Psychological Association.

Widiger, T. A., & Samuel, D. B. (2005). Diagnostic categories or dimensions? A question for the *Diagnostic and statistical manual of mental health disorders* (5th ed.). *Journal of Abnormal Psychology, 4,* 494–504.

Zimbardo, P. G. (2007). *The Lucifer effect: Understanding how good people turn evil.* New York: Random House.

Chapter 2
The Deadly Drama Triangle and Relational Competence Theory

This chapter illustrates, conceptually and empirically, how the deadly drama triangle (DT) can be explained and understood through its link with relational competence theory (RCT). As discussed in Chap. 1, expanding from a model to a theory can facilitate an understanding of the four select models of psychopathology discussed in Chaps. 3–6: namely, parentification, parental alienating behavior, bullying, and Stockholm syndrome. Together, the deadly DT and RCT create a theoretical background that buttresses and informs these four models of psychopathology. This chapter focuses on 14 components of RCT and their association with the deadly DT (see Table 2.1).

All individuals have seeds of the deadly DT and thus can assume any of its three major roles: victim, rescuer, or persecutor (Karpman, 1968). The origins of the deadly DT can be found in intimate relationships—in close, committed, and interdependent relationships—and sometimes in relationships of questionable duration. When one person meets another—whether they are of the same or opposite gender—one may feel that the other person will fulfill and even distract oneself from past hurts and sorrows, including loneliness and past abusive relationships, parental or romantic (L'Abate, 2011a). Consequently, in meeting and mating with someone else, most if not all individuals assume the role of the rescuer for the other person in the relationship—hereafter termed an intimate for the purposes of this discussion. That is, falling in love with someone else contains the implicit role of rescuer: whether recognized or not and whether preferred or not. The word *intimate* may also describe a person with whom someone has a close relationship but not a romantic relationship (e.g., a mother can be described as an intimate of her daughter).

Nonetheless, irrespective of how powerful and relevant the deadly DT may be, some scholars contend that the deadly DT by itself is insufficient as an explanation. RCT may offer a theoretical framework in which a deadly DT can be embedded successfully (L'Abate, 2012a). The three roles of the deadly DT model[14] (see Table 2.1)—victim, rescuer, and persecutor—are fundamental to the four models of psychopathology discussed in this book (i.e., parentification, parental alienating behavior, bullying, and Stockholm syndrome). All four models represent various manifestations of the

L.M. Hooper et al., *Models of Psychopathology: Generational Processes and Relational Roles*, DOI 10.1007/978-1-4614-8081-5_2,
© Springer Science+Business Media New York 2014

Table 2.1 Summary of the theory of relational competence in intimate relationships

Requirements	Verifiability	Applicability	Redundancy	Fruitfulness		
		Width	**Depth**	**Settings**		
Meta-theoretical assumptions about relationships						
Models		Emotionality, rationality, activity, awareness, and context[1]	Levels of interpretation[2]	Settings[3]	Both abilities[6]	Triangle of living[7]
		Emotionality	Description	Home	Functionality	Modalities
		Rationality	*Presentation*	School/work	High/middle/low	Being/doing/having
		Activity	*Phenotype*	Transit	GAF (100 to 0)	Sexual deviations
		Awareness	Explanation	Transitory		Driven personalities
		Context	*Genotype*			
			Generational–developmental			
Theoretical assumptions about relationships						
Models		Ability to love[4]	Ability to control and regulate[5]			
Dimensions		Distance	Control			
		Approach/avoidance	Discharge/delay			
DSM-IV-TR		Axis II, Cluster C	Axis II, Cluster B			
Normative models of the theory						
Models		Self-identity differentiation[8]	Styles in intimate relationships[9]	Interactions[10]	Selfhood[11]	Priorities[12]
Dimensions		Likeness continuum	AA/RR/CC	Functionality	Importance	Survival/enjoyment
		Symbiosis/alienation	Abusive/apathetic	Divisive	No-self	Vertical: self/intimates
		Sameness/oppositeness	Reactive/repetitive	Subtractive/static	Selfless/selfish	Horizontal: settings
		Similarity/differentness	Conductive/creative	Additive/multiplicative	Self-full	
			Codependencies/addictions	Below 39 on GAF		
			Conflict high	69 to 40 on GAF		
			Conflict low	100 to 70 on GAF		
DSM-IV-TR		Axis I				
		Axis II, Cluster B				
		No diagnosis				
Clinical applications of the theory						
Models		Distance regulation[13]	Deadly drama triangle[14]	Intimacy[15]	Negotiation[16]	
Dimensions		Pursuer/distancer/regulator	Victim/persecutor/rescuer	Sharing joys, hurts, and fears of being hurt	Structure/process	

Note: GAF=Global Assessment of Functioning

deadly DT. One could also argue that these four models, if deriving from the deadly DT, represent a branching-out from that model, an insight that also widens the scope and expansion of RCT that surrounds the deadly DT model[14] (Cusinato & L'Abate, 2012; L'Abate, 1997, 2005, 2009a, 2009b, 2009c, 2009d; L'Abate & Cusinato, 2007; L'Abate, Cusinato, Maino, Colesso, & Scilletta, 2010).

The deadly DT model[14] has been explained in previous publications in extensive detail (see L'Abate et al., 2010). Moreover, its presence in fiction as well as in the realities of legal systems, national and international politics, various religions, and wars has been supported (L'Abate, 1986, 2009d). Each member of the triangle plays all three roles contemporaneously, without any awareness of how one switches instantaneously from one role to another, depending on how one responds to the other two roles played by intimates. For example, a parent who punishes a child may be seen as a persecutor of the child, who is the victim. However, the other parent may intervene to lessen the punishment, thereby becoming a rescuer, at which point the seemingly persecuting parent may now feel victimized by the other parent.

In addition to the commonalities among the four models of psychopathology, reviewed in Chap. 1, all four models are characterized by role reversals and role changes. For instance, in parentification (see Chap. 3) the child assumes the role of parent (reversal). In the process the child changes from a child to an adult role; and at any time during the parentification process, the child may serve in the role of victim, rescuer, or persecutor. In parental alienation behavior (see Chap. 4), the parent changes from the role of parenting and nurturing to a role of feeling victimized and assumes the role of persecutor of the other parent, while rescuing the children as perceived victims of the "bad" parent. Many individuals who are bullies (see Chap. 5) were victimized before assuming the role of persecutors. Finally, nowhere is role change more evident than in Stockholm syndrome (see Chap. 6), where the victim assumes the roles of rescuer and persecutor.

Even though it is extremely difficult to validate the deadly DT model[14] empirically unless the observer or evaluator is outside the context in which the triangle exists, its presence has been illustrated anecdotally by case examples (see L'Abate, 2011c). For example, the victim in the deadly DT can respond internally—that is, physiologically, through biological changes and somatization. Or the victim in the deadly DT can respond externally—developing symptoms, overusing medications, or developing addictions as rescuers for being and feeling victimized. Here is where the body (or the physical self) is used as a rescuer through destructive pleasures found in addictions. Of course, the deadly DT is present in intimate and close relationships where parents may be seen as persecutors by their children but may consider themselves as rescuers of their children (victims).

The reasons for difficulties in empirically evaluating the deadly DT model[14] lie in its overlapping, simultaneous roles played by those involved in the triangle. Furthermore, in addition to longstanding theories such as psychoanalysis, learning theory, or symbolic interactionism, no theory has sufficiently validated and accounted for the complexity of the deadly DT given that the transactions and roles develop out of a seemingly normal and functional background (L'Abate, 2012b). RCT is an ideal theory to form a context or foundation for fully understanding the deadly DT.

A Comprehensive Theory for the Deadly Drama Triangle: Relational Competency Theory

The process of explaining the deadly DT according to various models of RCT uses requirements of verifiability, applicability, redundancy, and fruitfulness. Complex and multidimensional concepts are explained by various models of RCT according to different meanings and definitions of a construct (see Table 2.1). Applicability is an important requirement of RCT because each RCT model spans normative as well as nonnormative extremes. Abnormal or deviant extremes yield dimensions instead of categories for disorders described in the *Diagnostic and Statistical Manual of Mental Disorders* (4th ed., text rev.; *DSM–IV–TR*; American Psychiatric Association [APA], 2000) classification. RCT, therefore, is isomorphic with psychiatric classification given its focus on dimensions rather than categories (APA, 2000).

Even though the deadly DT is listed as model[14] in RCT (Table 2.1), its theoretical antecedents go back to the 13 preceding models (i.e., models[1–13]; see Table 2.1). Together, these multiple descriptions and links among RCT models (i.e., models[1–16]; see Tables 2.1 and 2.2) provide a coherent and rich explanation for the deadly DT and the theoretical foundations for the four models of psychopathology considered in this volume: parentification, parental alienating behavior, bullying, and Stockholm syndrome.

Meta-theoretical Assumptions

As illustrated in Table 2.1, three models (i.e., models[1–3]) include and represent psychological knowledge that is determined by assumptions that go above and beyond RCT. These three models are the emotionality, rationality, activity, awareness,

Table 2.2 Relationships among four models (self-identity differentiation[8], style in intimate relationships[9], interactions[10], selfhood[11]) and psychiatric categories

Model[8]: self-identity differentiation				
Symbiosis	Sameness	Similarity/differentness	Oppositeness	Alienation
Model[9]: styles in intimate relationships				
Abusive	Reactive	Conductive	Reactive	Abusive
Apathetic	Repetitive	Creative	Repetitive	Apathetic
Model[10]: interactions				
Divisive/subtractive	Static/positive	Multiplicative/additive	Static/negative	Divisive/subtractive
Model[11]: selfhood				
No-self	Selfless	Self-full	Selfish	No-self
Psychiatric categories (DSM-IV-TR)				
Axis I and Axis II	Axis II	No diagnoses	Axis II	Axis I and Axis II
Cluster A	Cluster C		Cluster B	Cluster A

and context model[1] (ERAAwC model[1]); the levels of interpretation model[2] (LoI model[2]); and the settings model[3]. One way or another, these first three RCT models furnish the fundamental background and underpinning for the hierarchical structure of RCT. Therefore, their assumptions form the foundation for the complete pyramidal structure of RCT and inform the deadly DT model[14].

Emotionality, Rationality, Activity, Awareness, and Context Model[1] (ERAAwC Model[1]): Horizontal Information Processing

This horizontal (flat) model attempts to encapsulate previous knowledge about how individuals receive (input), process (throughput), and express (output) neutral, pleasurable, and painful events according to what was originally a five-component RCT model: emotionality, rationality, activity, awareness, and context. This original ERAAwC model[1], however, was found to be existentially and empirically inadequate (Cusinato & L'Abate, 2012). After 10 years of research with a 50-item questionnaire, this model was expanded to include eight different components (see Cusinato, 2012; Nisbett et al., 2012) based on Cusinato's (2012) conceptualization:

1. $E_{feelings}$ represents an assessment of experiencing feelings.
2. $E_{expressed}$ includes how feelings are expressed both verbally and nonverbally.
3. Rationality considers how individuals think (including level of intelligence) in the present and plan for the future.
4. Activity represents nonverbal, motoric, and symbolic expressions and outcomes of the first three components.
5. Awareness$_{meta}$ represents the extent to which individuals are aware of their own awareness.
6. Awareness$_{feedback}$ assesses how an individual's awareness serves as a change agent in a recursive loop.
7. Context$_{suffered}$ includes how the proximal or distal surroundings are subjectively perceived negatively or positively.
8. Context$_{fitting}$ represents how immediate human and physical surroundings are perceived as relevant to overall functioning in interaction with ever-changing circumstances.

This newly expanded model, the ERAAwC model[1], is basic to an understanding of the deadly DT when the components' functioning is inordinate and inadequate. For example, component 3, rationality, may be impaired, so stronger emphasis may be given to component 2, expressing feelings ($E_{express}$) immediately and impulsively in destructive actions, with a limited awareness of how this expression may affect the individual as well as those who are recipient of that expression. It is plausible that individuals involved in the deadly DT may be deficient in experiencing positive feelings and, as a result, in experiencing all the other components of the model — inconsistent with normal functioning as described by Cusinato (2012) in the case of alexithymia. Individuals involved in the deadly DT would be unreliable and faulty in their awareness of past hurts and of how to improve upon previous feelings, thoughts, and actions by reducing them to normative levels. One characteristic of psychopathology is that inadequate awareness of context leads to its denial. Furthermore, Sommers (2011), among others—including Cohen and Siegel (1991) and McNulty and Fincham (2012)—well summarized the powerful effects of contexts on behavior above and beyond personality influences or traits. Its denial is a major aspect of psychopathology (Bergman, Magnusson, & El-Khouri, 2003, Engle, Sedek, von Hecker, & McIntosh, 2005; Mesquita, Feldman-Barrett, & Smith, 2010; Rottenberg & Vaughan, 2008; Shoda, Cervone, & Downey, 2007).

Levels of Interpretation Model[2] (LoI Model[2])

As explained above, the first model, the ERAAwC model[1], is horizontally flat in structure. The LoI model[2], in contrast, is vertical, in that it is composed of two major layers or levels of description and explanation (see Table 2.1). *Description* means that the individual's behavior can be videotaped at a public facade, impression-management sublevel, as well as at a private sublevel and in one's place of residence in intimate and close relationships. *Explanation*, however, has to rely on inferred levels from the genotypical self-identity differentiation model[8] (Self-ID model[8]), the selfhood model[11], and the generational sublevel (see Chap. 1).

Consider one example of parental conflict related to power struggles and decision making in the family system. A mother—depressed all her life—favors her same-gendered child, allowing her daughter to have or do whatever she wants without limits, as a victim; that is, the daughter plays the role of victim, and the mother plays the role of rescuer. Meanwhile, the father may attempt unsuccessfully to set limits by becoming the persecutor of the family system, although he believes that he is a victim of his wife's preference for the daughter. This triangle—in part—creates a dependent personality in the daughter, who goes on to conceive her own daughter out of wedlock, raising her daughter as a single mother while being fully supported by her own mother. In the context of this deadly DT, the father eventually gives up trying to set limits with the daughter. The daughter has no need to seek employment or worry about the future, because the mother pays for all housing expenses and sets up a college fund for her granddaughter. From this deadly DT and personality outcome, the much beloved granddaughter, still in middle school, becomes a parentified child, learning to take care of her grandmother and eventually of her own mother, who is by this point completely unemployable.

Of significance, the deadly DT-involved individuals in this family system may behave perfectly well in public settings (e.g., work or school) but have become involved in the deadly DT in the privacy of their home. No one outside of their family system is aware of the possible discrepancies between the presentational and private levels of functioning unless some behaviors become public. As is the case with personality disorders described in the *DSM-IV-TR* (APA, 2000), many individuals involved in the deadly DT may be aware of this discrepancy, but to them it seems natural and therefore "normal" (i.e., ego syntonic), with no need for professional help.

Settings Model[3]

Instead of general and nonspecific terms such as environment or situation, RCT differentiates among diverse types of settings according to their functions, such as (a) long-term settings like (e.g., home, school, work); (b) temporary or transitory settings (e.g., barber, hair salon, grocery store, mall); and (c) transit settings (e.g., bus, car, road, street). In contrast to subjectively perceived contexts of the ERAAwC model[1], settings are objectively and statically present. They can be photographed and subdivided into smaller units. For example, a home can be subdivided into a kitchen for cooking, bedrooms for sleeping, a dining room for eating, a living room for entertaining or watching TV, and an office for working. Normatively speaking, arguments and discussions among intimates may occur in any subdivision of a house, but most rational arguments would likely occur in the living room or office. However, rationality is not a characteristic of individuals involved in the deadly DT. They can argue practically anywhere and without appointments, with great repetition, and without solution or resolution, as presented by the negotiation model[16] (see Table 2.1).

Theoretical Assumptions

This section examines four additional RCT models. Even though they are derived from the previous meta-theoretical assumptions, these RCT models theoretical assumptions are also foundational for and critical to subsequent models of RCT.

Ability to Love Model[4] (AtL Model[4])

Love, of course, is a multidimensional construct that can be explained by various models of RCT. The ability to love is defined by a dimension of space that underlies distance between intimates and non-intimates. Distance is evaluated by extremes in approach (e.g., in dependent personality disorders of Cluster C in the *DSM-IV-TR*; APA, 2000) and by extremes in avoidance (e.g., in avoidant personality disorders also found in Cluster C). Individuals approach who and what they like, and they avoid whom and what they do not like. This is one of the first established psychological principles—except that sometimes individuals must approach who and what they do not like, such as some authority figures or death. Normatively, one's ability to love is located in the middle of this dimension of space between oneself and others, according to the appropriate age and developmental stage in one's own life cycle.

Dix and Buck's (2012) model of approach and avoidance motivation may be informative across the lifespan. They contended that "…parent–child interactions in the first 2 to 3 years of life may play an initial formative role… that may stabilize children's early approach and avoidance tendencies" (p. 53). Additionally, these scholars reviewed research on the biological component of such motivation as well as its environmental component and the interactions of children's predispositions and experience with their parents. Dix and Buck concluded their review by empha- sizing that:

> "few aspects of human social relationships are more central than whether individuals seek or avoid social contact. The origins of this motivation are evident in infant social reactivity and responsiveness and appear central to adjustment and well-being throughout life" (p. 72).

Within the supposedly normative limits of the approach–avoid distance dimen- sion, at least five different but greatly overlapping processes form the basis for the beginning and eventual emergence of the deadly DT: alliances, coalitions, collu- sions, favoritisms, and parental overprotection. As important as these five processes are for family functioning, it is interesting to note that very few references to them have been evidenced in family-related discourses. Only a handful of treatises (described below) have referred to one or more of these terms. All five processes involve a stronger, more frequent, or more intense approach toward another, usually an intimate partner, child, relative, or friend. This stronger approach toward one selected individual in and of itself implies avoidance of another intimate—usually at the expense (emotional, practical, or financial) of that intimate.

Alliance

Even though the *APA Dictionary of Psychology* (VandenBos, 2007) has curiously limited this interactive process and definition to animal behavior, its definition is equally applicable and perhaps even more relevant to humans in intimate relation- ships. As a construct, *alliance* is defined as "an association between two or more individuals that allows them collectively to control resources that one individual could not control alone" (VandenBos, 2007, p. 17). As Chap. 1 mentioned, under- standing how alliances are formed and maintained in intimate relationships is important. This construct constitutes one building block from which the overall, deleterious process of the deadly DT (Karpman, 1968) emerges. The deadly DT process can be derived from seemingly normal but probably dysfunctional alli- ances. Alliances may be positive, as when both parents work in unison to nurture themselves and their children; or they may be negative, as when one parent shows an intense bond with one child at the expense of the other parent or of other siblings. Karpel and Strauss (1983) provided a comprehensive review of therapeutic alliances between families and professionals, as well as alliances and coalitions among fam- ily members.

Minuchin, a seminal family systems scholar, emphasized the importance of alliances in his theoretical and clinical writings. He included appealing, joining, supporting, and recruiting on the positive side of the process, with disaffiliation and opposition on the negative side of the process (Minuchin, 1974; Minuchin, Rosman, & Baker, 1978). The empirical literature has also reported how alliances have been operationalized and measured.

For example, Favez, Scaiola, Tissot, Darwiche, and Frascarolo (2011) presented the first steps in the validation of an observational tool for father–mother–infant interactions: the Family Alliance Assessment Scales (FAAS; Favez et al., 2011). The researchers acknowledged family-level variables to be unique contributors to the understanding of the socioaffective development of the child, yet producing reliable assessments of family-level interactions posed a methodological challenge. This validation study was carried out on three samples: one nonreferred sample of families taking part in a study on the transition to parenthood (normative sample; $n = 30$), one sample referred for medically assisted procreation (infertility sample; $n = 30$), and one sample referred for a psychiatric condition evidenced in one parent (clinical sample; $n = 15$). Results showed that the FAAS scores had good interrater reliability and good validity.

In a related study, Lavadera, Laghi, and Togliatti (2011) developed an observational method of family relationships and interactions—the Lausanne trilogue play (LTP)—and adapted it to typical observed clinical situations. The major objective of their study was to assess whether this procedure is useful in distinguishing among the levels of complexity and characteristics of divorced families who are being followed by a court expert in child custody cases. Sixty high-conflict divorced families participated in this research study. The families were observed through clinical LTP during a counseling session. The families displayed different relational characteristics, and the sample included a significant number of families with dysfunctional alliances. The association between the clinical diagnosis of family alliance and the structural reading scores highlighted that families with dysfunctional alliances obtained lower scores than families whose alliances were functional.

To identify alliance-related behavior patterns in more and less successful family therapy, Friedlander, Lambert, Valentín, and Cragun (2008) analyzed two cases with highly discrepant outcomes. Both families were seen by the same experienced clinician. Results showed that participants' perceptions of the alliance, session impact, and improvement at three points in time were congruent with the families' differential outcomes and with observer-related alliance behavior as measured by the System for Observing Family Therapy Alliances (Friedlander et al., 2006). In this measure, therapist behaviors contributed to the alliance. Client behaviors revealed the strength of the alliance on four dimensions: engagement in the therapeutic process, emotional connection with the therapist, safety within the therapeutic system, and shared sense of purpose within the family. In the case with poor outcome, observer ratings and self-reported alliance scores revealed a persistently split alliance between family members. This family dropped out midtreatment. Only in the case with good outcomes did clients follow the therapist's alliance-building interventions with positive alliance behaviors.

Coalition

The process of building coalitions is similar to the process of building alliances. VandenBos (2007) provided a clear definition of a *coalition* with relevance to the AtL model[4]:

> a temporary alliance formed by two or more individuals in order to gain a better outcome (e.g., power and influence) that can be achieved by each individual alone. Coalitions tend to be adversarial in that they seek outcomes that will benefit the coalition members at the expense of non-members. They also tend to be unstable because (a) they include individuals who would not naturally form an alliance but are obliged or encouraged to do so by circumstances and (b) members frequently abandon one alliance to form a more profitable one. (VandenBos, 2007, p. 184)

From this definition it follows that alliances and coalitions may be similar or even synonymous processes. Indeed, Broderick (1993) is one of the few theorists who directed a great deal of effort to discuss the terms jointly. One possible, still tentative way to differentiate between the two processes is to determine the degree to which the process is voluntary or involuntary, as well as conscious or unconscious. For instance, an alliance may be more formally offered and consciously agreed upon than a coalition. Nonetheless, more research is required to see whether it is possible or necessary to differentiate between alliances and coalitions. Unlike the alliance construct, limited empirical research has been conducted on the process and outcomes associated with coalitions.

Collusion

The *APA Dictionary of Psychology* (VandenBos, 2007) defines collusion in the context of the psychotherapy "…process in which a therapist consciously or unconsciously participates with a client or third party to *avoid* an issue that needs to be addressed" (p. 195, italics added). Collusions are also described in the context of the family and couple systems (Bagarozzi, 2013). That is, a "collusional marriage" is defined as "a marriage in which one partner instigates or engages in inordinate, deficient, irregular, or illegal conduct, and the other covertly endorses it or covers it up, while ostensibly being in the role of passive victim or martyr." This process is often seen in cases of incest (Kirschner & Kirschner, 1996) when a molested child reports the behavior of one caretaker to a second caretaker, who discounts such a report by blaming the child. This process is also evident in addictions, where one partner or parent allows addictive behavior to occur and to persist.

For example, Furniss (1983) proposed a treatment approach on the basis of clinical experience with 27 families where incest was present. He suggested that work on intergenerational boundaries in the family system is the initial step. Problems in the mother–daughter dyad, for example, often influence incest that may occur between father and daughter and must be addressed. The relationship between mother and father must be worked through after the parenting issues of protection and competition have been acknowledged. Once these steps have been taken, it is easier to work on the father–daughter dyad.

In another study, Joyce (2007) qualitatively examined the perspectives of clinical social workers regarding nonoffending mothers of sexually abused children. The study examined whether clinicians still considered a process of collusion as one explanation for the mothers' denials of the abused children's reports. The mothers' behavior indicates the absence of awareness and also the strong needs of these women to rely or depend on men, despite research refuting the effects of collusion. Findings revealed that, although social workers did not consider whether collusion was a factor, they still viewed the mothers negatively. Multiple contexts of agency practice influenced considerations of collusion. Because of the agency's (i.e., context of the study) role as a teaching site in graduate social work, field instructors transmitted the belief that incest typifies severe family difficulties and poses complex assessment and intervention problems.

Hylander, Krabbe, and Schwartz (2005) developed a clinical approach to work with families with one or two parents diagnosed with mental disorders. The interactions between parents and child can be disturbed in such contexts, and collusion often takes place. The child becomes either invaded or forgotten, depending on the needs of the parent, and the child is therefore forced to adapt to each parent's perspective to preserve the relationship with each parent. One important issue is the need to coordinate the efforts of different professional agents. The most important principles in this clinical approach are as follows: The parent's mental illness excludes parent change as a goal, and thus the objective is to compensate for the lack of parental support. The therapy, therefore, must focus on differentiation between child and parent. This approach must mirror, contain, and clarify healthier processes. Unfortunately, no supporting evidence is described in this study to allow this approach to be replicated within the same setting or in different clinical settings.

Finally, Bullock and Dishion (2002) explained that sibling collusion is a process by which siblings form coalitions that promote deviance and the undermining of parents. These researchers contended that collusive sibling processes can be identified and measured using macro ratings of videotaped family interactions. Bullock and Dishion tested their hypotheses with a multiethnic sample of urban youth (males and females, ages 12–14)—with a target child identified as either high risk ($n = 26$) or normative ($n = 26$)—and their families. Siblings in families with a high-risk target child showed reliably higher rates of collusion than those in families with a normative target child. Sibling collusion also accounted for variance in problem behavior after controlling for involvement with deviant peers. Findings suggested that deviant conduct forms a common ground among siblings, potentially amplifying risk of mutuality in problem behavior during early adolescence. These results also indicated that attention to sibling relationship processes is relevant to family interventions designed to mitigate the development of behavior problems.

Favoritism

In a recent book, Kluger (2011) showed how favoritism for one sibling over another sibling forms what could be framed as the normative bases of the deadly DT. This favoritism is also found in parent–child alliances that are typically denied by most parents, indicating that these processes are evidenced below the level of awareness. The favoring parent is usually counterbalanced by another parent who favors another sibling—the normative beginning of the deadly DT. In the deadly DT's various intensities and types, within so-called normal limits, lie the seeds for future psychopathology among siblings. According to Kluger, many nonfavored siblings suffer negative, lifelong results from such favoritism. Indeed, the favoritism process—as with processes involving alliances, coalitions, and collusions—is replete with the denial of its existence among parents who practice it completely and unwittingly. Therefore, favoritism could be conceived as being the basis, albeit normatively, of psychopathology. Its nonnormative, deviant, and extreme expressions need to be evaluated in much greater depth than Kluger did through interviews. This process supports the position that the deadly DT can only be observed from the outside but not from the inside.

Even though the evidence produced by Kluger (2011) might have been anecdotal, empirical evidence of the negative effects of favoritism is available. Toward this end, to distinguish between mothers who do and do not report favoring some of their adult children, Suitor, Sechrist, and Pillemer (2007) used data from the Within-Family Differences Study (Suitor & Pillemer, 2000), in which older mothers ($n = 553$) were interviewed about each of their children. Multivariate analyses revealed that mothers' values and mother–child value similarity predicted which mothers differentiated among their children regarding closeness and confiding, whereas mothers' and children's demographic characteristics predicted which mothers differentiated regarding preferred caregivers. Black American mothers were less likely than White American mothers to differentiate when seeking a confidant; however, race played no role in mothers' likelihood of differentiating regarding emotional closeness or help during illness. These findings indicated that differentiating among adult children is common. Further, family-level predictors of mothers' differentiating mirror the patterns shown in dyad-level analyses of mothers' favoritism.

In another study, Suitor and colleagues (2009) collected data from 708 adult children nested within 274 later-life families from the Within-Family Differences Study (Suitor & Pillemer, 2000) to explore the role of perceived maternal favoritism in the quality of sibling relations in midlife. Mixed-model analyses revealed that regardless of which sibling was favored, perceptions of current favoritism and recollections of favoritism in childhood reduce closeness among siblings. Recollections of maternal favoritism in childhood were found to be more important than perceptions of current favoritism in predicting tension among adult siblings, regardless of age. These findings are consistent with childhood studies (Sutton-Smith & Rosenberg, 1970; Walsh, 1993) showing that siblings have better relationships when they believe that they are treated equitably by their parents.

Coldwell, Pike, and Dunn (2008) studied whether difference scores or favoritism scores demonstrate stronger links with child outcomes. They evaluated this association by replicating previous links with children's adjustment as well as using children's reports of maternal differential treatment (MDT). Their study tested for a unique prediction of children's adjustment from distinct aspects and informants of MDT. The sample consisted of 173 working-class and middle-class English families with two children between the ages of four and eight. Mothers provided reports of the mother–child relationship, and both mothers and fathers provided reports of the children's problematic behavior. The children also provided reports of parent–child relationships and perceived favoritism via a puppet interview. Results confirmed moderate links between MDT and children's adjustment and showed that difference scores better predict adjustment than do favoritism scores. Finally, the results showed that mothers' reports of differential positive feelings were the most salient aspect of MDT for older siblings, whereas mothers' reports of negative feelings and positive discipline were the most salient aspects of MDT for younger siblings.

Finally, Chinese adolescents from Hong Kong ($N = 317$; ages 13–17) participated in a study of the relationship between perceived parental favoritism (in terms of affection and control) and suicidal ideation (De Man, Wong, & Leung, 2003). Correlation analyses showed that adolescents who believed that children in their families were treated differently, in terms of affection from and control by their mothers and fathers, reported greater suicidal ideation. Whether they personally were the favored or nonfavored child made no difference.

Parental Overprotection

Parker (1983) originally reviewed the parental overprotection process extensively using clinical cases about maternal and paternal overprotection with empirical evaluations. Parker defined *overprotection* as a process of control, intrusion, encouragement of dependence on the caretaker, and exclusion of outside influence. He contended that this pernicious process serves as the antecedent cause for a significant portion of psychopathologies, including socialization difficulties, anxiety, depression, and retributive aggression (Parker, 1983). To explore parental overprotection, Parker used psychological evaluations in his case studies including factor analyses, a first in his field. To measure this process, the Structural Family Interaction Scale (SFIS; Grotevant & Carlson, 1989) was developed. The 76-item SFIS is composed of eight subscales about overprotection and autonomy. However, the psychometric properties of the SFIS scores lacked rigor.

More recently, Rork and Morris (2009) examined the association between parenting behaviors and social anxiety in children. Three parental factors—parental socialization, control, and warmth—were investigated in a sample of 31 two-parent families. Rather than relying solely on retrospective self-report questionnaires, this study incorporated direct observation and a daily activity log to assess the qualities of social interaction. Moderate associations between parental control and child anxiety symptoms were found. More specifically, maternal overprotection and observed negative commands were found to be related to child social anxiety, and paternal overprotection was related to child general anxiety. Several gender differences were found regarding the impact of parent behaviors on child anxiety. No support was found for the association between parental warmth and child anxiety.

In another study, Carr and Francis (2010) tested the hypothesis that early maladaptive schemas (EMSs) mediate the relationship between retrospectively reported childhood experiences and avoidant personality disorder (AVPD) symptoms. In this study, 178 nonclinical participants completed questionnaires measuring childhood experiences, EMSs, and AVPD symptoms. Path analyses showed that the EMSs of subjugation, abandonment, and emotional inhibition fully mediated the relationship between retrospectively reported childhood experiences (i.e., mother overprotection and family sociability) and AVPD symptoms. The abandonment and subjugation EMSs were found to fully mediate the relationship between family sociability and AVPD symptoms, whereas the subjugation and emotional inhibition EMSs fully mediated the relationship between maternal (but not paternal) overprotection and AVPD symptoms. Finally, retrospective reports of childhood maltreatment were found to be associated with all EMSs within the disconnection and rejection domain, apart from the abandonment EMS—although EMSs did not significantly account for AVPD symptoms. This study was the first to show that EMSs mediate the relationship between childhood factors and AVPD features.

Parental behaviors (e.g., parental overprotection) and family environment appear to play a role in the suicidal behavior of adolescents. Freudenstein et al. (2011) assessed the relation between parental bonding and suicidal behavior in suicidal ($n = 53$) and nonsuicidal ($n = 47$) adolescent inpatients. Two dimensions of parental bonding—namely, care and overprotection—were assessed using the Parental Bonding Instrument (PBI; Parker, Tupling, & Brown, 1979). Results showed that adolescents with severe suicidal behavior tend to perceive their mothers as less caring and more overprotective compared to the perceptions of those adolescents with mild or no suicidal behavior. A discriminant analysis distinguished significantly between adolescents with high suicidality and those with low suicidality in 71 % of the cases. The perception of the quality of maternal bonding may be an important correlate of suicidal behavior in adolescence and may guide therapeutic strategies and prevention.

The aim of a study by Karukivi et al. (2011) was to explore the associations of perceived social support and parental attitude with alexithymia in a Finnish adolescent population sample. Of the initial sample of 935 adolescents, 729 (78 %) answered the questionnaire and formed the final sample. The mean age of participants was 19 years (range 17–21 years). The 20-item Toronto Alexithymia Scale (TAS-20; Bagby, Parker, & Taylor, 1994) was used to assess alexithymia. Perceived social support from family, friends, and significant other people was measured using the Multidimensional Scale of Perceived Social Support (MSPSS; Zimet, Dahlem, Zimet, & Farley, 1988). Perceived parental care and overprotection were assessed using the PBI; mothers and fathers were assessed separately. After controlling for sociodemographic factors, alexithymia was found to be significantly associated with a lower degree of experienced social support and higher parental overprotection in both females and males. Maternal overprotection was associated with the TAS-20 total score as well as the difficulty identifying feelings subscale score and difficulty describing feelings subscale score. The lack of social support from friends appeared to predict alexithymia more strongly than lack of support from family and significant other people. Maternal care and paternal care were not directly associated with alexithymic features. The study by Karukivi et al. highlights the significance of intrusive and overprotective parental attitudes as a possible risk factor for development of alexithymia.

These five processes in the AtL model[4]—alliances, coalitions, collusions, favoritisms, and parental overprotection—may be titled differently and have varied empirical support. However, the overlap among them is so great that it requires an integrative model to show such an overlap within a distance of space encompassed by extremes in approach and avoidance. A too selective approach toward someone at the expense of someone else appears as the pathogenic background for psychopathology. How the AtL model[4] relates to the emergence of the deadly DT remains unclear at this time. However, it would not be surprising to find any of these five processes present differentially in the lives of individuals involved in the deadly DT.

Ability to Control and Regulate Self Model[5]

A great deal of information and research has focused on self-control or self-regulation, commonly known as willpower (Baumeister & Tierney, 2011)—to the point where Stafford and Bayer (1993) considered willpower to be one of the three basic variables needed to understand interactions between parents and children. (The other two basic variables they identified—that is, self-concept and negotiation—are covered by other models of RCT, such as the Self-ID model[8] and the negotiation model[16].)

The ability to control and regulate self model[5] is defined by a dimension of time evaluated by speed (how quickly or how slowly one approaches or avoids someone else) and perhaps by a dimension of force (how strongly, intensely, or nonintensely one approaches or avoids someone or something else). Both dimensions, if independent of each other, are defined by two extremes. At one end is the extreme of *discharge*, too little or inadequate control as an immediate response to an internal or external stimulus or event; this extreme is seen in impulsive behavior and is apparent in Cluster B personality disorders in the *DSM-IV-TR* (APA, 2000). At the other extreme is *delay*, too much control, as seen in procrastination, shown by some Cluster C personality disorders. Ample evidence supports the validity and importance of the ability to control and regulate self model[5].

In their novel work on emotion regulation and immune functions, Diamond and Facundes (2012) described a possible link between emotional regulation and health. They also outlined a possible link among close relationships (both detrimental and beneficial), emotional regulation, and health. Diamond and Facundes suggested "Whereas most prior research has conceptualized the experience and regulation of such emotions [related to social threat], as intraindividual processes, we emphasize instead their embeddedness in day-to-day dyadic interchanges with our most intimate and important social partners" (p. 95).

Clearly, deadly DT-involved intimates tend to react thoughtlessly without paying attention to the consequences of their impulsive actions and demonstrate limited awareness of the context in which these ultimately destructive actions occur.

When one considers the association between the deadly DT model[14] and both the AtL model[4] and the ability to control and regulate self model[5], a combined model may be more useful and the most parsimonious.

Both Abilities Combined Model[6]

By combining both the AtL model[4] and the ability to control and regulate self model[5]—and the dimensions of space and time that define them, including whether these dimensions are optimal or extreme—it is possible to obtain a both abilities combined model[6] that covers functionality and dysfunctionality. When distance and speed of responding are appropriate, nonextreme, and positive (if not optimal), functional and positive behavior will occur. When one extreme is high and the other is low, one can predict borderline functionality. When both dimensions are extremely negative, one can predict dysfunctionality. The latter two combinations are present in all types of alliances, coalitions, collusions, favoritism, and parental overprotection—the processes of the AtL model[4] reviewed above. If and when any of these extremes is present, one can predict borderline to severe dysfunctionality, as in the case of family members involved in the deadly DT. The deadly DT, therefore, would not be found when distance and speed are both optimal, but it would be present when the ability to love or the ability to control and regulate self is either extreme or inadequate.

Triangle of Living Model[7]

The triangle of living model[7] is derived from the six resources of status or importance (selfhood model[11]) and love or intimacy (intimacy model[15]) that when combined produce a modality of being or presence. That is, a combination of information and services produces a modality of doing or performance. A combination of money and goods or possessions produces a modality of having or production (Foa & Foa, 1974). Finally, a combination of the doing and having modalities results in a supermodality of power (Guinote & Vescio, 2010).

Each modality implies different ascribed or assumed roles, such as daughter or son, partner, husband or wife, parent, grandparent, and other roles included in one's presence in one's family of origin and the way in which those roles are transferred to other generations. *Doing* involves working and performing jobs or professional responsibilities in work and home settings (settings model[3]). *Having* involves how one deals with money and possessions and how one contributes to personal and family well-being as a provider. Functionality results when all three modalities—doing, having, and being—are balanced according to appropriate age and stage criteria along the lifespan. Dysfunctionality occurs when one modality is expanded at the expense and diminution of the other two modalities. For instance, in the case of the deadly DT, the modalities of doing or having, or their combination, may assume a hegemonic position over being. Being available emotionally to self and intimates in the deadly DT may be much more difficult to achieve than modalities of doing or having.

Developmental and Normative Models

Even though the models in this section are considered developmental and normative, that does not mean that psychopathology or dysfunction is absent. As stated from the outset of this chapter, each model in RCT (see Table 2.1) is required to possess both normative *and* nonnormative qualities and applications.

Self-Identity Differentiation Model[8] (Self-ID Model[8])

Differentiation is an important construct that has been the subject of a great deal of research and theorizing (Leary & Tangney, 2012; Morf & Mischel, 2012; Oyserman, Elmore, & Smith, 2012; Schwartz, Luyckx, & Vignoles, 2011a, 2011b). The result is a variety of well-researched models without an integrative theory to link them together. Furthermore, with few exceptions (see Dunning, 2012), many of these propositions have failed to include a relational perspective. Therefore, to correct for this limitation, a curvilinear, developmental, dialectical model may be useful.

The Self-ID model[8] starts with the same–dissimilar dichotomy in infancy, according to a continuum of likeness or resemblance. This continuum includes how one follows life roles in ways that are similar to or different from one's family of origin, according to three steps in the sameness side of the continuum (from similarity to sameness to symbiosis) and three steps on the dissimilar side (from differentness to oppositeness to alienation) (Cusinato & L'Abate, 2008). The curvilinear and developmental nature of this continuum of likeness has been supported by Cusinato and Colesso (2008), L'Abate et al. (2010), Colesso (2012), and Colesso, Cusinato, and L'Abate (in press). The degrees of differentiation occur below the level of awareness and consciousness. One may predict that individuals involved in the deadly DT are functioning at underlying levels of either symbiosis–alienation or sameness–oppositeness (see Table 2.1).

Styles in Intimate Relationships Model[9]

Dialectically and behaviorally combining symbiosis with alienation produces apathetic–abusive (AA) and neglectful styles in intimate relationships, representing the most extreme level of psychopathology, as seen in individuals diagnosed with schizophrenia and identified as criminals (L'Abate, 2011b). Combining sameness with oppositeness produces reactive–repetitive (RR) styles at a borderline level of functionality. Combining similarity with differentness produces an optimal level of functionality characterized by creative–conductive (CC) styles. Although limited research has supported these assertions, one may predict that most individuals involved in the deadly DT function according to either the AA or the RR style (Cusinato & L'Abate, 2012; L'Abate et al., 2010).

Interaction Model[10]

A broader expansion of the two previous models — the Self-ID model[8] and the styles in intimate relationships model[9] — can be found in an arithmetical model of interaction that distinguishes among multiplicative, additive, positive static, negative static, subtractive, and divisive interactions. The interaction model[10] has been expanded by Colesso and colleagues (in press) using complex log logarithms functions. Most multiplicative and additive interactions are visible in CC intimate relationship styles. Most positive and negative static interactions are visible in RR styles. Most subtractive and divisive interactions are characterized by AA styles. One most likely finds the deadly DT in positive and negative static as well as subtractive and divisive interactions. However, empirical evidence for the existence of this triangle in severe psychopathology has been absent from the literature base thus far.

Selfhood Model[11]

The selfhood model[11] deals with how one attributes a sense of importance to self and others. When attribution and bestowal processes are positive toward self and intimate others, a relational propensity called *self-fullness* and optimal functioning tends to emerge. In contrast, when a sense of importance is positive toward self and negative toward others, a relational propensity called *selfishness* tends to emerge. In its extremes the propensity toward selfishness can lead one to act out, engage in inappropriate behaviors, engage in criminal behavior, and even commit murder (L'Abate & Cusinato, 2011). A third relational propensity called *selflessness* tends to emerge when a sense of importance is negative toward self and positive toward others. In its extremes this selfless propensity can lead to depression and possibly suicide (L'Abate et al., 2010). Finally, when this attribution is negative toward both self and others, a relational propensity called *no-self* tends to emerge. In its extremes the no-self propensity can lead to severe psychopathologies evidenced in the *DSM-IV-TR* (APA, 2000), such as Axis I disorders: dissociative disorders, severe depression, bipolar disorder, and schizophrenia disorders.

One may predict that most individuals involved in the deadly DT are likely to function at selfish and selfless as well as no-self relational propensities. Self-oriented relationships among the four preceding models and psychiatric categories are illustrated in Table 2.2. Potentially selfish and selfless individuals would attract each other and as a result mate and marry in what may even start as a seemingly loving relationship. With time and closeness, eventually, their failure to share similar interests, values, and commonalities will start to produce significant differences that eventually emerge as eventual alienation, as discussed in Model[8] and as illustrated by the other models reviewed in this book.

Priorities Model[12]

The priorities model[12] deals with how priorities are ranked or ordered over and above all models summarized thus far. Priorities include desires, expectations, goals, motivations, and understandings of what is important in individuals' lives, besides self and intimate others (selfhood model[11]). These priorities include what settings (settings model[3]) are more important than other ones (e.g., whether work is more important than home), what modalities (triangle of living model[7]) are more important than other modalities, which intimates are more important than others, whether survival is more important than enjoyment, and so on. For example, if enjoyment is important, how do individuals go about obtaining it, legitimately or illegitimately? All of the above priorities imply choices that individuals must make in ranking who and what to choose according to an order that they follow practically every day, likely automatically. When one translates this model to everyday living and applies it to intimates involved in the deadly DT, the most likely prediction one can make is that priorities might be inaccurate, incomplete, unclear, ill-defined, mixed, and even missing. Within RR or AA styles of responding (styles in intimate relationships model[9]), immediacy and reactivity are the most likely reaction, whereas rationality (ERAAwC model[1]) may take second or third place in ranking the eight components of that model.

Clinical or Deviancy Models

The three models described in this section deal directly with deviant and nonnormative relationships that might be evidenced in dysfunctional rather than in functional ones.

Distance Regulation Model[13]

The distance regulation model[13] is a further expansion of the AtL model[4] because it deals with how distance is regulated according to three different roles: (a) the pursuer, that is, the one who seeks closeness or intimacy (intimacy model[15]), be it emotional, physical, or sexual; (b) the one who does not want and denies the importance of and need for closeness by withdrawing at least temporarily from the request; and (c) the distance regulator, that is, the one who asks for closeness but when refuses it when offered ("Come here, I need your help…Go away, your help is not needed or wanted anymore because it is inadequate, incorrect, or insufficient"). The deadly DT could be conceived as one way for its players to achieve closeness and decrease distance among intimates.

Deadly Drama Triangle Model[14] (Deadly DT Model[14])

The Deadly DT model[14] was described earlier in this chapter and has been covered well elsewhere in the literature (L'Abate, 1986, 2009a). However, in previous publications it did not expand and explain the deadly DT in light of RCT as this chapter does. For more detailed descriptions and applications of the deadly DT see Chaps. 3–6.

Intimacy Model[15]

When *intimacy* is defined as the sharing of joys as well as hurts and fears of being hurt, the previously discussed RCT models makes clear that this process is rarely found in deadly DT-involved individuals. It may be present in clearly circumscribed public events, such as marriages and funerals, but not in the privacy of one's home (L'Abate, 2011a).

Conclusive Model

Negotiation Model[16]

The ability to negotiate is required for successful relationships. As long as the deadly DT is present, it is practically impossible for intimates to negotiate anything successfully, because a modicum of functionality is required to do so. As long as the deadly DT in its various manifestations is present, any kind of negotiation is doubtful.

Implications for Future Research

This chapter explains how the deadly DT is evident in most models of RCT. In that respect, one can see how a theory such as RCT can explain why the deadly DT is important: especially how it exists in the gap between functionality and dysfunctionality, as well as at the underpinnings of most psychopathologies. Research exists to support many of the 16 RCT models, but much more research is needed. In particular the RCT models associated with clinical deviancy require additional testing and validation research. The research presented in this chapter was based on theory-derived, relational tests and psychometric applications. In addition to these methods, RCT models can be evaluated dynamically, directly and indirectly, through experimental workbooks and interactive practice exercises (L'Abate, 2011c). Toward this end, the appendices of this book offer workbooks to assess different expressions of the deadly DT. For example, one workbook (Appendix A) was developed to help participants understand the specific nature of the deadly DT. A second workbook (Appendix B) was developed to help individuals who experience behavioral, psychological, and characterological distress.

References

American Psychiatric Association. (2000). *Diagnostic and statistical manual of mental disorders* (4th ed., text rev.). Washington, DC: Author

Bagarozzi, D. J. (2013). *Couples in collusion: Short-term, assessment-based strategies for helping couples disarm their defenses.* New York: Taylor & Francis.

Bagby, R., Parker, J., & Taylor, G. (1994). The 20-item Toronto alexithymia scale. I. Item selection and cross-validation of the factor structure. *Journal of Psychosomatic Research, 38*, 23–32.

Baumeister, R. F., & Tierney, J. (2011). *Willpower: Rediscovering the greatest human strength.* New York: Penguin.

Bergman, L. R., Magnusson, D., & El-Khouri, B. (2003). *Studying individual development in an Individual context: A person-oriented approach.* Mahwah, NJ: Erlbaum.

Broderick, C. B. (1993). *Understanding family process: Basics of family systems theory.* Newbury Park, CA: Sage.

Bullock, B. M., & Dishion, T. J. (2002). Sibling collusion and problem behavior in early adolescence: Toward a process model for family mutuality. *Journal of Abnormal Child Psychology, 30*, 143–153. doi:10.1023/A:1014753232153.

Carr, S. N., & Francis, A. J. P. (2010). Do early maladaptive schemas mediate the relationship between childhood experiences and avoidant personality disorder features? A preliminary investigation in a non-clinical sample. *Cognitive Therapy and Research, 34*, 343–358. doi:10.1007/s10608-009-9250-1.

Cohen, R., & Siegel, A. W. (Eds.). (1991). *Context and development.* Hillsdale, NJ: Erlbaum.

Coldwell, J., Pike, A., & Dunn, J. (2008). Maternal differential treatment and child adjustment: A multi-informant approach. *Social Development, 17*, 596–612. doi:10.1111/j.1467-9507.2007.00440.x.

Colesso, W. (2012). The continuum of likeness scales: A proposal for evaluating self-identity differentiation. In M. Cusinato & L. L'Abate (Eds.), *Advances in relational competence theory: With special attention to alexithymia.* New York: Nova Science.

Colesso, W., Cusinato, M., & L'Abate, L. (in press). Self-identity differentiation: A supermodel expanded into two other models. In E. L. Anderson & S. Thomas (Eds.), *Socialization: Theories, processes, and impact.* New York: Nova Science.

Cusinato, M. (2012). Understanding alexithymia through an information processing model. In M. Cusinato & L. L'Abate (Eds.), *Advances in relational competence theory: With special attention to alexithymia.* New York: Nova Science.

Cusinato, M., & Colesso, W. (2008). Validation of the continuum of likeness in intimate relationships. In L. L'Abate (Ed.), *Toward a science of clinical psychology: Laboratory evaluations and interventions* (pp. 337–352). Hauppauge, NY: Nova Science.

Cusinato, M., & L'Abate, L. (2008). Likeness: A hidden ingredient in family therapy. *American Journal of Family Therapy, 36*, 116–125. doi:10.1080/01926180701189812.

Cusinato, M., & L'Abate, L. (Eds.). (2012). *Advances in relational competence theory: With special attention to alexithymia*. New York: Nova Science.

De Man, A. F., Wong, I. N., & Leung, P. W. L. (2003). Perceived parental favoritism and suicidal ideation in Hong Kong adolescents. *Social Behavior and Personality, 31*, 245–252. doi:10.2224/sbp.2003.31.3.245.

Diamond, L. M., & Facundes, C. P. (2012). Emotion regulation in close relationships: Implications for social threat and its effects on immunological functioning. In L. Campbell & T. J. Loving (Eds.), *Interdisciplinary research on close relationships: The case for integration* (pp. 83–106). Washington, DC: American Psychological Association.

Dix, T., & Buck, K. A. (2012). The emergence of social approach and avoidance motivation in early parent-child relationships. In L. Campbell & T. J. Loving (Eds.), *Interdisciplinary research on close relationships: The case for integration* (pp. 53–81). Washington, DC: American Psychological Association.

Dunning, D. (2012). The relation of self to social perception. In M. R. Leary & J. P. Tangney (Eds.), *Handbook of self and identity* (2nd ed., pp. 481–501). New York: Guilford.

Engle, R. W., Sedek, G., von Hecker, U., & McIntosh, D. N. (Eds.). (2005). *Cognitive limitations in aging and psychopathology*. New York: Cambridge University Press.

Favez, N., Scaiola, C. L., Tissot, H., Darwiche, J., & Frascarolo, F. (2011). The family alliance assessment scales: Steps toward validity and reliability of an observational assessment tool for early family interactions. *Journal of Child and Family Studies, 20*, 23–37. doi:10.1007/s10826-010-9374-7.

Foa, U., & Foa, E. (1974). *Societal structures of the mind*. Springfield, IL: C. C. Thomas.

Freudenstein, O., Zohar, A., Apter, A., Shoval, G., Weizman, A., & Zalsman, G. (2011). Parental bonding in severely suicidal adolescent inpatients. *European Psychiatry, 26*, 504–507. doi:10.1016/j.eurpsy.2011.01.006.

Friedlander, M. L., Escudero, V., Horvath, A. O., Heatherington, L., Cabero, A., & Martens, M. P. (2006). System for observing family therapy alliances: A tool for research and practice. *Journal of Counseling Psychology, 53*, 214–224.

Friedlander, M. L., Lambert, J. E., Valentín, E., & Cragun, C. (2008). How do therapists enhance family alliances? Sequential analyses of therapist-client behavior in two contrasting cases. *Psychotherapy: Theory, Research, Practice, Training, 45*, 75–87. doi:10.1037/0033-3204.45.1.75.

Furniss, T. (1983). Family process in the treatment of intrafamilial child sexual abuse. *Journal of Family Therapy, 5*, 263–278. doi:10.1046/j.1983.00622.x.

Grotevant, H. D., & Carlson, C. I. (1989). *Family assessment: A guide to methods and measures*. New York: Guilford.

Guinote, A., & Vescio, T. K. (Eds.). (2010). *The social psychology of power*. New York: Guilford.

Hylander, L., Krabbe, E., & Schwartz, R. (2005). Metoder og dilemmaer i langvarige behandlingsforløb for børnefamilier med psykisk syge forældre [Methods and dilemmas in long-term therapy for families with mentally ill parents]. *Psykologisk Paedagogisk Rådgivning, 42*, 177–204.

Joyce, P. A. (2007). The production of therapy: The social process of construction of the mother of a sexually abused child. *Journal of Child Sexual Abuse, 16*, 1–18. doi:10.1300/J070v16n03_01.

Karpel, M. A., & Strauss, E. S. (1983). *Family evaluation*. New York: Gardner.

Karpman, S. (1968). Fairy tales and script drama analysis. *Transactional Analysis Bulletin, 7*(26), 39–43.

Karukivi, M., Joukamaa, M., Hautala, L., Kaleva, O., Haapasalo-Pesu, K.-M., Liuksila, P.-R., et al. (2011). Does perceived social support and parental attitude relate to alexithymia? A study in Finnish late adolescents. *Psychiatry Research, 187*, 254–260. doi:10.1016/j.psychres.2010.11.028.

Kirschner, S., & Kirschner, D. A. (1996). Relational components of the incest survivor syndrome. In F. W. Kaslow (Ed.), *Handbook of relational diagnosis and dysfunctional family patterns* (pp. 407–419). New York: Wiley.

Kluger, J. (2011). *The sibling effect: What the bonds among brothers and sisters reveal about us.* New York, NY: Riverhead.

L'Abate, L. (1986). *Systematic family therapy.* New York: Brunner/Mazel.

L'Abate, L. (1997). *The self in the family: A classification of personality, criminality, and psychopathology.* New York: Wiley.

L'Abate, L. (2005). *Personality in intimate relationships: Socialization and psychopathology.* New York: Springer-Science.

L'Abate, L. (2009a). The drama triangle: An attempt to resurrect a neglected pathogenic model in family therapy theory and practice. *The American Journal of Family Therapy, 37,* 1–11. doi:10.1080/01926180701870163.

L'Abate, L. (2009b). In search of a relational theory. *American Psychologist, 64,* 779–788. doi:10.1037/0003-066X.64.8.779.

L'Abate, L. (2009c). Paradigms, theories, and models: Two hierarchical frameworks. In L. L'Abate, P. De Giacomo, M. Capitelli, & S. Longo (Eds.), *Science, mind, and creativity: The Bari symposium* (pp. 107–156). New York: Nova Science.

L'Abate, L. (2009d). A theory-derived structured interview for intimate relationships. *The Family Psychologist, 25,* 12–14.

L'Abate, L. (2011a). *Hurt feelings: Theory, research, and applications in intimate relationships.* New York: Cambridge University Press.

L'Abate, L. (2011b). Self-control: An orphan construct in search of a theory? In A. Durante & C. Mammoliti (Eds.), *Psychology of self-control* (pp. 37–67). New York: Nova Science.

L'Abate, L. (2011c). *Sourcebook of interactive practice exercises in mental health.* New York: Springer.

L'Abate, L. (2012a). *Clinical psychology and psychotherapy as a science: An iconoclastic perspective.* New York: Springer.

L'Abate, L. (Ed.). (2012b). *Paradigms in theory construction.* New York: Springer.

L'Abate, L., & Cusinato, M. (2007). Linking theory with practice: Theory-derived interventions in prevention and family therapy. *The Family Journal: Counseling and Therapy for Couples and Families, 15,* 318–327. doi:10.1177/1066480707303745.

L'Abate, L., & Cusinato, M. (2011). Selfhood: A theory-derived relational model for mental illness and its applications. In L. L'Abate (Ed.), *Mental illnesses: Understanding, prediction, and control* (pp. 439–358). Rijeka, Croatia: InTech Open Access Publisher.

L'Abate, L., Cusinato, M., Maino, E., Colesso, W., & Scilletta, C. (2010). *Relational competence theory: Research and mental health applications.* New York: Springer.

Lavadera, A. L., Laghi, F., & Togliatti, M. M. (2011). Assessing family coordination in divorced families. *American Journal of Family Therapy, 39,* 277–291. doi:10.1080/01926187.2010.539479.

Leary, M. R., & Tangney, J. P. (Eds.). (2012). *Handbook of self and identity* (2nd ed.). New York: Guilford.

McNulty, J. K., & Fincham, F. D. (2012). Beyond positive psychology? Toward a contextual view of psychological processes and well-being. *American Psychologist, 67,* 101–110. doi:10.1037/a0024572.

Mesquita, B., Feldman-Barrett, L., & Smith, E. R. (Eds.). (2010). *The mind in context.* New York: Guilford.

Minuchin, S. (1974). *Families and family therapy.* Cambridge, MA: Harvard.

Minuchin, S., Rosman, B. L., & Baker, L. (1978). *Psychosomatic families: Anorexia nervosa in context.* Cambridge, MA: Harvard.

Morf, C. C., & Mischel, W. (2012). The self as a psycho-social dynamic processing system: Toward a converging science of selfhood. In M. R. Leary & J. P. Tangney (Eds.), *Handbook of self and identity* (2nd ed., pp. 21–49). New York: Guilford.

Nisbett, R. E., Aronson, J., Blair, C., Dickens, W., Flynn, J., Halpern, D. F., et al. (2012). Intelligence: New findings and theoretical developments. *American Psychologist, 67,* 130–159. doi:10.1037/a0026699.

Oyserman, D., Elmore, K., & Smith, G. (2012). Self, self-concept, and identity. In M. R. Leary & J. P. Tangney (Eds.), *Handbook of self and identity* (2nd ed., pp. 69–104). New York: Guilford.

Parker, G. (1983). *Parental overprotection: A risk factor in psychosocial development.* New York: Grune & Stratton.

Parker, G., Tupling, H., & Brown, L. (1979). A parental bonding instrument. *British Journal of Medical Psychology, 52,* 1–10.

Rork, K. E., & Morris, T. L. (2009). Influence of parenting factors on childhood social anxiety: Direct observation of parental warmth and control. *Child and Family Behavior Therapy, 31,* 220–235. doi:10.1080/07317100903099274.

Rottenberg, J., & Vaughan, C. (2008). Emotion expression in depression: Emerging evidence for emotion context-insensitivity. In A. Vingerhoets, I. Nyklicek, & J. Denollet (Eds.), *Emotion regulation: Conceptual and clinical issues* (pp. 125–139). New York: Springer-Science.

Schwartz, S. J., Luyckx, K., & Vignoles, V. L. (Eds.). (2011a). *Handbook of identity theory and research: Domains and categories.* New York: Springer-Science.

Schwartz, S. J., Luyckx, K., & Vignoles, V. L. (Eds.). (2011b). *Handbook of identity theory and research: Structures and processes.* New York: Springer-Science.

Shoda, Y., Cervone, D., & Downey, G. (Eds.). (2007). *Persons in context: Building a science of the individual.* New York: Guilford.

Sommers, S. (2011). *Situations matter: Understanding how context transforms your world.* New York: Riverhead.

Stafford, L., & Bayer, C. L. (1993). *Interaction between parents and children.* Newbury Park, CA: Sage.

Suitor, J. J., & Pillemer, K. (2000). Did mom really love you best? Exploring the role of within-family differences in developmental histories on parental favoritism. *Motivation and Emotion, 24,* 104–119.

Suitor, J. J., & Pillemer, K. (2000). Did mom really love you best? Exploring the role of within-family differences in developmental histories on parental favoritism. *Motivation and Emotion, 24,* 104–119.

Suitor, J. J., Sechrist, J., & Pillemer, K. (2007). When mothers have favourites: Conditions under which mothers differentiate among their adult children. *Canadian Journal on Aging, 26,* 85–100. doi:10.3138/cja.26.2.085.

Suitor, J. J., Sechrist, J., Plikuhn, M., Pardo, S. T., Gilligan, M., & Pillemer, K. (2009). The role of perceived maternal favoritism in sibling relations in midlife. *Journal of Marriage and Family, 71*(4), 1026–1038.

Sutton-Smith, B., & Rosenberg, B. G. (1970). *The sibling.* New York: Holt, Rinehart, & Winston.

VandenBos, G. R. (Ed.). (2007). *APA dictionary of psychology.* Washington, DC: American Psychological Association.

Walsh, F. (1993). *Normal family processes.* New York: Guilford.

Zimet, G. D., Dahlem, N. W., Zimet, S. G., & Farley, G. K. (1988). The multidimensional scale of perceived social support. *Journal of Personality Assessment, 52,* 30–41.

Chapter 3
Parentification

Chapters 1 and 2 discussed the conceptual underpinnings or active ingredients of relational competence theory (RCT; L'Abate, Cusinato, Maino, Colesso, & Scilletta, 2010), as well as the deadly drama triangle (DT; Karpman, 1968, 2009; L'Abate, 2009) and how and to what extent the deadly DT may relate to select roles and generational and relational psychopathologies. Chapters 3–6 now turn to specific models of psychopathology, namely, parentification, parental alienating behavior, bullying, and Stockholm syndrome.

This chapter explores how RCT and other theories can serve as a foundation to explain multiple and divergent outcomes (e.g., pathological and normative) of parentification. The deadly DT also elucidates roles, responsibilities, and processes related to parentification (Hooper 2012a, 2012b).

Defining Parentification

This chapter begins with a working definition of parentification based on the contributions of several seminal scholars (Boszormenyi-Nagy, & Spark, 1973; Hooper, 2003; Jurkovic, 1997; Kerig, 2005; Minuchin, Montalvo, Guerney, Rosman, & Schumer, 1967). *Parentification* is characterized by a relational and interactive family systems process whereby adult members of the family abdicate their roles and responsibilities to a child or children in the family. As a result, children take on roles and responsibilities usually reserved for adults. This process typically requires a family structure that allows generational boundaries to be crossed and permits family members to join or exist in subsystems at different generational levels than those to which they belong (Kerig, 2005).

In these families, children have a scope or degree of power that enables them to participate in subsystems to which they also should not belong. In addition, the boundaries between subsystems (e.g., parental, spousal, child, and sibling) where parentification occurs are reduced, blurred, or nonexistent. For instance, boundaries

L.M. Hooper et al., *Models of Psychopathology: Generational Processes and Relational Roles*, DOI 10.1007/978-1-4614-8081-5_3,
© Springer Science+Business Media New York 2014

evidenced in these families are inconsistent with a well-functioning family system. The hierarchical structure is often inverted, such that the children compose the executive subsystem, where the power exists and family decisions take place (Hooper, Doehler, Wallace, & Hannah, 2011; Kerig, 2005). Consequently, parents or adult members exhibit very little power and control in the family system. Although this process can begin with the parent's temporary abdication of roles, responsibilities, and power, at some point this relational process becomes ingrained or fixed, such that everyone in the family is invested in and even comfortable with maintaining the family structure—even a potentially pathological, dysfunctional one.

Family systems scholars have long lamented that the roles and responsibilities associated with parentification have the potential to be normative and useful in developing parenting skills, healthy romantic attachments, and leadership and organizational skills. Moreover, some have argued that relational competencies could result from parentification, which could have a positive and beneficial effect in adulthood (Boszormenyi-Nagy, & Spark, 1973; Byng-Hall, 2008b; East, 2010; Hooper, 2007b; Jurkovic, 1997; Smyth, Cass, & Hill, 2011). However, researchers have been slow to examine the potential positive aftereffects of parentification (Smyth et al., 2011). Because the psychology and ecology of many of these families is such that the parentification process fills a significant need for most if not all family members—even for the children of the family—it is often maintained and perceived as normal even when it is not.

As a result, when parentification exists, the empirical research has often suggested that the parentified roles and responsibilities exceed what can be considered developmentally, emotionally, and age-appropriate. Moreover, the clinical literature has proposed that the extent to which parentification engenders pathogenic outcomes is contingent upon age of onset, duration, frequency, and the direction of the roles and responsibilities (Telzer & Fuligni, 2009). However, some of these propositions—primarily based on clinical reports—have rarely been empirically examined or tested (Chase, 1999).

The Clinical and Empirical Research Base

Two distinct bodies of literature on parentification have accumulated since the 1960s: clinical and empirical. Although not all the reported clinical observations have been investigated empirically, the empirical literature is rich with evidence about the associations between parentification in childhood and negative outcomes in childhood and adulthood (Chase, 1999; Hooper, DeCoster, White, & Voltz, 2011; Jurkovic, 1998). These associations have been fairly consistent across populations and over time (since the 1960s). However, only a few studies have examined the relation among these variables longitudinally (see East & Weisner, 2009; Stein, Rotheram-Borus, & Lester, 2007) or in randomized clinical trials. Overwhelmingly, the accumulated findings have been derived from cross-sectional survey studies. Many of these studies have been undergirded by the formative and substantive theoretical conceptualizations of prominent scholars: Minuchin, Boszormenyi-Nagy, and Jurkovic. Several groups of researchers have empirically tested these scholars' theoretical theses and clinical observations. These investigations have uncovered several factors that have shown to predict, mediate, and moderate the outcomes associated with parentification.

In general, these aforementioned studies have been supported by family systems theory (Hooper, 2007a; Jurkovic, 1997), attachment theory (Byng-Hall, 2008a; Hooper, Marotta, & Lanthier, 2008), social identity development theory (Hardway & Fuligni, 2006), psychodynamic theory (Wells & Jones, 2000), and more recently trauma-based theories, such as posttraumatic growth theory (Hooper, 2007b; Hooper et al., 2008). Guided by these theoretical conceptualizations of parentification, the investigations offer unique perspectives from which to examine the developmental trajectory and outcomes of the parentified child and the adult he or she becomes.

Childhood parentification has been shown to predict poor functioning in adult relationships. Thus, conceptualizing parentification within the framework of attachment theories is useful in examining this association. Attachment theory emphasizes the importance of secure attachments to parents during childhood, because early attachment patterns serve as the basis for interpersonal relationships throughout one's life (Bowlby, 1969). Because parentification is characterized by the dissolution of boundaries and insecure attachment patterns within the family system, attachment theory predicts that the parentified child may exhibit insecure attachment in adult relationships. Indeed, researchers have found that insecure attachment patterns of parentified children do persist into adult relationships, in the form of excessive caretaking and parental attitudes toward one's romantic partner (Byng-Hall, 2008a).

According to social development theorists, the family is the primary social group to which children belong. Providing developmentally appropriate and sufficiently acknowledged helping may therefore increase the child's sense of competencies, connection, and mattering to the family (Telzer & Fuligni, 2009). However, parentification confers helping responsibilities that are beyond the developmental abilities of the child and can be unreciprocated and unacknowledged. The child's sense of belonging and mattering to the family suffers, and the child may begin to view herself or himself as inadequate. It is through this process that social development theorists propose pathological outcomes of parentification occur.

Wells and Jones (2000) presented a psychodynamic conceptualization of parentification and psychopathology in which childhood parentification predicts proneness to shame in adulthood. From a psychodynamic perspective, children internalize an ego ideal through a parent's projection of expectations during childhood, and permeating feelings of shame emerge when an individual fails to live up to his or her ego ideal. Parentification occurs when parents project developmentally premature and unrealistic expectations upon children. Thus, pathological feelings of shame develop as a result of the child's perceived failure to live up to these expectations. Parentified children continue to be more prone to feelings of shame and guilt in adulthood, resulting in masochistic personality traits (Jones & Wells, 1996). In a study of 197 university students, Wells and Jones administered the Parentification

Questionnaire (Sessions & Jurkovic, 1986) and the Test of Self-Conscious Affect (Tangney, Wagner, & Gramzow, 1989) to examine this association empirically. They found that parentification and proneness to shame were significantly correlated ($R^2 = 0.19$, $p = 0.01$).

Although much of the literature has presented a destructive developmental model of childhood parentification, recently researchers have begun to focus on potential adaptive outcomes for the parentified child (Telzer & Fuligni, 2009). One conceptual model for examining positive outcomes is that of posttraumatic growth theory (Hooper, 2007b). Within this model, one may conceptualize parentification as a traumatic experience in which a child does not receive sufficient support to develop secure attachments and achieve self-differentiation. However, positive developmental outcomes may result from childhood parentification if the child is able to adapt the skills developed through parentification responsibilities to successfully transition to adulthood (Hooper et al., 2008). This theory is rooted in a model of resiliency, in which skills acquired to carry out parentification roles and responsibilities foster competency in adulthood.

Jurkovic and many of his colleagues and students have substantially contributed to the clinical and empirical literature base by publishing numerous nonoverlapping studies on parentification (Jurkovic et al., 2004; Jurkovic & Thirkield, 1998a, 1998b; Jurkovic, Thirkield, & Morrell, 2001; Kuperminc, Jurkovic, & Casey, 2009; Sessions & Jurkovic, 1986). Jurkovic's research has been instructive, in that it opened the door to considering that parentification may be experienced or perceived as a destructive *or* constructive process (see Jurkovic, 1997). Although a significant portion of Jurkovic and colleagues' research has examined the link between parentification and psychological distress, his conceptualization of the parental child and the parentification process has extended and added to the work of seminal scholars Salvador Minuchin and Boszormenyi-Nagy (see Jurkovic, 1997). Toward this end, Jurkovic and his colleagues have focused on the ethicality of the perpetual, crossgenerational process of parentification. In addition, his theorizing about the multifactorial nature of parentification and the extent to which the process may be perceived as ethical or fair is assessed in his self-report measures of parentification, the Parentification Questionnaire (Jurkovic & Thirkield, 1998a, 1998b). Overall, the substantive work of Jurkovic and his colleagues have informed much of the research on parentification that continues today.

Research led by Hooper with colleagues and students has produced an expanded view of parentification in childhood and outcomes in adulthood. In the past decade, Hooper has examined parentification in rural families (Hooper, Doehler, Jankowski, & Tomek, 2012) and nonclinical community adults and families, along with several cross-national studies composed of racially and geographically diverse college students (Hooper et al., 2008; Hooper & Wallace, 2010). Grounded by family systems and attachment theories, the findings in these studies have been for the most part consistent with the long-held view that parentification in childhood relates to negative outcomes in adulthood. However, to ensure balanced consideration and measurement of diverse outcomes, Hooper's contribution to the empirical literature base has also focused on when and for whom parentification may lead to positive outcomes.

Toward this end, in 2012 study Hooper and colleagues (Hooper et al., 2012) reported on the buffering effects parentification had in their rural family sample composed of parents and adolescents. Hooper's body of research is primarily informed by cross-sectional survey investigations using several measures to assess parentification, pathology, and wellness or posttraumatic growth (Hooper, Marotta, & Depuy, 2009). Findings in these studies have demonstrated that parentification can serve as a mediating and moderating factor in some populations (see Hooper & Doehler, 2011b; Jankowski, Hooper, Sandage, & Hannah, 2011). A consistent finding is the possibility for bimodal outcomes in adulthood when parentification is experienced in childhood.

Fuligni and his colleagues have examined several aspects of parentification, including racial and cultural factors that may relate to antecedents and outcomes of parentification. His research has also taken a balanced approach to clarifying the implications of parentification among racially diverse adolescents and their families. For example, Telzer and Fuligni (2009) examined how parentification may influence the positive and negative psychological sequelae among Mexican American, Asian American, and White American adolescents ($n = 752$). The researchers found that daily caregiving or parentification-related behaviors did not have a negative impact on the adolescents. Their unexpected finding was that higher levels of parentification were associated with higher levels of happiness. Telzer and Fuligni also hypothesized that the strength and direction of the association between parentification and study outcomes might be different based on the racial or cultural background of the participants. However, the study's findings were fairly consistent, irrespective of self-reported race, although Mexican Americans reported engaging in slightly more parentification behaviors than their Asian American or White American counterparts did. The White American participants spent the least amount of time providing caregiving behaviors to their family than participants in other racial groups. Although they hypothesized that gender might make a difference, Telzer and Fuligni (2009) found no gender differences in this study. Finally, consistent with the study's hypotheses, the identity of the person for whom the adolescents cared did have an impact on outcomes. Parentification involving care for parents was associated with feelings of distress, whereas parentification involving care for siblings was associated with feelings of happiness—although both of these significant relations were small. Telzer and Fuligni (2009) concluded that parentification can be a meaningful and positive activity for racially diverse adolescents.

Another study conducted by Fuligni, Tseng, and Lam (1999) examined the extent to which attitudes and beliefs about parentification (family obligations and duties) among adolescents ($n = 800$) might vary based on race, gender, and school grade. In this study composed of Asian, Latino, and White American backgrounds, Asian and Latino Americans expressed stronger values, expectations, and positive beliefs about family caregiving than those expressed by their White American counterparts. In addition, for all racial groups, attitudes and beliefs about caregiving were positively related to family and peer relationships, time spent studying, and academic behaviors (e.g., academic aspirations). Attitudes and beliefs about family caregiving were not found to be related to academic grades. Fuligni et al. (1999)

concluded that in general, family caregiving and obligations do not appear to have a negative impact on adolescents' relational and academic development.

In one of the few longitudinal studies, Stein and colleagues (1999, 2007) examined the extent to which parentification had a long-term impact on outcomes (psychological distress, substance use, and behavior) among adolescents with a parent diagnosed with HIV/AIDS ($n=213$). This study collected data at two points in time: baseline (Time 1) and 6 years later (Time 2). Results showed that severity of parents' presenting symptomatology and parentification are associated with both negative and adaptive outcomes over time. Specifically, Stein et al. found that parentification is associated with negative outcomes (e.g., sexual behavior, alcohol, and marijuana use) in the short term (Time 1) but positive coping skills and less alcohol use and tobacco use in the long run (Time 2). Moreover, parentification was not associated with *long-term* negative outcomes measured in the study (e.g., emotional distress, adolescents' parenting attitudes, and adolescents' parentification of their own children). Stein et al. (2007) concluded that parentified youth are not fated to the commonly assumed negative outcomes later in life. In addition, these researchers underscored the feasibility of resilience and positive outcomes even when significant risk factors are present.

Many scholars, including Fuligni and Hooper, have expanded the research base and clinical conversations to investigate racial and cultural aspects of parentification (see East, 2010; East & Weisner, 2009; Fuligni et al., 1999; Fuligni, Yip, & Tseng, 2002; Gilford & Reynolds, 2011; Hardway & Fuligni, 2006; Hooper & Moore, 2012; Hooper, 2012a, 2012b; Hooper, Wallace, Doehler, & Dantzler, in press; Kam, 2011; McMahon & Watts, 2002; Nebbitt & Lombe, 2010; Telzer & Fuligni, 2009). In her study on the development and cross-validation of the Parentification Inventory (Hooper, 2009), Hooper and colleagues attempted to infuse additional culturally relevant items in the development of the survey, such as language brokering (see Hooper, Doehler, et al., 2011). Kam (2011) similarly examined the effects of language brokering on Mexican-heritage adolescents' ($n=684$) mental health, substance use, parentification-like roles and responsibilities, and behaviors, including risky behaviors. Although Kam's results were limited by the use of incomplete measures to capture parentification fully, Kam found that the frequency with which the adolescents serve as cultural brokers for family members is not associated with parentification (roles and responsibilities). In addition, positive perceptions about language brokering are positively related to parentification. In this study, higher levels of parentification are not related to negative psychological sequelae or risky behaviors.

To date, only one meta-analysis assessing parentification has been conducted. In their meta-analysis study, Hooper, DeCoster, et al. (2011) examined the strength of the relation between parentification in childhood and psychological distress and psychopathology in adulthood. The results produced a significant positive relation, but the effects were small ($r=0.14$; 95 % confidence interval $= 0.10$–0.18). Several study factors moderated this association, including type of psychological distress, self-reported race, type of parentification measure used, and sample demographics (clinical, community, and student). As expected in this meta-analysis, the studies composed of clinical participants showed higher levels of parentification compared to studies involving college students or community participants. Surprisingly, this meta-analysis found that depression and substance use symptomatology have weaker associations with parentification than do eating, anxiety, and personality disorders. Finally, two of the most widely used scales produced differential effects: that is, the Parentification Questionnaire (Jurkovic & Thirkield, 1998b) produced stronger associations among the measured factors than did the Parentification Scale (Mika, Bergner, & Baum, 1987).

Although parentification is often measured at the individual level (see Hooper & Doehler, 2011a), it is an interactive and systemic process evidenced between at least two family members. Further, although a dyadic subsystem is required for the parentification process to emerge, parentification typically involves numerous family members. Therefore, it is important to consider the physical and relational context and the family systems structure in which it exists. In addition, researchers have more recently considered the differential effects of the family members who are directly involved in the parentification process: father, mother, and siblings (see Telzer & Fuligni, 2009). RCT may assist researchers, clinicians, and educators in expanding or adding to the literature base on parentification.

Relational Competence Theory and Parentification

As previously mentioned, several theoretical models have been suggested to better understand parentification and to explain the processes and outcomes associated with it. For example, attachment theory (Byng-Hall, 2002, 2008a; Hooper, 2007a), family systems theory, trauma theory (Hooper, 2007b), and psychodynamic theory have long been used to help understand parentification and the commonly observed antecedents, precipitating events, family contexts, and clinical outcomes (Byng-Hall, 2008b; Dallos & Vetere, 2012). Although absent from the literature, RCT could be a useful framework to understand the paradoxical, cultural, and diverse processes and outcomes associated with parentification.

In some ways, parentification can be seen as a relational paradox. For example, parentification exists because there is a disruption or fracture in the adult family members' serving in appropriate parenting roles and carrying out parental responsibilities. Thus, the child (or children) cannot get age-appropriate needs met (e.g., functional, instrumental, emotional, and relational). In turn, the child attempts to fix, attach, or make a connection with the parent by engaging in the very roles and responsibilities that the parent is not. To maintain connection and proximity to the parent, the child offers to parent the parent or siblings, thereby meeting the needs of the entire family, including the child's own. In this context, the child also parents himself or herself. Even though the parent is not meeting the child's parental needs, the parentified child gets his or her relational needs met from the parent in a counterintuitive or paradoxical way through the parentification process. Consequently, parentification becomes or *is* the relational process or method for the family.

Because of the relational, systemic, and interactive nature of parentification, RCT may be an exemplar framework in further clarifying the oft-observed pathological roles and responsibilities that engender and maintain the parentification process across multiple generations. Importantly, RCT can also help clarify when and for whom relational competence is engendered by parentification. Although it is important to underscore that RCT has informed or undergirded only a few empirical studies thus far, it may nonetheless afford researchers a promising framework to use in future clinical conceptualizations and empirical research investigations.

RCT provides an alternative theoretical model that underscores elements of relational, generational, and interactional ways of being among systems and subsystems (Ngu & Florsheim, 2011). Four tenets of RCT may have relevance for parentification. First, RCT suggests that "socialization and relationships in one's family of origin may sculpt and leave indelible effects" on family members' relational competence (L'Abate et al., 2010, p. 6). Second, relational competence reflects the extent to which individuals in stressful times can effectively navigate, both intrapersonally and interpersonally, with people with whom we do and do not have close relationships. Third, relational competence is developed in the context of long-lasting, significant, interactive, and involved relationships. Finally, relational competence has relevance "to dyadic and multi-relational systems, such as couples, families, parents, and children, siblings, and in-laws" (L'Abate et al., 2010, p. 12).

Roles and Responsibilities Associated with Parentification

The original conceptualization of parentification outlined associated roles that include functional and emotional roles carried out by children long before they are ready, competent, or prepared to do so (Boszormenyi-Nagy & Spark, 1973; Minuchin, 1974; Minuchin et al., 1967). The *functional* roles have been described as including those of adult, parent to one's parent, parent to one's siblings and other family members, parent to self, housekeeper, financial manager, financial provider, caregiver, and in some cases a partner (intimate or romantic) to the parent. The *emotional* roles have been described as including those of confidant, secret keeper, emotional substitute, financial manager (differentiated as a functional role and an emotional role), family mediator, and emotional supporter.

Since 2000, the roles of the parentified child have been expanded, clarified, and updated for twenty-first-century demographics to include such roles as language broker, medical provider, and medicine manager (Smyth et al., 2011). Unfortunately, the existing measures to assess for parentification lack items that include these present-day issues, roles, and responsibilities. The Parentification Inventory (Hooper, 2009) is a promising new instrument that may begin to fill this gap, although results from the initial construct validation study (Hooper, Doehler, et al., 2011) suggested that the Parentification Inventory requires additional refinement, as well as additional psychometric-focused studies with diverse populations (e.g., clinical and racial).

Role Abdication and Role Reversal

Parentification clearly and indisputably involves the abdication of parentlike and adultlike roles to children and youth in the family. Parents or other adult caregivers relinquish their role to the children of the family. The reasons for the abdication and scope of the roles in which the child or children engage may vary. Nonetheless, the overarching role is often the same. Parentified children are serving in adult and parentlike roles that are usually developmentally and emotionally inappropriate— roles they are not prepared to take on. Commonly reported reasons for the abdication of parental roles (Hooper, 2012a, 2012b) include the following: (a) a serious medical condition (e.g., HIV/AIDS, cancer, Alzheimer's), (b) substance use and dependence, (c) a serious mental health disorder, (d) caregivers' nonexistent ability to parent well, and (e) environmental or contextual factors, such as low resources or poverty, military culture, divorce, unexpected death of a family member, and family system discord (Hooper & Moore, 2012).

Role reversal or in some cases role corruption (Garber, 2011) happens when an individual exchanges roles with another individual (or individuals) in order to experience or produce alternative interactions, relations, or outcomes. Role reversal is one of the active and seminal ingredients of parentification and being parentified. Without role reversal, parentification does not happen.

Role Taking

As is the case with attachment systems, the process of parentification is bidirectional. As much as parents and other adult members of the family influence the roles and relations in the family, so too do the children and adolescents. Thus, when adults abdicate their roles as parent, executor, and decision maker in a family, some scholars, practitioners, and researchers contend that some children and adolescents are also willingly taking on the role of parentified family member, consciously or unconsciously. Because of this role taking, parentified youth get their needs met. Dallos and Vetere (2012) contended that "there may be cases where children become concerned and involve themselves without explicitly being invited to do so by the parents" (p. 129). The notion of role taking by no means blames youth for being parentified. Rather, this idea reflects the interactive, bidirectional, systemic aspect of parentification.

In other words, like other concepts in family systems theory, parentification is a product of both the adult and the child. The act of role taking is fostered by both adult and child and therefore requires mutual behaviors by multiple individuals. The adult abdicates his parental or adult roles and responsibilities in the family, and the child or adolescent takes on those roles and responsibilities. This bidirectional, interactive process of abdicating and taking on roles continues in a systemic, circular manner that meets the needs of individuals and the family as a whole, irrespective of how pathological and deleterious it may be. Moreover, one or more of the family members may attempt to reframe this process as normal, appropriate, and positive for the family and its individual members (Smyth et al., 2011). This reframing may be appropriate and accurate in some families where the role taking is infrequent, temporary, acknowledged, and overtly and explicitly supported (Byng-Hall, 2008b; Hooper, 2007b).

Responsibilities

The responsibilities involved in parentification are often distinguished by the emotional and instrumental (logistical) needs of the family. That is, youth participate in emotional or instrumental caregiving responsibilities (or both) directed toward parents or siblings (or both) that go unrewarded and unrecognized (Boszormenyi-Nagy & Spark, 1973; Jurkovic, 1997; Minuchin et al., 1967). The emotional parentification role requires participation in the "socioemotional needs of family members and the family as a whole," according to Jurkovic, Morrell, and Thirkield (1999), who described responsibilities that include "serving as a confidant, companion, or mate-like figure, mediating family conflict, and providing nurturance and support" (p. 94). In recent years, responsibilities related to parentification have been extended to include the cultural context in which parentification takes place. For example, literature regarding the link between the responsibility of language brokering and positive and negative outcomes has been explored (see Kam, 2011). Similarly, responsibilities regarding instrumental parentification have been expanded to include caring for sick family members and activities such as medication management for parents and other family members (Smyth et al., 2011). Although these new parentification-like responsibilities have emerged—likely tied to increased levels of immigration and the expanded life expectancy of parents, grandparents, and other family members—it is significant that questionnaires and inventories to assess for parentification have been slow to include items related to these new responsibilities.

Deadly Drama Triangle and Parentification

Family systems theorists have long suggested that the deadly DT is a seminal construct in family systems theory and therapy (Bowen, 1978; Haley, 1967; Minuchin, 1974; Satir, 1972). The triangulated relationships evinced in families are often representative of the level of functionality and dynamics in the family system (Bowen, 1978). The regulatory function that the triangle serves for many poorly functioning families cannot be overstated.

Parentification as a construct can be viewed from a noun-based framework and a verb-based framework. It may represent the extent to which an individual experiences the phenomenon of parentification (noun-based framework). That is, individuals who have been parentified can identify as or be assessed for belonging to a group or category (noun). It may also refer to the processes or dynamics that involve family members and family systems in parentifying youth (verb-based framework). Relationship triangles can be viewed in the same way (Dallos & Vetere, 2012). Dallos and Vetere (2012) asserted, "We can speak of dynamic triangular relationships between intimates (noun) and processes of triangulation that draw a third person into consideration with a dyad (verb)" (p. 118). Dallos and Vetere further suggested that triangles should not be viewed as neutral; rather, they can serve both to benefit and to harm family systems and functioning. This point is relevant for understanding multiple outcomes related to parentification. Likewise, just as parentification includes an explicit and predictable intergenerational component, so too does triangulation in many cases.

The deadly DT outlines three roles that may have relevance to being parentified, the structure of the family system, and the systemic parentification process: victim, persecutor, and rescuer. Karpman (1968) and others (L'Abate, 2009) described these deadly DT roles in the following way. The *rescuer* is a helper and provides support when it is not indicated and even when the rescuer is not asked to do so. The *victim* believes he or she is incapable and needs to be rescued. Individuals in the victim role also have a propensity to catastrophize and demonstrate a lack of insight into the contribution they make to maintain the victim role. Finally, the *persecutor* tends to be unrealistic, demanding, and unforgiving. Individuals who engage in this role and related behaviors also tend to be controlling and critical of others. As drama or anxiety enters into the triangle, roles shift and change, and the anxiety or drama may increase (Burgess, 2005). Moreover, the individual who engages in the rescuer role is highly likely to serve in the victim role at some point.

In his careful review of the deadly DT literature, L'Abate (2009) outlined how the deadly DT may be applied to the roles evinced in the family system wherein parentification takes place. The family members involved in the parentification process can engage in each of the three deadly DT roles at different times for some unacknowledged or covert purpose (e.g., maintaining homeostasis and equilibrium, maintaining proximity to an adultlike figure, or angling for a perceived benefit or payoff). L'Abate suggested that each family member may engage in overlapping roles; for example, "the Victim can be perceived as a Persecutor or Rescuer at the same time, depending on who does or says what" (p. 2). With regard to the parentification process, the parentified child could be seen as the victim. The parent of the parentified child could be viewed as the prosecutor, and another family member (sibling or parent) serves as the rescuer. These roles are not fixed or static; they can change based on the needs and interactions of family members, as proposed by Karpman (1968). For example, the parentified child could just as easily be seen as the rescuer, with the parent viewed as the victim, and another family member (sibling or another parent) perceived as the persecutor. Thus, at any time, the parentified child—as well as other family members—can move through multiple roles in the deadly DT. Figure 3.1 illustrates the parentified child or adolescent in the victim role, but as previously mentioned, he or she—as well as other family members—could engage in other roles evinced in the deadly DT.

Fig. 3.1 Parentified child or
adolescent: starting position
as victim

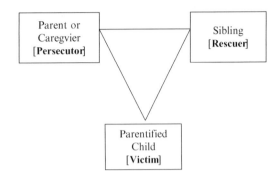

Karpman (1968) suggested that the drama begins when these roles are first established. The drama is minimized if roles are constant and anticipated; but if the roles
are shifting and unexpected, the drama in the system—in this case, the family—is
heightened. Drama, anxiety, and individual- and family-level functioning likely
inform when these roles change or alternate among family members. Although most
family members have a preferred role, these roles are nonetheless interchangeable.
Some family members may carry out these different roles concurrently or simultaneously. Similar to the notion that the family is always in the room, even when family
members are not physically present, the deadly DT roles and scripts associated with
the parentified member and the family members are always in the room. That is,
these roles and scripts are always present even when the parentified family member
is in another context and away from family members. Thus the deadly DT can be
played out with other individuals.

Certainly, culture influences the deadly DT process. For example, how parentification is introduced, how it is maintained, and whether it is perceived as fair (Jurkovic,
1997; Jurkovic & Thirkield, 1998a, 1998b) or beneficial (Hooper, 2009; Hooper,
Doehler, et al., 2011) are all likely tied to the culture of the system in which it takes
place. The cultural context may also inform and relate to the degree to which the
drama associated with parentification foretells severe and significant pernicious outcomes (East, 2010; Hooper, 2012a, 2012b; Kam, 2011; Smyth et al., 2011)—although
how and to what extent remains unclear and has yet to be fully and empirically examined. Few studies provide some preliminary evidence to buttress the relevance of the
association between cultural context and outcomes when the three roles (victim, persecutor, and rescuer), responsibilities, and scripts of the deadly DT exist.

Figure 3.1 illustrates the interactive and interchangeable nature of the deadly DT.
Significantly, for the recent momentum to develop a balanced view of parentification,
the deadly DT framework—in conjunction with RCT—also allows for alternative
views and perceptions of the interactions by family members irrespective of the
overwhelming negative outcomes. The deadly DT allows for reframing or alternative ways of viewing these roles (Choy, 1990)—important for extending the parentification literature. In addition, the deadly DT is useful in elucidating the interactions
and patterns that have engendered and maintained parentification in the family.
Therefore, the individuals who engage in these roles are not fated to pathological
and deleterious interactions and outcomes (Hooper, 2007b; Hooper et al., 2012).

Triangles are not always problematic. They can have a stabilizing function, just as parentification can (Bowen, 1978; Hooper, 2007b). Consequently, the deadly DT and its associated roles may have utility. In other words, although one family member may describe his or her role and responsibilities as burdensome, overwhelming, or abusive, another family member may perceive that role as appropriate, fostering autonomy and skill development. This deadly DT process of reframing, which may be used—purposefully or unintentionally—by family members, may account for how the family can characterize negative transactions as positive (even when they are not) and thereby sustain these transactions across generations.

That said, these triangulated family behaviors are typically not in the family's best interest—particularly if they persist for a long time. The deadly DT framework can be used to determine intervention and adjustment points in the family system to aid in detriangling family members, roles, and responsibilities—similar to the triangle as it is often discussed in the family systems literature (Bowen, 1978). For example, adjusting the role of one family member in the triangle could change other parts of the system. Without any intervention, the deadly DT roles are likely maintained or exacerbated based on the chronicity and level of anxiety, intensity, or pathology in the family system.

Implications for Practice

Parentification is a ubiquitous phenomenon seen in many families. The aftereffects can be severe and long-lasting, sometimes evidenced across many generations. Regardless of the commonly experienced negative outcomes frequently reported in the empirical literature on parentification, therapists must recognize that the parentification process is often the glue that holds together the family—and family *relationships*. When therapists and other healthcare providers work with individuals and families where parentification is present, several specific interventions and strategies derived from family systems theory, attachment theory, and RCT theory may be useful (Engels, Finkenauer, Meeus, & Dekovic, 2001; Johnson & Brock, 2000). For example, the treatment process can explore relational concepts and processes such as differentiating within the family of origin, detriangling, reframing boundaries, and establishing alternate and updated relational images of self and other family members.

Bowen's (1978) theorizing on the clinical importance of triangles, detriangulation, and differentiation of self may be helpful when parentification exists in families. Focusing on how the family members have triangled others, in addition to being triangled by others, is one way to clarify how triangles are being established in the family. Differentiation is closely linked with triangulation. Because differentiation within the family of origin requires a lifetime of effort, this process has relevance across the lifespan, life stages, and family life cycle (Fishbane, 2001). Therapists can help adolescents make a relational claim from parents so that the adolescents can resume or reclaim age-appropriate roles in the family system. In so doing, children, adolescents, and parents alike can work toward functioning autonomously while maintaining relationships and staying emotionally connected even during times of stress. This process of increasing differentiation of self can help all family members be more relationally competent. Family therapists and other mental healthcare providers can therefore use the parentification process to increase differentiation of self (Jankowski & Hooper, 2012) and reframe the transactions, interactions, and triangles seen in the family (Johnson & Brock, 2000).

Moreover, parentification can be reframed as a positive way of being that was appropriate for the family at one point in time but is no longer functional for individuals or the family. Therapists can help family members clarify their relational images of self and others. The primary goal is to teach the family to have clearer, more permeable boundaries, with the adults serving in the executive subsystem and the children serving in an age-appropriate subsystem—thereby creating a new relational narrative for the family and its members. When one applies the deadly DT to parentification, one clearly sees how the parent or adult caregiver who parentifies the child can serve all three roles (i.e., victim, rescuer, and persecutor)—in the context of one interaction, in some cases. The parentified child, too, can serve all three roles in the context of the family where parentification takes place. Other family members can be pulled into the triangle and serve one of the three roles; they can maintain the role of bystander as well. Finally, the parentified child can easily vacillate between rescuer and persecutor. For example, the parentified child rescues the parent and family by competently handling the tasks of the family and meeting everyone's needs. At the same time, the parentified child can become angry, frustrated, and resentful about being placed in the role of caring for the family. Then the parentified child may switch into the role of persecutor.

In RCT (L'Abate et al., 2010), similar to Bowen's (1978) theory, the individual and the family system must be considered. The therapist will have to help each family member clarify what the roles of victim, rescuer, and persecutor have afforded him or her as well as the family. Then the therapist can help the family see how these roles are no longer useful for all involved. Establishing new roles and getting the family and its members to challenge the utility of these old roles is another primary goal to address in therapy. To restore the parent–child hierarchy is paramount, including the restoration of parental authority and responsibility. Also important is the task of teaching the family how to develop relational resources and competencies in the younger family members without parentifying them and the next generation. In this way, the process of transmitting parentification can cease. This relational corrective experience has the potential to foster relational competence in the younger family members, as well as the adults and parents they will become (Fishbane, 2001). This process could also incorporate the technique of authoring a different relational story with self and parents that includes new and updated roles and responsibilities, rather than those of victim, rescuer, and persecutor. As Bowen discussed in his theory, the goal is not for the therapist to change each family member but rather to get each family member to change his or her own actions, roles, and responsibilities in the context of the relationship—as Fishbane suggested, the differentiation of self within the family of origin, also termed *relational autonomy*. This approach and process may allow an adult who was parentified as a child to become unstuck from this childhood relationship and stop continuing these relational processes and roles in his or her current relationships.

Conclusion

Although parentification is often measured at the individual level, it is an interactive and systemic process evidenced between at least two family members. Although a dyadic subsystem is required for the parentification process to emerge, parentification typically involves numerous family members. Therefore, it is important to consider the physical and relational context and the family systems structure in which it exists. In addition, researchers have begun to consider the differential effects of the family members who are directly involved in the parentification process (father, mother, and siblings). RCT may assist researchers, clinicians, and educators in expanding or adding to the literature base on parentification.

RCT (L'Abate et al., 2010) in conjunction with deadly DT (Fulkerson, 2003; Karpman, 1968, 2009; L'Abate, 2009) may help add to an understudied, underdeveloped area related to parentification, namely, interventions and treatment models. Because much of the research on parentification has focused on describing the link between parentification and pathology, RCT may serve as a framework to inform new and innovative research in the twenty-first century. In particular, RCT may help researchers and practitioners to clarify how parentification and positive interpersonal relationships, growth, thriving, and competence can coexist across the lifespan and even across multiple generations. Moreover, understanding paths and mechanisms that underlie positive relational, generational, and cultural factors would significantly benefit the clinical and research literature base. Relational competence in the individual family member could be more important than relational quality between family members—in particular among parentified adolescent family members.

References

Boszormenyi-Nagy, I., & Spark, G. (1973). *Invisible loyalties: Reciprocity in intergenerational family therapy*. Oxford: Harper & Row.

Bowen, M. (1978). *Family therapy in clinical practice*. New York: Jason Aronson.

Bowlby, J. (1969). *Attachment and loss: Vol. 1. Attachment*. New York: Basic Books.

Burgess, R. C. (2005). A model for enhancing individual and organisational learning of 'emotional intelligence': The drama and winner's triangles. *Social Work Education, 24*, 97–112. doi:10.1 080/0261547052000325008.

Byng-Hall, J. (2002). Relieving parentified children's burdens in families with insecure attachment patterns. *Family Process, 41*, 375–388. doi:10.1111/j.1545-5300.2002.41307.x.

Byng-Hall, J. (2008a). The crucial roles of attachment in family therapy. *Journal of Family Therapy, 30*, 129–146. doi:10.1111/j.1467-6427.2008.00422.x.

Byng-Hall, J. (2008b). The significance of children fulfilling parental roles: Implications for family therapy. *Journal of Family Therapy, 30*, 147–162. doi:10.1111/j.1467-6427.2008.00423.x.

Chase, N. D. (1999). *Burdened children: Theory, research, and treatment of parentification.* Thousand Oaks, CA: Sage.

Choy, A. (1990). The winner's triangle. *Transactional Analysis Journal, 20,* 40–46.

Dallos, R., & Vetere, A. (2012). Systems theory, family attachments and processes of triangulation: Does the concept of triangulation offer a useful bridge? *Journal of Family Therapy, 34,* 117–137. doi:10.1111/j.1467-6427.2011.00554.x.

East, P. L. (2010). Children's provision of family caregiving: Benefit or burden? *Child Development Perspectives, 4,* 55–61. doi:10.1111/j.1750-8606.2009.00118.x.

East, P. L., & Weisner, T. S. (2009). Mexican American adolescents' family caregiving: Selection effects and longitudinal associations with adjustment. *Family Relations, 58,* 562–577. doi:10.1111/j.1741-3729.2009.00575.x.

Engels, R. C. M. E., Finkenauer, C., Meeus, W., & Dekovic, M. (2001). Parental attachment and adolescents' emotional adjustment: The associations with social skills and relational competence. *Journal of Counseling Psychology, 48,* 428–439. doi:10.1037/0022-0167.48.4.428.

Fishbane, M. D. (2001). Relational narratives of the self. *Family Process, 40,* 273–291. doi:10.1111/j.1545-5300.2001.4030100273.x.

Fuligni, A. J., Tseng, V., & Lam, M. (1999). Attitudes toward family obligations among American adolescents with Asian, Latin American, and European backgrounds. *Child Development, 70,* 1030–1044. doi:10.1111/1467-8624.00075.

Fuligni, A. J., Yip, T., & Tseng, V. (2002). The impact of family obligation on the daily activities and psychological well-being of Chinese American adolescents. *Child Development, 73,* 302–314. doi:10.1111/1467-8624.00407.

Fulkerson, M. (2003). Integrating the Karpman drama triangle with choice theory and reality therapy. *International Journal of Reality Therapy, 23,* 12–14.

Garber, B. D. (2011). Parental alienation and the dynamics of the enmeshed parent-child dyad: Adultification, parentification, and infantilization. *Family Court Review, 49,* 322–335. doi:10.1111/j.1744-1617.2011.01374.x.

Gilford, T. T., & Reynolds, A. (2011). "My mother's keeper": The effects of parentification on Black female college students. *Journal of Black Psychology, 37,* 55–77. doi:10.1177/0095798410372624.

Haley, J. (1967). Family experiments: A new type of experimentation. *Family Process, 1,* 265–293. doi:10.1111/j.1545-5300.1962.00265.x.

Hardway, C., & Fuligni, A. (2006). Dimensions of family connectedness among adolescents of Mexican, Chinese, and European backgrounds. *Developmental Psychology, 42,* 1246–1248. doi:10.1037/0012-1649.42.61246.

Hooper, L. M. (2003). Parentification, resiliency, secure adult attachment style, and differentiation of self as predictors of growth among college students. *Dissertations Abstracts International, 64,* 1493.

Hooper, L. M. (2007a). The application of attachment theory and family systems theory to the phenomena of parentification. *The Family Journal, 15,* 217–223. doi:10.1177/1066480707301290.

Hooper, L. M. (2007b). Expanding the discussion regarding parentification and its varied outcomes: Implications for mental health research and practice. *Journal of Mental Health Counseling, 29,* 322–337.

Hooper, L. M. (2009). *Parentification inventory.* Available from L. M. Hooper, Department of Educational Studies in Psychology, Research Methodology, and Counseling, The University of Alabama, Tuscaloosa, AL 35487.

Hooper, L. M. (2012a). Parentification. In R. J. R. Levesque (Ed.), *Encyclopedia of adolescence* (Vol. 4, pp. 2023–2031). New York: Springer. doi:10.1007/978-1-4419-1695-2.

Hooper, L. M. (2012b). Parentification. In K. Keith (Ed.), *Encyclopedia of cross cultural psychology.* New York: Springer.

Hooper, L. M. (2012). Assessing parentification in South American college students: A factor analytic study of a Spanish version of the parentification inventory. *Journal of Multicultural Counseling and Development.*

Hooper, L. M., DeCoster, J., White, N., & Voltz, M. L. (2011). Characterizing the magnitude of the relation between self-reported childhood parentification and adult psychopathology: A meta-analysis. *Journal of Clinical Psychology, 67,* 1028–1043. doi:10.1002/jclp.20807.

Hooper, L. M., & Doehler, K. (2011a). Assessing family caregiving: A comparison of three retrospective parentification measures. *Journal of Marital and Family Therapy, 38*, 653–666. doi:10.1111/j.1752-0606.2011.00258.x.

Hooper, L. M., & Doehler, K. (2011b). The mediating and moderating effects of differentiation of self on body mass index and depressive symptomatology among an American college sample. *Counseling Psychology Quarterly, 24*, 71–82. doi:10.1080/09515070.2011.559957.

Hooper, L. M., Doehler, K., Jankowski, P. J., & Tomek, S. (2012). Patterns of self-reported alcohol use, body mass index, and depressive symptoms in a rural family sample: The buffering effects of parentification. *The Family Journal: Counseling and Therapy for Couples and Families, 20*, 165–179. doi:10.1177/1066480711435320.

Hooper, L. M., Doehler, K., Wallace, S. A., & Hannah, N. J. (2011). The parentification inventory: Development, validation, and cross-validation. *The American Journal of Family Therapy, 39*, 226–241. doi:10.1080/01926187.2010.531652.

Hooper, L. M., Marotta, S. A., & Depuy, V. (2009). A confirmatory factor analytic study of the posttraumatic growth inventory among a sample of radically diverse college students. *Journal of Mental Health, 18*, 335–343. doi:10.1080/09638230802522502.

Hooper, L. M., Marotta, S. A., & Lanthier, R. P. (2008). Predictors of growth and distress following childhood parentification: A retrospective exploratory study. *Journal of Child and Family Studies, 17*, 693–705. doi:10.1007/s10826-007-9184-8.

Hooper, L. M., & Moore, H. (2012). Parentification in military families. *Children and Youth Services Review*.

Hooper, L. M., & Wallace, S. (2010). Evaluating the parentification questionnaire: Psychometric properties and psychopathology correlates. *Contemporary Family Therapy, 32*, 52–68. doi:10.1007/s10591-009-9103-9.

Hooper, L. M., Wallace, S. A., Doehler, K., & Dantzler, J. (in press). Parentification, ethnic identity, psychological health in Black and White American college students: Implications of family of origin and cultural factors. *Journal of Comparative Family Studies*.

Jankowski, P., & Hooper, L. M. (2012). Differentiation of self: A validation study of the Bowen theory construct. *Couple and Family Psychology: Research and Practice, 1*, 226–243. doi:10.1037/a0027469.

Jankowski, P., Hooper, L. M., Sandage, S., & Hannah, N. J. (2011). Parentification and mental health symptoms: The mediating effects of perceived unfairness and self-regulation. *Journal of Family Therapy, 35*, 43–65. doi:10.1111/j.1467-6427.2011.00574.x.

Johnson, A. H., & Brock, C. D. (2000). Exploring triangulation as the foundation for family system thinking in the Balint group process. *Families, Systems, and Health: The Journal of Collaborative Family Healthcare, 18*, 469–478. doi:10.1037/h0091871.

Jones, R. A., & Wells, M. (1996). An empirical study of parentification and personality. *The American Journal of Family Therapy, 24*, 145–152. doi:10.1080/01926189608251027.

Jurkovic, G. J. (1997). *Lost childhoods: The plight of the parentified child*. New York: Brunner Mazel.

Jurkovic, G. J. (1998). Destructive parentification in families: Causes and consequences. In L. L'Abate (Ed.), *Family psychopathology* (pp. 237–255). New York: Guilford.

Jurkovic, G. J., Kuperminc, G., Perilla, J., Murphy, A., Ibanez, G., & Casey, S. (2004). Ecological and ethical perspectives on filial responsibility: Implications for primary prevention with immigrant Latino adolescents. *The Journal of Primary Prevention, 25*, 81–104. doi:10.1023/B:JOPP.0000039940.9463.eb.

Jurkovic, G. J., Morrell, R., & Thirkield, A. (1999). Assessing childhood parentification: Guidelines for researchers and clinicians. In N. Chase (Ed.), *Burdened children* (pp. 92–113). New York: Guilford.

Jurkovic, G. J., & Thirkield, A. (1998a). *Parentification questionnaire*. Available from G. J. Jurkovic, Department of Psychology, Georgia State University, University Plaza, Atlanta, GA 30303.

Jurkovic, G. J., & Thirkield, A. (1998b). *Parentification questionnaire—adult*. Available from G. J. Jurkovic, Department of Psychology, Georgia State University, University Plaza, Atlanta, GA 30303.

Jurkovic, G. J., Thirkield, A., & Morrell, R. (2001). Parentification of adult children of divorce: A multidimensional analysis. *Journal of Youth and Adolescence, 30,* 245–257. doi:10.102 3/A:1010349925974.

Kam, J. A. (2011). The effects of language brokering frequency and feelings on Mexican-heritage youth's mental health and risky behaviors. *Journal of Communication, 61,* 455–475. doi:10.1111/j.1460-2466.2011.01552.x.

Karpman, S. B. (1968). Fairy tales and script drama analysis. *Transactional Analysis Bulletin, 7,* 39–43.

Karpman, S. B. (2009). Sex games people play: Intimacy blocks, games, and scripts. *Transactional Analysis Journal, 39,* 103–116.

Kerig, P. K. (Ed.). (2005). *Implications of parent-child boundary dissolution for developmental psychopathology: "Who is the parent and who is the child?".* New York: Hawthorne.

Kuperminc, G. P., Jurkovic, G. J., & Casey, S. (2009). Relational filial responsibility to the personal and social adjustment of Latino adolescents from immigrant families. *Journal of Family Psychology, 23,* 14–22.

L'Abate, L. (2009). The drama triangle: An attempt to resurrect a neglected pathogenic model in family therapy theory and practice. *The American Journal of Family Therapy, 37,* 1–11. doi:10.1080/01926180701870163.

L'Abate, L., Cusinato, M., Maino, E., Colesso, W., & Scilletta, C. (2010). *Relational competence theory: Research and mental health applications.* New York: Springer-Science.

McMahon, S. D., & Watts, R. J. (2002). Ethnic identity in urban African American youth: Exploring links with self-worth, aggression, and other psychosocial variables. *Journal of Community Psychology, 30,* 411–431. doi:10.1002/jcop.10013.

Mika, P., Bergner, R. M., & Baum, M. C. (1987). The development of a scale for the assessment of parentification. *Family Therapy, 14,* 229–235.

Minuchin, S. (1974). *Families and family therapy.* Cambridge, MA: Harvard University Press.

Minuchin, S., Montalvo, B., Guerney, B., Rosman, B., & Schumer, F. (1967). *Families of the slums: An exploration of their structure and treatment.* New York: Basic Books.

Nebbitt, V. E., & Lombe, M. (2010). Urban African American adolescents and adultification. *Families in Society, 91,* 234–240. doi:10.1606/1044-3894.4000.

Ngu, L., & Florsheim, P. (2011). The development of relational competence among young high-risk fathers across the transition to parenthood. *Family Process, 50,* 184–202. doi:10.1111/j.1545-5300.2011.01354.x.

Satir, V. (1972). *Peoplemaking.* Palo Alto, CA: Science and Behavior Books.

Sessions, M. W., & Jurkovic, G. J. (1986). *The parentification questionnaire.* Available from G. J. Jurkovic, Department of Psychology, Georgia State University, University Plaza, Atlanta, GA 30303.

Smyth, C., Cass, B., & Hill, T. (2011). Children and young people as active agents in care-giving: Agency and constraint. *Children and Youth Services Review, 33,* 509–514. doi:10.1016/j.childyouth.2010.05.009.

Stein, J. A., Riedel, M., & Rotheram-Borus, M. J. (1999). Parentification and its impact on adolescent children of parents with AIDS. *Family Process, 38,* 193–208. doi:10.1111/j.1545-5300.1999.00193.x.

Stein, J. A., Rotheram-Borus, M. J., & Lester, P. (2007). Impact of parentification on long-term outcomes among children of parents with HIV/AIDS. *Family Process, 46,* 317–333. doi:10.1111/j.1545-5300.2007.00214.x.

Tangney, J. P., Wagner, P. E., & Gramzow, R. (1989). *The test of self-conscious affect.* Fairfax, VA: George Mason University.

Telzer, E. H., & Fuligni, A. J. (2009). Daily family assistance and the psychological well-being of adolescents from Latin American, Asian, and European backgrounds. *Developmental Psychology, 45,* 1177–1189. doi:10.1037/a0014728.

Wells, M., & Jones, R. (2000). Childhood parentification and shame-proneness: A preliminary study. *The American Journal of Family Therapy, 28,* 19–27. doi:10.1080/019261800261789.

Chapter 4
Parental Alienation Behaviors

This chapter summarizes the literature related to the oft-reported destructive interactions, behavior patterns, and deleterious effects of the phenomenon typically called *parental alienation syndrome*, more recently described as *parental alienation disorder* (see Bernet, 2008; Houchin, Ranseen, Hash, & Bartnicki, 2012). According to Gardner (1987a), parental alienation syndrome is a "disorder" in which the child is "programmed" (or brainwashed) by one parent in an effort to "denigrate the other parent" (p. xix). In addition, this phenomenon involves mothers, fathers, and sometimes other family members or guardians (e.g., grandparents, aunts or uncles, or nonbiological caregivers) who deny a parent access to a child or keep the child physically distant from a parent, for example, when one parent or caregiver abducts and transports a child from his or her country of origin. Such enforced distance or denial of access typically has three aims: (a) to coach and manipulate the child to have a negative view of and limited attachment with one parent; (b) to create an environment in which one parent can distort positive memories and behaviors and attempt to instill new, inaccurate, and destructive ones; and (c) to exclude one parent from the child's daily life, including educational, medical, and social events and activities (Gottlieb, 2012). (As noted above, the parental alienation process sometimes involves another relative, a nonbiological caregiver, or other guardian instead of one or both biological parents. For the sake of simplicity, this chapter will use the word *parent* to denote all such parent-like roles.)

An introductory discussion on parental alienation is incomplete without considering the work of Richard A. Gardner. Gardner, a child psychiatrist, is credited as the first person to recognize distinct patterns of parental alienation, which he considered a divorce-specific psychological distress and labeled parental alienation syndrome (Gardner, 1987a, 1987b, 1991, 1992, 2001). Gardner described several transactions and maneuvers involved in the alienation process that implicated both the parent and child in carrying out and contributing to the parental alienation process. Behaviors carried out by the *parent* who alienates often include:

(a) Demonizing the other parent or caregiver
(b) Describing the other parent as worthless

L.M. Hooper et al., *Models of Psychopathology: Generational Processes and Relational Roles*, DOI 10.1007/978-1-4614-8081-5_4,
© Springer Science+Business Media New York 2014

(c) Advancing meritless claims about the other parent (e.g., physical abuse; excessive use of alcohol and drugs)
(d) Manipulating and coaching the child to believe the child chooses to alienate the other parent

Meanwhile, behaviors observed in the *child* who is involved in parental alienation include:

(a) Expressing an aversion toward the left-behind parent
(b) Failing to express a reason for rejecting or not wanting to see the parent who is alienated
(c) Appearing to align with the alienator
(d) Failing to express guilt about events and outcomes related to parental alienation
(e) Expressing strong dislike for the left-behind parent's family members

A seminal thesis in Gardner's descriptions of parental alienation syndrome is the notion of brainwashing. Gardner (1987a, 1987b, 1991, 1992, 2001) outlined specific examples of common techniques and themes used to brainwash children. For example, the alienating parent might systematically discuss negative topics and untruths about the victim parent (or left-behind parent), such as issues of infidelity or a lack of child or family financial support. The alienator (or persecutor) especially might complain about how little money he or she receives from the victim parent to support the children. Parents who engage in alienating behaviors frequently accuse the left-behind parent of having abandoned the family, and the accusing parent may even resort to exaggerating issues and accusing the victim parent of abuse or addiction to alcohol or drugs, even when no basis exists for the accusations.

Gardner (1987a, 1987b, 1991, 1992, 2001) also described how some parents accuse the left-behind parent of having said something he or she never said, which puts the left-behind parent in the position of having to clarify inaccuracies with the child to overcome the child's skepticism. Falsifying the appearance of violence, subjectively selecting photographs that depict the victim parent in a negative light, and making sarcastic comments are some methods or maneuvers used to destroy a child's love for the victimized parent, who sometimes lives in the home but more often is too far away to defend himself or herself from such attacks (Gardner, 1987a). Another common maneuver used by alienators is to instruct their children to tell the victim parent that the alienating parent is not available or not at home when the victim parent calls. These children are not only being taught to be dishonest but are being used as accomplices in the discord and fighting between parents. In this way the child becomes a partner in the alienation process (Gardner, 1987a).

Gardner (1987a, 1991, 1992) referred to the mother as often being the primary perpetrator of verbal attacks and untruths. More recently, however, it has become clearer that males and females are equally capable of inflicting verbal harm and alienation (Reay, 2007). For example, one father who abducted his children to Europe in 2003 employed the tactics and behaviors described by Gardner. The father successfully employed alienating maneuvers. For example, his youngest child accused the mother of never having called during their first year abroad. Meanwhile, the mother stated that whenever she called, she was always told the children were unavailable. It was the father who said they were too busy to talk, and the mother was unaware of the father's other alienating and brainwashing behaviors.

Ever since the original descriptions were put forward by Gardner (1985, 1987a), the controversy surrounding parental alienation syndrome has been unwavering (see Gardner, 2001; Houchin et al., 2012; Kelly & Johnston, 2001; Levesque, 2012; Rand, 2011). The controversy has been informed in part by the difficulties in operationalizing, measuring, and evaluating the complex behavior patterns evinced in family systems and family members where parental alienation is present (Baker, 2007a, 2007b; Gottlieb, 2012; Mone & Biringen, 2012). At least two major points have emerged from the literature on parental alienation syndrome. First, scholars and practitioners have questioned the legitimacy of parental alienation syndrome and its associated processes and behaviors. Specifically, many researchers and practitioners have questioned the extent to which parental alienation syndrome is valid and reliable (Emery, Otto, & O'Donohue, 2005; Houchin et al., 2012; Kelly & Johnston, 2001; Walker & Shapiro, 2010). The second important point emerging from the literature reveals that only limited empirical research has examined parental alienation syndrome to support the proposition that parental alienation is indeed a syndrome (Burrill, 2006; Gardner, 2001; Rand, 2011). As a result, scholars have questioned whether parental alienation is a syndrome, a disorder, or a constellation of normal behaviors in response to abnormal or dysfunctional familial relationships, roles, and interactions (e.g., parents' characterological difficulties, divorce, abductions, and interpersonal and intergenerational conflict, adversity, and trauma; Gottlieb, 2012). Because of the multilayered outcomes that may result from parental alienation—such as divorce, abduction, psychological distress, or multigenerational abuse—many professionals from different disciplines have informed the research base and the recommendations for treatment of family members who have experienced parental alienation.

Consequently, in addition to examining parental alienation, this chapter also describes the lack of consensus among scholars, practitioners, nonmental health professionals (e.g., lawyers and child protective services personnel), and family members regarding parental alienation syndrome and how the discourse related to parental alienation syndrome has been emotionally charged and fiercely debated (Bernet, 2008; Houchin et al., 2012; Kelly & Johnston, 2001; Walker & Shapiro, 2010). Child abduction is one commonly reported pathway to or aftereffect of parental alienation behavior. For example, in an effort to alienate children from one parent—and often from other family members—the alienating parent might abduct and transport children to unknown places, never to be seen again. Because of the dearth of empirical research on parental alienation syndrome and its relation to child abductions, this chapter reviews several prominent cases—in addition to the few studies that exist—to bring some clarity to the complex behaviors, family systems, and interaction patterns that appear to coexist with parental alienation.

Finally, in light of the controversies described here, in addition to the lack of accumulated empirical support, this chapter uses an alternate descriptor to refer to parental alienation syndrome (Walker & Shapiro, 2010). Specifically, consistent with Baker and Chambers (2011), we use the descriptor *parental alienation behaviors* to describe this phenomenon when possible. Some scholars, not without debate, have used the term *parental alienation disorder* (see Houchin et al., 2012), although recent reports from psychological and psychiatric association's suggest that parental alienation disorder will not be included in the revised version of the current *Diagnostic and Statistical Manual of Mental Disorders*—IV (4th ed., text rev.; *DSM-IV-TR*; American Psychiatric Association, 2000). In response to the accumulated controversies, researchers and practitioners have suggested the alternative descriptor *parental alienation behaviors* as a term that is possibly more accurate and less pathologizing compared to parental alienation syndrome (Hands & Warshak, 2011; Levesque, 2012; Walker & Shapiro, 2010) or parental alienation disorder (Houchin et al., 2012).

Parental Alienation and Alienators: Definitions and Characteristics

Recent Definitions

Typically, parental alienation is not a one-time event. Rather, it is an ongoing, complex process that involves at least three family members (two parents or caregivers, plus a child) in which one parent vilifies the other, even subtly, in order to rupture normal family relationships. Thus, parental alienation is supported by a pathogenic triangle among family members. In addition, there appears to be some consensus among scholars that parental alienation involves, at a minimum, some form of brainwashing and possibly some form of emotional, physical, verbal, or sexual abuse by the parent (Reay, 2007). In some cases, one parent alienates children from the other parent by abducting the child. This complicated process may involve other family members and individuals as well. For example, grandparents, extended family members, and nonbiological caregivers may collude with one parent or guardian against another and thereby contribute to and engage in parental alienation behaviors. Nonfamily members such as therapists and lawyers may unknowingly contribute to the processes that underpin parental alienation (Gottlieb, 2012). In addition to creating current individual and family discord, adversity, and trauma, parental alienation can even have a long-lasting impact on multiple generations. Several possible long-term aftereffects, described later in this chapter, have been reported in the literature.

Gordon, Stoffey, and Bottinelli (2008) provided a useful definition of parental alienation syndrome: A childhood disorder caused when an alienating parent methodically and frequently engages in and shares primitive defenses and often meritless claims about one parent with a child. Primitive defenses include brainwashing, coercion, and negative, vicious, and inappropriate comments about one parent of the child; these defenses help maintain a pathological symbiosis between the child and the idealized alienating parent, who attempts to portray him- or herself as all good and the target parent as all bad (Gordon et al., 2008). Warshak (2010) described the parental alienation process as insidious, unhindered, and continuous. Consistent with other scholars, Warshak contended that at some point the parental alienation process becomes "brainwashing" (p. 24).

Characteristics

Typically, the parental alienator—or the persecutor, as defined by the deadly drama triangle (DT; see Chaps. 1 and 2)—possesses identifiable personality types or traits. Three such personality types include ego-driven, hostile, or bullying. Individuals with the first personality type, ego-driven ("egoist"), often cannot compromise and instead see the world through egocentric lenses. Such people believe their ideas are always correct. They do not want to hear other perspectives nor will they empathize with what others feel or explain about their own feelings. As much as one tries to change the egoist, he or she most likely will not change (Marano, 2012).

Those with the second personality type, hostile, typically exude aggression and demonstrate a lack of cooperation. Such individuals use coercion to manipulate and hurt those with less power (Marano, 2012). They typically do not back down, at least not when in front of a group. If someone seeks to moderate the encounter or the interactions, he or she will not be able to change the hostile individual. Someone who marries an abusive person can prevent his or her punishing behavior only by seeking counseling or involving the court system. In such a deadly DT, it even becomes difficult for outsiders to identify who is the alienator and who is the victim parent. The victim, persecutor, and rescuer roles in this deadly DT can change throughout the process of resolving conflicts. In some cases, the individual turns violent, as can sometimes be seen in postdivorce trauma motivated by separation and acting out the deadly DT. Thus, it is essential for clinicians, mental healthcare providers, and other professionals to explore the varying degrees of alienation and whether that alienation leads to violence.

The bully is the third common personality characteristic or type of alienator (see Chap. 5 for more discussion of bullying as a psychopathology). Such an individual enjoys playing the role of persecutor; but when it becomes advantageous, he or she shifts to the role of rescuer. If necessary, the bully may assume the victim role, despite not knowing how to play that role well. The complexity and applicability of the three deadly DT roles and related processes to parental alienation behaviors is clear in the bullying personality scenario. The receiver of the bullying behaviors and tactics is the victim; however, once the real victim finds help, his or her liberator takes on the role of rescuer. Those who support victims may unknowingly encourage victims to remain victims or end up enabling the victims to become persecutors in the deadly DT.

Parental Alienation: A Syndrome or Behavior?

The purpose of this chapter is not to debate the extent to which parental alienation is a syndrome. Whether parental alienation is indeed a syndrome remains a topic of such heated controversy that scholars and researchers on both sides of the debate often refuse to even consider alternate or competing perspectives (see Rand, 2011 for a comprehensive review). To further complicate the discourse, numerous professional disciplines or groups (e.g., mental health and law), in addition to individual families, have informed the debate on whether parental alienation should be viewed as a syndrome or a set of inappropriate behaviors. Some scholars have dismissed parental alienation as junk science or popular psychology, because the behaviors and interactive processes that represent this phenomenon enable the parent (often the mother) to manipulate children to turn against their fathers with erroneous facts and information with the ultimate goal of gaining full custody of the children (Keeshan, 2004). Although, parental alienation can be carried out by both mothers and fathers (Reay, 2007), some of the arguments that divide groups are often gender-focused, portraying the mother as a victim and casting the father as the alienator and in some cases as an abuser of family members. Other arguments that complicate whether parental alienation ought to be considered a syndrome or cluster of overlapping behaviors are related to the fact that many of the complaints or charges put forward by the victim parent are later found to be meritless and manufactured. Significantly, the research and clinical communities have failed to disentangle the link between original propositions about parental alienation, divorce, and parental alienations possible link with sexual abuse in the family system (Gardner, 1987b). More recently, scholars and professionals have recognized that parental alienation may exist without divorce or a history of sexual abuse in the family system. However, the original ideas put forward by Gardner persist irrespective of a lack of empirical support.

Rand (2011) noted that at least two groups have opposed the use of the terms *parental alienation syndrome* and *parental alienation*. The first group includes numerous mental health professionals, researchers, and others working in the area of legal custody, whereas the second group includes advocates for abused women. Among the first group, the developing consensus is that the left-behind parent (i.e., also known as the *victim parent* or *rejected parent*; Walker & Shapiro, 2010) may indeed be guilty of abuse (Garber, 2011). The second group, informed by a feminist perspective, has opposed the way courts have minimized mothers' allegations of sexual abuse by fathers (Rand, 2011). As part of that discussion, substantial criticism has focused on Gardner's (1987b) Sex Abuse Legitimacy Scale formerly used to determine whether fathers were offenders (Rand, 2011).

Currently, however, many agree that various forms of abuse (e.g., emotional, physical, or sexual)—to the extent abuse is happening—are perpetrated by parents of both genders, just as alienators can be of either gender. It is likely that the many will continue to believe that a significant link exists between parental alienation and sexual abuse, until empirical research establishes the validity, scope, and magnitude of this longheld proposition originally put forward by Gardner.

Parental Alienation Behaviors and the Deadly Drama Triangle

The deadly DT (Karpman, 1968, 2009) has implications for parental alienation behaviors. The inescapable fact is that the child is a victim, because he or she is often being victimized by the alienating parent. Thus, it is informative to consider the intersection or overlap between the relationships, roles, and processes of the deadly DT and of parental alienation (L'Abate, 2009; L'Abate, Cusinato, Maino, Colesso, & Scilletta, 2010).

The three deadly DT roles—victim, persecutor, and rescuer—can be seen in parental alienation. L'Abate (2009) described the deadly DT as follows:

> This pathogenic triangle is constituted by three intrinsically and simultaneously connected roles found in most if not all individuals involved in family dysfunctions. In such relationships, all three roles are enacted by self and other parties at the same time, without an awareness of or control over their damaging consequences. Each participating intimate (close, committed, interdependent, and prolonged) plays the victim, and can be perceived as a Persecutor or Rescuer at the same time, depending on who does or says what.

The roles evidenced in the deadly DT, as described by L'Abate, can be seen in and assumed by all members in a family where parental alienation takes place. Although the left-behind parent perceives himself or herself as the victim, the alienator perceives himself or herself as the rescuer who is best able to rescue the children from the other parent, viewed as the persecutor. Yet the left-behind parent also perceives himself or herself as the rescuer who saves the children who have been denied access to him or her. The children find themselves involved in this triangle in all three roles—victims, persecutors, and rescuers—whereas each parent perceives the other parent as the persecutor. The children may see themselves as rescuers of the parental alienator, often a parent with narcissistic personality traits who has taught the children that it is their duty to care for him or her (Rand, 1997).

As mentioned in Chap. 3, parentification may occur when the alienating parent's abuse is at its worst (see Godbout & Parent, 2012). In this parentification scenario, the roles are reversed: The child becomes the alienator's caretaker, and the alienated parent becomes dependent upon the victimized child. Fights ensue in many cases, and the child, adolescent, or even emerging adult sees himself or herself as both victim and rescuer. Nevertheless, when the survivor of alienation addresses the left-behind parent, he or she may act as a persecutor toward this truly victimized parent, who wishes to save the family by reuniting with the children. It is easy to see how each of the individuals involved with parental alienation behaviors cycle through the three deadly DT roles (Karpman, 1968, 2009).

As in other dysfunctional family systems, conflict between the alienator parent and the victim parent exists on a continuum that ranges from simple hurt feelings to ferocious anger, hostility, and disagreement (Garber, 2011; Hartson & Payne, 2006). In this type of family system, adults tend to give their children too much information about private matters. Fidelity and finances should remain out of the conversation when parents interact with children. Parents must take time to consider whether impulsive complaints are really worth the damage done to children caught in the middle of conflict (Hartson & Payne, 2006).

The deadly DT in the context of parental alienation has implications for other people outside the family system. Other people outside the family may also serve in the roles of victims, persecutors, and rescuers: for example, child protective service authorities, lawyers, and mental health professionals who try to intervene on behalf of the children or parents. Later in this chapter, we present several case examples from the clinical and research literature base as well as the print and nonprint media. The link between the deadly DT and parental alienation behaviors can be observed in those case examples.

Parental Alienation Syndrome Research Base

Much research on parental alienation syndrome is based on anecdotal self-reports and is mostly qualitative, although a few quantitative empirical studies have been conducted. The quantitative studies, although useful, are limited by their retrospective nature and sample, composed primarily of college student populations. Likewise, short- and long-term outcome research has been sparse. Nonetheless, recent research has been informative. Researchers have examined the relation between parental alienation syndrome and long-term psychological correlates (Baker & Chambers, 2011; Ben-Ami & Baker, 2012), professionals' views on parental alienation syndrome (Rand, 2011), and the links among parental alienation syndrome and personality characteristics, family typology, and personality disorders (Baker, 2007a; Gordon et al., 2008). This section briefly summarizes these studies.

Hands and Warshak (2011) described the long-term aftereffects evidenced in their sample, composed of 50 undergraduate psychology students. Their study revealed that alienating behaviors occur equally between females and males. However, not all participants who were exposed to alienating parents became alienated children. Of the college students who participated in the survey study, 29 % were from divorced families and reported experiencing alienation that the researchers contended could have been overcome through early intervention. The researchers also observed a higher degree of alienating behavior by divorced parents compared to nondivorced parents, and students who were alienated from one parent reported higher levels of alienating behaviors on the part of their parents. Hands and Warshak questioned to what extent becoming alienated from a parent is a normal reaction to divorce and family adversity rather than an abnormal response.

Baker (2007a) examined the extent to which unique patterns or identifiable characteristics exist among parents when parental alienation is present in families. Results revealed three family patterns among parents where parental alienation is found: (a) narcissistic mothers in divorced families, (b) narcissistic mothers in intact families, and (c) rejecting/abusive alienating parents. In most cases, the custodian was the alienating mother, who was diagnosed with a narcissistic personality disorder, and the father was the targeted or left-behind parent (Baker, 2007a). In the second pattern, in which the family remained intact, the narcissistic mothers made efforts to convince the children that their father was inadequate in many ways, giving the children no opportunity to question misinformation (Baker, 2007a). The similarity between the patterns that emerged in the study sample was the strong emotional bond the child made with the mother (Baker, 2007a). Families who demonstrated the third pattern comprised rejecting and alienating parents, whose abusive behavior ranged from fear to denigration. Baker (2007a) stated:

> One way to understand why the children in these pattern 3 families aligned themselves with their violent alienating parents against the targeted parent is within the context of identification with the aggressor, a psychological defense mechanism whereby individuals (often children) cope with the anxiety associated with feeling or being powerless by taking on the characteristics of the more powerful person—even if that person is aggressive or abusive toward them. (p. 33)

In the context of families who demonstrated the third pattern—that is, rejecting/abusive alienating parents—the parents tended to be diagnosed with narcissistic personality disorder or antisocial personality disorder as well as demonstrating related characteristics, such as deceitfulness and arrogance (Baker, 2007a). Baker also found that alcoholism often coexisted with personality disorders and patterns of parental alienation in these families. Based on these findings, professionals (e.g., mental health providers and lawyers) should explore the presence of personality disorders when working with families clinically and when establishing visitation rights and other court-ordered conditions.

Gordon and colleagues (2008) also considered the personality characteristics of individuals with a history of parental alienation syndrome. They administered the Minnesota Multiple Personality Inventory-2 (MMPI-2) to 158 individuals (76 parental alienation syndrome cases; 82 non-parental alienation syndrome cases) involved in court-ordered custody evaluations. The researchers used the MMPI-2 to determine the presence of primitive defenses in parental alienation syndrome cases and to assess the extent to which personality disorders existed for those individuals seeking custody of their children, compared to a control group of parents. The data were derived from three sets of mother–father pairs that included alienating mothers with father targets, alienating fathers with mother targets, and control mothers with control fathers. They found that alienating mothers and fathers had high MMPI-2 scores (i.e., in the clinical range), whereas control parents had MMPI-2 scores in the normal range. Victim or target parents were more similar to control parents than to alienating parents, whereas alienators had higher clinical range scores. These findings supported Gardner's (1987a) original descriptions of parental alienation syndrome.

Ben-Ami and Baker (2012) examined the long-term psychological aftereffects of parental alienation in childhood. In their study of 118 college students, they operationalized parental alienation as a history of having one parent who tried to undermine the child's relationship with the other parent. Participants were divided into two groups: (a) history of parental alienation in childhood and (b) no history of parental alienation in childhood. The researchers examined differences in psychological wellness, distress, and self-sufficiency based on group membership. Results revealed significant differences based on group membership. As expected, participants who reported a history of parental alienation in childhood reported higher levels of depressive symptoms, lower levels of self-sufficiency, lower levels of self-esteem, and insecure attachment styles, compared to those participants who had no self-reported history of parental alienation. The researchers concluded that parental alienation resulted in noticeable vulnerabilities that differed from those vulnerabilities resulting from divorces where parental alienation coexists (Ben-Ami & Baker, 2012).

In another quantitative study, Baker and Chambers (2011) examined the extent to which undergraduate and graduate students ($N = 133$) could recall 20 unique parental alienation behaviors experienced in childhood. The researchers also assessed the link between history of parental alienation behaviors in childhood and current levels of psychological distress—namely, depression and self-esteem. Of these student participants, 80 % ($n = 106$) recalled experiencing at least one type of parental alienation behavior or tactic in childhood, and 11 % ($n = 15$) reported experiencing 11 or more of the 20 parental alienation behaviors or tactics measured in the study. In addition, the results showed a link between prevalence of parental alienation and time of divorce. Students whose parents divorced before they were 18 years of age reported higher levels of parental alienation behaviors than those students whose parents divorced after the participants turned 18. No relation was found between recall of parental alienation behaviors in childhood and psychological distress in adulthood.

Results from Hands and Warshak's (2011) retrospective survey study provided support for the long-reported link between parental alienating behaviors and families who have experienced divorce. Hands and Warshak surveyed 50 college students to assess their perceptions of parental alienating behaviors. Results revealed higher levels of alienating behavior by divorced parents compared to nondivorced parents. Student-participants reported that mothers and fathers were equally guilty of alienating children, although the occurrence was higher in divorced homes. In addition, not all participants reported deleterious effects, although some participants who were caught in the middle of parental alienation did experience some harmful effects. Although Hands and Warshak's study added to the literature base, it was limited by its use of self-reporting only and by its college-age student sample.

Although theirs was not an empirical study, Johnston and Kelly (2001) established a task force of mental health professionals to examine the psychological and legal issues involving parental alienation syndrome. In response to a range of criticisms of Gardner's theories and descriptions of parental alienation syndrome, the task force developed a model known as the "alienated child," recognizing that a parent who engages in brainwashing techniques and behaviors contributes to a child's alienation from a victim parent. In their systematic review and task force findings, Johnston and Kelly suggested that a reformulation of parental alienation is warranted, because Gardner's formulations focused on the parent. The researchers argued that an alternative and preferred formulation of parental alienation should commence with and focus on the child (Johnston & Kelly, 2001).

Results accumulated from studies conducted by Owusu-Bempah (2007) suggested that knowledge about and contact with the nonresident parent is essential to the psychological health of children in divorced families. Children who lack continuity with the left-behind parent (victim parent) experience social problems. Vilifying the parent who lives apart from the child results in negation of the child's needs and well-being (Owusu-Bempah, 2007). For example, children often wish to spend time with the parent who is separated from the family through divorce or separation, but alienating behaviors make being together more difficult. As much as the child appears to be alienated, he or she "masks an inner world of grief and bewilderment" (Owusu-Bempah, 2007, p. 119):

> Research evidence suggests that when one parent enlists a child in a vendetta against the other, the bond between the child and the other parent can be ruthlessly undermined or destroyed. This is strange in view of attachment theorists' insistence that the tie formed between child and parent endures over time. However, when this happens, it is at considerable emotional and psychological cost to the child and eventually all concerned. (Owusu-Bempah, 2007, p. 119)

Finally, based on her clinical observations, Lowenstein (2006) described 16 specific individual-level outcomes experienced by brainwashed children as a result of alienation:

- Anger
- Loss of control
- Loss of self-confidence
- Separation anxiety
- Fears
- Depression
- Sleep disorders
- Eating disorders
- Academic problems
- Bed-wetting
- Drug abuse
- Obsessive–compulsive behaviors
- Anxiety and panic attacks
- Sexual identity issues
- Poor relationships with peers
- Excessive feelings of guilt

Case Examples: Parental Alienation Behaviors

Several published accounts and historical cases well describe parental alienation (see Connelly, 2009; McGlothin, 2005; White, 2005). As a first example, White, an attorney specializing in parental alienation behaviors, consulted on a case involving a father who had custody of a child. Intent on alienating the child, the father wanted to videotape the child's refusal to visit the mother. However, the father's tactic or maneuver had the opposite of the intended effect. In response, White, as the lawyer in the case, pointed out that the father's alienating behavior evidenced on the videotape could be used against him in court. The mother had moved in with her boyfriend in another state and was able to visit the child only once a month. This distance made it easier for the father to brainwash the child. A therapist recognized the father's brainwashing behaviors, which enabled the mother to obtain custody. White wrote, "The child cried and would not get into the car with the mother. However, I told the father and his attorney that this actually makes the case for the mother's alienation" by the father (p. 100). Although some researchers and practitioners believe cases like this only involve mothers who alienate their children against fathers, the same parental alienation behaviors occur among fathers as well.

Connelly (2009), an author and a former child victim who was alienated, wrote about his own experience in which his father constantly spoke negatively about his mother and eventually abducted Connelly and his brother to live far from their mother in the United States. To entice the boys, the father offered them various gifts. The father's extended family also helped him hide the boys and supported the father's belittling and negative remarks about the mother. Such behaviors are extraordinarily common within the families of parental alienators. It is also not unusual for the parents, extended family, children, and professionals to alternate between the roles evinced in the deadly DT: victim, persecutor, and rescuer. Connelly provides an example of one extended family's victimization and coercion of a child: "Everyone did his or her part letting us know how much a tramp, whore and slut Mother was. She was a bad parent, a drug user from the '60s. She was going to hell one day for every sin she committed on my poor Father. I heard these words daily. Like a mantra or prayer spoken by my father" (p. 32).

McGlothin (2005), another author and former child victim, described having heard a similar alienating discourse. His personal accounts centered on his childhood. He described how he searched for his mother 30 years after an incident of parental kidnapping and alienation in the United States. In perpetrating the alienation, his father absconded with the car in which he was riding. Realizing what was happening, the mother pursued the car on foot, in vain. Ultimately, his father spent decades using parental alienation behaviors to prevent him from missing his mother. McGlothin reported: "I was silent as my heart tumbled to my stomach: Here I am, only a kid; I just learned I have a mother, her name is Angie, and she's demonized. At that moment I knew I would never see my mother. I knew what it meant to be demonized, and it scared me" (p. 5). If a parent uses shame to humiliate a child, the results will likely be destructive and in some cases may be associated with abusiveness across multiple generations. Males may be particularly vulnerable to using violence in the context of their future adult relationships.

The use of shame in McGlothin's case appears to be a consistent aspect of parental alienation behavior and abuse seen in many cases, according to Dutton (2007). Without referencing any specific case, Dutton explained that alienators employ the cruel declaration that the child is unlovable: "Shame is targeted by three sets of actions that attack the global nascent self: public humiliation, random punishment, and direct verbal 'global attacks'" (Dutton, 2007, p. 203). It may be that shaming a child—a male in particular—prompts the transmission of bad behaviors to future generations, thereby enabling those future adults to proceed with parental alienation. Physical punishment combined with verbal abuse represents the most lethal mixture.

Depressive symptomatology including suicidal ideations and attempts seem to be likely among individuals who have been involved in parental alienation. For example, Connelly (2009) described past feelings of unhappiness as a result of his abduction by his father and of his father's alienation tactics: "I truly wanted to end my stupid life. I scanned the house for any object I could use to carry out this need... I understood it now. No matter what I did, it would always turn out wrong. There were little signs I should just die" (p. 206).

McGlothin (2005) expressed similar dismay and his sense of being unloved in response to his abusive father's words: "I felt like I had just been sucker punched and kicked in the stomach. I immediately withdrew" (p. 49). Not long afterward, he withdrew from school, as do many children who have been alienated from a parent. McGlothin posed a question that must run through the minds of many victims of parental alienation: "At times I feel as though my whole life has been stolen from me, wasted on the whim of a cultic fanatic set on being one-up on his ex. How might I be different if I had been allowed to experience the love of a mother as a child?" (p. 199).

Parental Alienation Syndrome, the Law, and International Abduction

The lack of agreement about parental alienation syndrome among legal and mental health professionals has long been reported and is an important consideration for any discussion on the possible implications of parental alienation syndrome (Garber, 2011; Kelly & Johnston, 2001; Rand, 2011). It still remains overwhelmingly difficult for the courts to determine the identity of an abusive parent and to assess whether any abuse has occurred at all. Clearly, perpetrators of alienation and violence against spouses and children are adept at hiding their behaviors; courts—and even therapists—often fail to recognize those actions. Parents and caregivers who are actually engaging in abuse claim that the custodial parent is attempting to turn the children against them. Exposure to abuse puts children at greater risk for later abuse, and in many cases the courts must understand the short- and long-term pernicious effects associated with sending those children to stay with an abuser who lives in a distant location.

According to Bancroft (2002), occasionally a parent who attempts to restrict his or her children from seeing the other parent is not engaging in alienating behavior but in fact seeking to protect the children, thereby acting out the role of rescuer. However, the seemingly protective parent might instead be attempting to alienate the child systematically for his or her own deleterious reasons. The difficulty in determining the veracity of abuse allegations is challenging even for mental health providers. Judging such a case is not easy, despite the fact that the existence of the parental alienator is more common than courts and professionals recognize.

This heated debate continues to create enemies in multiple systems: families, mental health, and the courts. According to Baker (2007a), with many more cases being seen than ever before, the time has come for mental health professionals and lawyers to acquire knowledge about and skill in assessing parental alienation. One might believe that a child's unwillingness to see a parent constitutes healthy self-protection, when in fact significant abuse could be enacted by a parent seeking to alienate the child from the target parent. Through various strategies such as limiting contact, belittling, and withdrawing love, the alienating parent creates the impression that the targeted parent is dangerous, unloving, or unworthy, thereby coaching the child to reject the targeted parent (Baker, 2007a; Baker & Andre, 2008; Baker & Darnall, 2007).

The context in which parental alienation takes place has implications for lawyers and mental health professionals as well. Parental estrangement and alienation have no boundaries. They form a global phenomenon, whose aftereffects can be long-lasting for everyone involved. It may be that parental alienation—coupled with international abduction, described below—remains one of the media's best-kept secrets, because very little coverage has typically been devoted to the process of parental and familial alienation. Mowbray (2003) offered an account of two children named Kevin and Kathleen, who were stolen from their mother and taken across international boundaries:

> Kevin and Kathleen were on an unsupervised visit with their father, a Syrian national living in the U.S., one weekend in 1993, when the father loaded his three- and six-year-old children on a flight bound for Syria. Since she [the mother] had full custody of the children and the father had broken the law kidnapping them—state and federal warrants were issued for his arrest, and he was listed on Interpol—Sarah believed the State Department would help her recover Kevin and Kathleen. But after five years, the State had not even arranged for her to see her children in Syria. The most "help" she received were a few phone calls over the years. (p. 46)

The implication of and evidence for the applicability of the deadly DT in the context of parental alienation behaviors are clear when international abductions take place. L'Abate (2009) pointed out that all legal and judicial interactions related to parental alienation behaviors are based primarily on the deadly DT. As part of the triangle, court personnel are typically the rescuers; the left-behind parent is the victim; the attorneys also serve as rescuers; and the alienating parent (or abducting parent) is the persecutor (L'Abate, 2009). Further, the roles of victim and persecutor may shift between the two parents as the courts or other jurisdictions attempt to determine who the real victim is. In the event the law has been broken by a parent who has, for example, kidnapped a child in violation of court orders, the perpetrator is obviously the persecutor.

In the context of international abductions, parental alienation behaviors are usually well planned. To succeed, the alienator frequently spreads misinformation about the victim parent, an activity that can begin when children are toddlers. For instance, one alienating father reinforced the idea that his children should not pay attention to anything their mother said, particularly when she tried to give them directions. She could not have predicted that he would eventually take them away to

Europe and deny her access for 8 years, even though the children had been born in the United States. What began as a seemingly imperceptible pattern was actually the first step in a long process of alienation that expanded until the children were taken to Europe. Further, their alienation from their mother expanded to include alienation from the rest of their family. In this case, the European courts remained unsympathetic to the mother's efforts to see the children return to their birthplace.

One Spanish mother, characterized as a persecutor, believed she needed to take matters into her own hands after not receiving the financial support she demanded within her marriage. After much planning, this alienating mother took her American-born infant to Spain and accused the left-behind father of being an inadequate financial provider. From her perspective, he was unworthy of retaining access to their daughter. Several years later, she posted her reasons for abducting their child on the Facebook social media platform. The woman noted that the father did not earn enough money and that his earnings were sporadic. She had left the United States despite court orders that sought to prevent her flight, and she absconded with the couple's daughter. The child did not see her biological father for 14 years until the father, bullied psychologically by the Spanish family, risked a trip to Spain. By May 2012, approximately 16 years had passed since the abduction, and the child had neither returned to the States nor met her half-sister. The father, the victim in this case, resided in Texas and received occasional messages from his child via Facebook. He continued to hope that the two would become closer over time.

In another well-known alienation case, Maureen Dabbaugh's daughter Nadia was taken away to Syria on November 3, 1992, by her husband. Dabbaugh tried a variety of means to obtain her daughter's return, including e-mail, Internet, and even a hunger strike (Detrich, 1998). Years later, in her book about her long ordeal, Dabbaugh (2012) wrote, "The child will forever be changed. Parents who abduct their children have little concern for the lifelong, devastating effects. Abducting parents operate under the mistaken belief that because a child is doing well in school, has friends, and appears to be developing normally, nothing is wrong" (p. 136).

Parental alienation has been observed in Japanese courts as well. Japanese courts typically empower one parent in the event of divorce. That parent is usually the Japanese mother; and if one of the parents is not Japanese, that parent often loses access altogether. Indeed, many American, Australian, Irish, and British citizens have lost access to their children after they divorced their Japanese partners or after their children were abducted by an alienating Japanese parent who refused to return the children. In such cases, not only are the children discouraged from speaking English, but also their memories of their left-behind parents may be expunged from their minds, or at least tainted, through incessant badmouthing from the alienating parent who maintains possession of the child.

As one example of alienation in cases involving one Japanese parent, David Morgan's (2012) children were abducted from Ireland and taken to Japan in 2008. He explained:

> My children have been alienated to such an extent that they no longer wish to speak to me. I can only hope that one day they will recall the memories of a caring and fun father that they once knew so well, a father that took them to karate and soccer, showed them how to

fish and loved and continues to love them unconditionally… Next month it will be 4 years since I have been allowed any contact with my children. Someday soon, perhaps my children's mother and her parents will see the sense in allowing Sean and Renee to have their dad back in their lives, or maybe Sean & Renee will see it for themselves.

In a similar case, the children of Matt Wyman, an Australian national, were taken to Japan on holiday and never returned. Wyman characterized Japan as a "black hole" for international abduction. In an attempt to see his children, Wyman moved to Japan, but the children's mother refused to let him see them. In television footage, the oldest child was clearly distressed by Wyman's attempt to gain access through the grandmother. Wyman explained to his own child, caught in the middle of a family argument, that the grandmother did not want him to have access to the child (Brockie, 2012). This provides yet another example of the deadly DT at work on an international scale with the roles of victim, persecutor, and rescuer switching between the child and the elders until it escalated into the courts.

Conclusion

Many valid reasons have been given to explain why children become alienated from a parent. Such alienation occurs in situations of domestic violence and abandonment (Burrill, 2006) and often in situations of divorce (Godbout & Parent, 2012; Hands & Warshak, 2011; Kelly & Johnston, 2001). In other words, a parent may have been responsible for alienating the child against himself or herself. In many cases, however, it has been left to the courts to judge the extent to which the described parental behavior is innocent or deleterious. Alienated children often display various traits described by Burrill, including denigration of the victim parent, a lack of ambivalence, guilt-free cruelty directed toward the victim parent, hostility, efforts to spread their animosity to others, and illogical rationalizations of the behavior (Burrill, 2006, p. 326). Burrill concluded that parental alienation should be considered to be a syndrome, consistent with the propositions originally put forward by Gardner in 1985.

The existence of parental alienation behaviors cannot be denied (Bernet, 2008). Whether or not it is a syndrome, parental alienation is certainly a phenomenon comprising well-planned, deliberate behaviors on the part of a parent who uses children to hurt and demean the other parent. Perhaps one of the worst alienating behaviors occurs when one parent abducts a child from the other parent while denying the victim parent any access to the child. Most people admit the existence of parental alienation and its detrimental effects on the growth of the child. Because parental alienation behaviors constitute an intergenerational phenomenon, more research should focus on how the deadly DT roles and interactions trigger or result in parental alienation behaviors. To aid further research, however, people must be able to speak openly and honestly about parental alienation behaviors without fear of being judged. Whether or not the research and practice communities accept the existence of parental alienation syndrome or parental alienation disorder, few may argue about the existence of parental alienation behaviors and how they are employed systematically by alienators (Bernet, 2008).

The research and clinical communities are a long way from empirically understanding the full, multifactorial nature of parental alienation behaviors. Thus far, the evidence for the phenomenon's existence is primarily anecdotal, supported by only a limited number of empirical studies and influenced by a great deal of emotionality. This shortcoming may be explained by the complexity of the described behavior, where continuously shifting roles are played out without any awareness on the part of the players about the behavior's destructiveness to themselves and their children.

References

American Psychiatric Association. (2000). *Diagnostic and statistical manual of mental health disorders* (4th ed., text rev.). Washington, DC: Author.

Baker, A. J. L. (2007a). *Adult children of parental alienation syndrome*. New York: W. W. Norton.

Baker, A. J. L. (2007b). Knowledge and attitudes about the parental alienation syndrome: A survey of custody evaluators. *American Journal of Family Therapy, 35*(1), 1–19. doi:10.1080/01926180600698368.

Baker, A. J. L., & Andre, K. (2008). Working with alienated children and their parents: Suggestions for sound practices for mental health practitioners. *The Annals of the American Psychotherapy Association, 11*, 10–17.

Baker, A. J. L., & Chambers, J. (2011). Adult recall of childhood exposure to parental conflict: Unpacking the black box of parental alienation. *Journal of Divorce & Remarriage, 52*, 55–76. doi:10.1080/10502556.2011.534396.

Baker, A. J. L., & Darnall, D. (2007). A construct study of the eight symptoms of severe parental alienation syndrome: A survey of parental experiences. *Journal of Divorce and Remarriage, 47*(1), 55–75. doi:10.1300/J087v47n01_04.

Bancroft, L. (2002). *Why does he do that?* (20th ed.). New York: Berkley Publishing Group.

Ben-Ami, N., & Baker, A. (2012). The long-term correlates of childhood exposure to parental alienation on adult self-sufficiency and well-being. *The American Journal of Family Therapy, 40*(2), 169–183. doi:10.1080/01926187.2011.601206.

Bernet, W. (2008). Parental alienation disorder and DSM-V. *The American Journal of Family Therapy, 36*, 349–366. doi:10.1080/01926180802405513.

Brockie, J. (Performer). (2012). Parental abductions [Television series episode]. In A. Llewelyn (Executive producer), *Insight*. Australia: SBS. Retrieved from http://www.sbs.com.au/insight/episode/watchonline/471/Parental-Abductions

Burrill, J. (2006). Reluctance to verify PAS as a legitimate syndrome. In R. Gardner, S. R. Sauber, & D. Lorandos (Eds.), *The international handbook of parental alienation syndrome* (pp. 323–330). Springfield, IL: Charles C. Thomas.

Connelly, K. (2009). *Throwing stones: Parental child abduction through the eyes of the child.* Bloomington, IN: iUniverse.

Dabbaugh, M. (2012). *Parental kidnapping in America: An historical and cultural analysis.* Jefferson, NC: McFarland.

Detrich, A. (1998). *Maureen Dabbaugh: Starving for her daughter's return.* Retrieved from http://www.allandetrich.com/maureenstory.htm

Dutton, D. G. (2007). *The abusive personality* (9th ed.). New York: Guilford Press.

Emery, R. E., Otto, R. K., & O'Donohue, W. T. (2005). A critical assessment of child custody evaluations: Limited science and a flawed system. *Psychological Science in the Public Interest, 6*(1), 1–29. doi:10.1111/j.1529-1006.2005.00020.x.

Garber, B. D. (2011). Parental alienation and the dynamics of the enmeshed parent-child dyad: Adultification, parentification, and infantilization. *Family Court Review, 49,* 322–335. doi:10.1111/j.1744-1617.2011.01374.x.

Gardner, R. A. (1985). Recent trends in divorce and custody litigation. In *Academy forum* (Vol. 29, No. 2, pp. 3–7).

Gardner, R. A. (1987a). *The parental alienation syndrome and the differentiation between fabricatedandgenuine*(10thed.).Cresskill,NJ:CreativeTherapeutics.doi:10.1177/1531244504268711.

Gardner, R. A. (1987b). *Sex abuse legitimacy scale.* Creskill, NJ: Creative Therapeutics.

Gardner, R. A. (1991). Legal and psychotherapeutic approaches to the three types of parental alienation syndrome families: When psychiatry and the law join forces. *Court Review, 28,* 14–21.

Gardner, R. A. (1992). *Parental alienation syndrome.* Cresskill, NJ: Creative Therapeutics.

Gardner, R. A. (2001). Commentary on Kelly and Johnston's "The alienated child: A reformulation of parental alienation syndrome". *Family Court Review, 39,* 611–621.

Godbout, E., & Parent, C. (2012). The life paths and lived experiences of adults who have experienced parental alienation: A retrospective study. *Journal of Divorce & Remarriage, 53,* 34–54. doi:10.1080/10502556.2012.635967.

Gordon, R. M., Stoffey, R., & Bottinelli, J. (2008). MMPI-2 findings of primitive defenses in alienating parents. *The American Journal of Family Therapy, 36*(3), 211–228. doi:10.1080/01926180701643313.

Gottlieb, L. J. (2012). *The parental alienation syndrome: A family therapy and collaborative systems approach to amelioration.* Springfield, IL: Charles C. Thomas.

Hands, A., & Warshak, R. (2011). Parental alienation among college students. *The American Journal of Family Therapy, 39*(5), 431–443. doi:10.1080/01926187.2011.575336.

Hartson, J., & Payne, B. (2006). *Creating effective parenting plans.* Chicago, IL: American Bar Association.

Houchin, T. M., Ranseen, J., Hash, P. A. K., & Bartnicki, D. J. (2012). The parental alienation debate belongs in the courtroom, not in DSM-5. *Journal of Academy Psychiatry Law, 40,* 127–131.

Johnston, J. R., & Kelly, J. B. (2001). Guest editorial notes in special issue: Alienated children in divorce. *Family Court Review, 39*(3), 246–248. doi:10.1111/j.174-1617.2001.tb00608.x.

Karpman, S. B. (1968). Fairy tales and script drama analysis. *Transactional Analysis Bulletin, 7,* 39–43.

Karpman, S. B. (2009). Sex games people play: Intimacy blocks, games, and scripts. *Transactional Analysis Journal, 39,* 103–116.

Keeshan, C. (2004). Divisive theory stirs up custody battles court orders challenges to 'parental alienation syndrome.' *The Daily Herald,* 1.

Kelly, J. B., & Johnston, J. R. (2001). The alienated child: A reformulation of parental alienation syndrome. *Family Court Review, 39,* 249–266. doi:10.1111/j.174-1617.2001.tb00609.x.

L'Abate, L. (2009). An attempt to resurrect a neglected pathogenic model in family therapy theory andpractice.*TheAmericanJournalofFamilyTherapy,37,*1–11.doi:10.1080/01926180701870163.

L'Abate, L., Cusinato, M., Maino, E., Colesso, W., & Scilletta, C. (2010). *Relational competence theory: Research and mental health applications.* New York: Springer.

Levesque, R. J. R. (2012). Parental alienation syndrome. In R. J. R. Levesque (Ed.), *Encyclopedia of adolescence* (Vol. 4, p. 1976). New York: Springer.

Lowenstein, L. F. (2006). The psychological effects and treatment of the parental alienation syndrome. In R. Gardner, S. R. Sauber, & D. Lorandos (Eds.), *The international handbook of parental alienation syndrome* (pp. 292–301). Springfield, IL: Charles C. Thomas.

Marano, H. E. (2012). The high art of handling problem people. *Psychology Today, 45*(3), 53–61.

McGlothin, B. L. (2005). *Have you seen my mother.* Kenner, LA: Taurleo.

Mone, G. J., & Biringen, Z. (2012). Assessing parental alienation: Empirical assessment of college student' recollections of parental alienation during their childhoods. *Journal of Divorce and Remarriage, 53,* 157–177. doi:10.1080/10502556.2012.663265.

Morgan, D. (2012, May 26). Video: Australian TV reports on parental child abduction to Japan [Web log post]. Retrieved from http://seanandrenee.wordpress.com/2012/05/26/video-australian-tv-reports-on-parental-child-abduction-to-japan/

Mowbray, J. (2003). *Dangerous diplomacy* (10th ed.). Washington, DC: Regnery Publishing.

Owusu-Bempah, K. (2007). *Children and separation*. New York: Routledge.

Rand, D. C. (1997). The spectrum of parental alienation syndrome. Part 1. *American Journal of Forensic Psychology, 15*, 23–52.

Rand, D. C. (2011). Parental alienation critics. *American Journal of Family Therapy, 39*, 48–71. doi:10.1080/01926187.2010.533085.

Reay, K. M. (2007). Psychological distress among adult children of divorce who perceive experiencing parental alienation syndrome in earlier years. Dissertation, Capella University, Minneapolis, Minnesota.

Walker, L. E., & Shapiro, D. L. (2010). Parental alienation disorder: Why label children with a mental diagnosis? *Journal of Child Custody, 7*, 266–286. doi:10.1080/15379418.2010.521041.

Warshak, R. A. (2010). *Divorce poison*. New York: Harper Collins.

White, G. J. (2005). *Child custody A to Z*. Lincoln, NE: iUniverse.

Chapter 5
Bullying

Bullying is characterized by aggressive behavior that is carried out repeatedly over time. Typically, bullying takes place in the context of an interpersonal relationship founded on an imbalance of power. This aggressive behavior may be verbal, physical, or relational. Considerable attention has been devoted to understanding the causes and consequences of children who are aggressive (i.e., bullies) as well as the victims of bullies in K-12 school systems. However, bullying in adulthood has been afforded less attention. Specifically, bullying in the workplace and in adult intimate relationships has received scant attention, even though bullying is often reported to take place in these contexts (Gianesini, 2010).

Both youth and adults who bully others tend to have difficulties with relationships, such as those with friends, parents, and colleagues. Many studies indicate that early bullying behavior in childhood is strongly associated with emotional and sometimes physical abuse in intimate relationships in adulthood and that bullying can be transmitted from one generation to another (Jacobson, 1992). The primary focus of the research base has been the dynamic interaction between the bully and the victim in both immediate and more distal contexts, leading to relationship attributes such as dependency and conflict. In addition, research has emphasized empirical examinations of the bully's individual characteristics in conjunction with the multiple social systems in which he or she is embedded.

This chapter addresses the issue of bullying from a relational perspective: hypothesizing that bullying involves a pathologic triangle, constituted by three intrinsically and simultaneously connected roles (i.e., victim, rescuer, and persecutor), which repeat from one relationship to another and from one generation to another. Bullying behavior may be better understood as a dysfunctional interaction, in relationship with others and self (e.g., deadly drama triangle [DT]; Karpman, 1968; L'Abate, 2009), whose dynamics are defined by three positions of victimhood (Forrest, 2008). Empirical investigations that explore dysfunctional and pathological triadic relational processes may offer ideas for sensitive and effective interventions at multiple contextual levels that foster or restore emotional and physical well-being.

L.M. Hooper et al., *Models of Psychopathology: Generational Processes and Relational Roles*, DOI 10.1007/978-1-4614-8081-5_5,
© Springer Science+Business Media New York 2014

Consequently, this chapter considers specific relational and interactive processes that may underpin bullying in both youth and adults.

Bullying Defined

Bullying is recognized as a relationship problem (Pepler et al., 2006). It can be described as comprising behaviors that harm others directly or indirectly through damage or threat to friendship or group inclusion (James et al., 2011). These include manipulation, controlling, belittling, demeaning, rejecting, and exclusionary behaviors in social contexts, as well as damage or threat to one's reputation. Engaging in or experiencing relational aggression may be an unconscious reaction to dynamics in relationships (James et al., 2011), stemming from family background and related to jealousy, malicious gossip, friendship exclusion, inappropriate remarks, feelings of humiliation, fear of rejection, loneliness, and anger (Nishina, Juvonen, & Witkow, 2005). Bullying does not end with adolescence. Bullying can be evidenced in adulthood; it may actually increase in adulthood. More specifically, bullying can be observed in workplace and romantic relationships, and in extreme cases it can lead to domestic abuse or violence (Goldstein, Young, & Boyd, 2008).

Bullying: The Criticality of Power

Like many other forms of violence, bullying is defined in terms of a power differential between victim and perpetrator, but little is known about the dynamics of power assertion by bullies and power abdication by victims (Nation, Vieno, Perkins, & Santinello, 2008). Power, by definition, is relationship dependent. So power inevitably varies across relationships, whereas empowerment is a more stable characteristic developed when individuals are in control of their environment, life, and resources (Perkins & Zimmerman, 1995). In the context of bullying, behavior, power, social rank, and dominance play an important role and can greatly vary by age (Pellegrini & Long, 2002). Popularity, meanness, and power are all forms of expression that facilitate hierarchical behavior within groups. Socially aggressive strategies aim to protect personal status and represent effective tools for achieving one's own needs. For example, disempowered relationships with teachers have consistently been found to predict bullying behavior in school; such relationships have been hypothesized to represent a compensation (bullying) or generalization (victimhood) of power differential (Nation et al., 2008). In peers' interactions as well as in adult relationships, when power inequality replaces mutual exchange, social dominance and bullying become visible (Pellegrini & Long, 2002). Research on social dominance and bullying has supported the idea that bullies do have a power advantage over their victims in their interpersonal relationships. However, consistent with the propositions of some scholars, this chapter (and this book) considers bullying to be rather a power *disadvantage* or power dependency, in peer relationships as well as in adult intimate relationships, that yields bullying behaviors.

Lawler and Yoon (1996), building on Emerson's theory (Emerson, 1972) of power dependence, developed a theory of relational cohesion that predicts when the structure of power, in terms of power dependence, fosters a cohesive relation and commitment. Although Emerson proposed that structural relations of dependency determine behavioral patterns, regardless of intentionality and awareness, Molm (1997) suggested that "coercive exchange provides reward in exchange for the other's withholding of expected punishment and can be used strategically creating contingencies that produce predictable consequences" (p. 113).

Two forms of power are defined structurally: *reward power*, which is based on control over positive outcomes; and *coercive power*, which is based on control over negative outcomes. Forms of coercion are more common among individuals who are disadvantaged in terms of reward power and who lack other means of influencing those on whom they depend for rewards (Molm, 1997). Drawing from theories of structural power and exchange and building on Molm's theory of coercive power in exchange, Gianesini (2000) corroborated the theoretical propositions regarding power and outcomes in her study using National Survey of Family and Households (NSFH) data. Specifically, her study found support for the hypothesis that the initiation of coercive power increases proportionally to the power disadvantage in a relationship. Gianesini found that a situation of power imbalance predicts the presence of violence in a dyad, whereas its direction is determined by the disadvantaged partner. The dynamic of relationships, in terms of power imbalance, was found to be the key factor in understanding the presence of violence, despite and beyond any typification or categorization of the individuals involved (Gianesini, 2000).

Although both explicit factors (e.g., overt submission behaviors) and implicit factors (e.g., greater competence, status, or influence) are involved in bullying, the role of perceived interpersonal power and empowerment in bullying is still unclear (Nation et al., 2008). In any given context, a perceived absence of power is crucial. A context without potential power inhibits personal individual planning and identity, incites feelings of anger, and favors the emergence of interpersonal aggression, mistrust, passivity, inability to construct long-term plans, and aggregation without specific goals. A combination of emotional connectedness (i.e., because anger acts as a form of bonding) and ambivalent and negative belonging (i.e., powerlessness) creates a distancing bond from others as a result of unsatisfied expectations and needs. Feeling powerless denies empowerment, may lead youth to distance themselves from the context, and ultimately results in rage and hopelessness (Arcidiacono, Procentese, & Di Napoli, 2007). A sense of community, place, and social identity contributes to a feeling of community trust that influences the social interaction between individuals, at both the micro and macro levels. Powerlessness is the key issue in understanding relationships, emotional and interpersonal connectedness, environmental and contextual factors, and a sense of belonging.

Bullying: Background Factors, Predictors, and Mediators

Most individuals are involved in a myriad of relationships—with parents, partners, and peers—involving interactions that both influence and are influenced by other individuals' behaviors and interactions (Scholte & van Aken, 2006). Evidence indicates

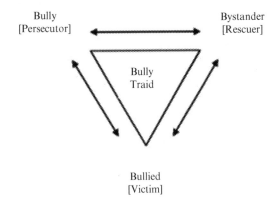

Fig. 5.1 Assimilation of the drama triangle with the bully triangle. Reproduced with permission from "Fairy Tales and Script Drama Analysis," by S. Karpman, 1968, Transactional Analysis Bulletin, 7(26), p. 39–43. Copyright 1968 by Stephen B. Karpman, M.D

(Reproduced with permission from Karpman)

that bullies and their victims often come from families where parenting is inconsistent, sometimes abusive, and often low in warmth (Bowes, Maughan, Caspi, Moffitt, & Arseneault, 2010). In a large sample ($n = 1,735$) of Japanese junior high school students, Komiyama (1986) found that bullying victims and perpetrators alike showed maladjustment in school, a desire for friendships, disagreeable experiences at home, a mother relationship characterized by lack of affection and rejection, low tolerance for frustration, and general lack of discipline. Rican, Klicperova, and Koucka (1993) found in their sample of young adolescents ($n = 168$) that fathers' behaviors were more closely related to active and passive participation in bullying than were mothers' behaviors.

Social desirability, social and interpersonal dominance, interpersonal empathy, depression, self-worth, self-esteem, and self-awareness have been hypothesized as mediators in bullying (Hoover, 2005), whereas family violence is directly and strongly related to bullying. Victimization always occurs in an interpersonal context that includes not only peers but also often parents, teachers, and other adults (Leadbeater & Hoglund, 2006). For example, relational aggression is modeled by parents, peers, and media and is often portrayed as effective (James et al., 2011). The participant role approach (Salmivalli, 1999) proposes that children can not only bully or be a bullying victim but also can also act as reinforcers (encouraging bullying), defenders (trying to stop it), or bystanders (observing without intervening). Coloroso (2005) conceptualized the differing roles of the bully, the bullied, and the bystander as the Bully Triad (see Fig. 5.1), a triangular interaction similar to Karpman's DT (1968) involving the use and misuse of power. These interactions imply the unconscious shifting of emotional role exchange between victim, rescuer, and persecutor, leading to psychological drama. When brought to a conscious level, these dysfunctional roles and interactions emphasize the power and a control issues previously described and raise awareness that may transform the dynamics.

Parental, Sibling, and Family Environment

Family relationships and dynamics, as well as teacher and peer interactions, are more potent predictors of bullying behaviors than are demographic variables such as family structure, social class, or race and ethnicity (Murray-Harvey & Slee, 2010). A productive and effective functioning social system, in the school, work, and family context, has an impact on the social, emotional adjustment of individuals, creating cohesiveness and supportiveness. Low levels of cohesiveness in the family and the presence of powerful and dominant fathers have been linked to bullying (Bowers, Smith, & Binney, 1992). The empirical research has established that parenting practices, style, and models affect children's relational competence and that relationship patterns may lead to bullying (Curtner-Smith, 2000). Moreover, both coercive authoritarian styles and compliant submissive responses have been hypothesized to result from generalized beliefs and strategies about power in relationships (Nation et al., 2008). Aggressive victims (bullied and bullying) often come from families where harsh and abusive discipline is present, whereas passive victims tend to have overprotective and overinvolved parents who undermine their child's assertive ability in peer relationships (Finnegan, Hodges, & Perry, 1998). In a nationally representative sample of 1,116 twin pairs and their families, Bowes et al. (2010) found that maternal and sibling warmth had an environmental effect in protecting children from the negative outcomes associated with bullying, supporting the notion that a positive environment at home promotes hardiness and resilience in the face of bullying.

Menesini, Camodeca, and Nocentini (2010) investigated the role of personality and relational variables in bullying among siblings. Their results highlighted several risk factors related to the sibling subsystem. For example, they found that the presence of an older brother, high conflict in the sibling dyad, low level of empathy in the dyad, high emotional instability, and friendliness all placed individuals at risk for bullying. Findings from their study underscored the need for a multicontextual approach to understanding and preventing bullying.

Other researchers have found that children with more siblings are more likely to bully others (Eslea & Smith, 2000), whereas maternal warmth, sibling warmth, and a positive atmosphere at home are important in promoting emotional and behavioral adjustment following bullying victimization (Bowes et al., 2010). In another study, maternal involvement, including monitoring and close supervision, predicted negatively both the initial value of bullying and its degree of change over time. However, both parent behavior and child behavior reciprocally influence each other, rather than one shaping the other in a unidirectional way (Nickerson, Mele, & Osborne-Oliver, 2010).

Teachers and School Environment

Power disadvantage and disempowerment in teacher–student relationships can be conjectured to contribute to bullying as well. Effective classroom management, students' autonomy, decision-making power, and the quality of teacher–student relationships all not only result in increased academic success (Roland & Galloway, 2002) but also foster students' self-determination and facilitate the creation of a positive environment where reciprocal respect and emotional support is encouraged. Important findings have started to accumulate on the relation between bullying and one's teachers and school environment. More specifically, findings from a study by Nation and colleagues (2008) showed that the factors having the greatest impact on bullying and victimization in school are teacher–student and parent–child relationships, albeit to differing degrees based on the age and gender of the child. The kind of behavior that parents and teachers adopt, with respect to coercive power, decision making, and fairness, may unintentionally promote, validate, or simply tolerate bullying rather than fostering more collaborative decision making and prosocial behavior. Scholars and researchers alike have contended that the role of teachers related to bullying is profound (Rowe & Rowe, 2002). Teachers may play a direct role by perpetrating bullying (Brendgen, Wanner, Vitaro, Bukowski, & Tremblay, 2007) or an indirect role by failing to provide a protective buffer for the victims of bullies. In a study on 4,331 elementary- and middle-school children, Flaspohler, Elfstrom, Vanderzee, Sink, and Birchmeier (2009) found that a positive school climate as well as peer and teacher support might mitigate the impact of bullying on the quality of life of victims.

Supportive and stressful relationships operate as protective or risk factors for bullying and for social, emotional adjustment in general. In a study on students in grades 5 through 9 in 22 South Australian schools, Murray-Harvey and Slee (2010) identified two significant factors for family, peer, and teacher relationships—one for supportive relationships and one for stressful relationships—noting that "support and stress operate independently of each other, despite the expected inverse association between the two, and have the potential to act in different ways to affect outcomes for students" (p. 279). Results in Murray–Harvey and Slee's study showed that supportive relationships have a direct influence on reducing reports of bullying. In addition, stressful relationships were found to have a direct effect on increasing reports of bullying.

Disempowered relationships with both parents and teachers have consistently been found to predict bullying and victimization behaviors (Andreou, 2004) in children and adolescents, confirming the idea that relationship problems are elicited by the power asserted to control the relationship (Schwartz, Dodge, Pettit, & Bates, 1997) and thus could be avoided by adopting a less directive parenting and teaching style. Leadbeater, Hoglund, and Woods (2003) found that classroom levels of emotional problems predict increases in relational and physical victimization, beyond individual differences in emotional and behavioral problems. They also found that a classroom level of social competence interacts with individual levels of emotional problems such that children with higher levels of emotional problems in classes with more socially competent children reported more relational and physical victimization in that study. Spriggs, Iannotti, Nansel, and Haynie (2007) found that parental communication, social isolation, and classmate relationships are similarly related to bullying across ethnic groups, but living with two biological parents protects against bullying involvement only for White American students.

In sum, the classroom context and environment is of particular relevance, because classroom compositions determine to whom children are exposed and with whom they continuously interact, directly or indirectly, over the course of the school year (Leadbeater & Hoglund, 2006). Classroom, playground, school, home, work, and neighborhood cultures vary widely in their level of tolerance for aggression. Thus, victimization can occur or co-occur at multilevel contexts. Undoubtedly, parents' and teachers' understanding of bullying dynamics and recognition of bullying incidents is crucial for subsequent interventions (Sawyer, Mishna, Pepler, & Wiener, 2011).

Bullying and Violence in Intimate Relationships and the Workplace

Within intimate relationships, victimhood or bullying is designed to ensure alienation—not only from others but also from self—because the intensity of the power dynamics and the degree of humiliation, shame, and rage become much greater than with peers as being rejected by a partner has very intense emotional implications. Because genuine intimacy requires vulnerability and honesty, it is incongruent with the roles and interactions evidenced in the drama triangle. Needing to hide unworthiness makes distance imperative; therefore, as long as partners maintain hidden agendas and deny their truth, intimacy is impossible. In adult romantic relationships, gender battles and games exacerbate the drama and anxiety, creating a context for intense emotional implications, humiliation, rejection, despair, and retaliation. Later this chapter presents a case study that illustrates how intergenerational and relational dysfunctional dynamics affect intimate relationships and how the deadly DT model[14] (see Chap. 2) can promote a better understanding of these dynamics in adult relationships and foster therapeutic awareness.

The pathogenic deadly DT comprises three intrinsically and simultaneously connected roles found in most individuals involved in family dysfunction, namely, victim, rescuer, and persecutor (see Fig. 5.1). In such relationships, all three roles in the deadly DT may be enacted by self and other parties at the same time, without awareness of or control over their damaging consequences. Each individual in this triadic relationship plays the roles of victim, rescuer, and persecutor. The reactive quality of this triangle leads individuals to repeat it from one relationship to another and from one generation to another (L'Abate, 2009). Each person involved in the triangle typically has a primary or preferred role, that is, the position at which he or she first "got hooked" on the triangle, the one he or she most likely learned in the family of origin. However, it is possible to rotate through all the positions, going completely around the triangle. The triangle has been referred to as a "shame generator" because, through the process of taking on these roles, individuals unconsciously reenact life themes that create shame and reinforce old, painful beliefs, keeping them stuck in a limited version of reality and therefore in a specific role or roles (see Forrest, 2008).

Finally, although the research is sparse, the same power dynamics that foster bullying in schools and intimate relationships are present in the workplace and within organizations as well (see Branch & Murray, 2008; Giorgi, Ando, Arenas, Shoss, & Leon-Perez, 2013). Branch and Murray (2008) reported a strong link between organizational policies and workplace bullying, which includes harassment, intimidation, and other aggressive and violent behaviors. Branch and Murray suggested that a positive and trustworthy organizational climate depends upon management's ability to address inappropriate behaviors and deal effectively with bullying, especially when the perpetrator is a supervisor.

Case Example

This section synthesizes and applies assessment and treatment recommendations—based on relational competence theory (RCT) and the deadly DT—to a specific case. The client was a 42-year-old divorced woman living in an abusive heterosexual relationship, with no children. She had a full-time job as secretary, was very content with her working conditions, enjoyed the company of friends, and took great pleasure and satisfaction from her hobby, martial arts, which she practiced as junior instructor at the gym owned by her male partner, a 54-year-old body-building trainer with a black belt in a karate. The client was referred to the therapist by a friend who was concerned about her situation, having observed this client try numerous times to end her abusive relationship, all unsuccessfully. Using a mix of stalking behaviors, intimidation, retaliation, and manipulative cries for help, the male partner was always able to win the client back. In the end, after initially accepting his sexual preferences of cross-dressing along with his verbal, physical, and psychological abuse, the client decided to end the relationship after discovering he was having homosexual relationships, including seeing male prostitutes in her apartment. The client's initial concern, in fact, exclusively focused on her sexuality and transgender issues, as she came to doubt her own sexual orientation, was concerned about health issues and her reputation, and just wanted her partner to leave her house. To accomplish her primary aim of getting her partner to leave her house, she offered him money and considered even transferring her property (the apartment) to him.

The client's genogram (see Fig. 5.2) depicts three generations: 25 families, overall comprising 75 individuals. The genogram shows a family difficulty in sustaining positive and lasting intimate relationships with few and superficial contact between generations (i.e., 46 relatives were recalled by their roles not by names and six marriages are childless) and a tendency toward aggressive and abusive behaviors. The client reported the following number (see parentheses) of emotional links among relatives: friendship (2), harmony (2), love (2), manipulation (2), hostility/conflict (7), abuse (2), fusion/violence (2), and cutoff (4). However, in those relationships directly involving the client—harmony (6), cutoff (1), hostility/conflict (1), fusion/violence (1), and abuse (2)—positive relationships outnumbered the negative ones. In particular, the client's reported difficulties with male figures started from the client's conflicts and abusive relationships with both her father and older brother. The genogram clearly illustrates that the family of origin was

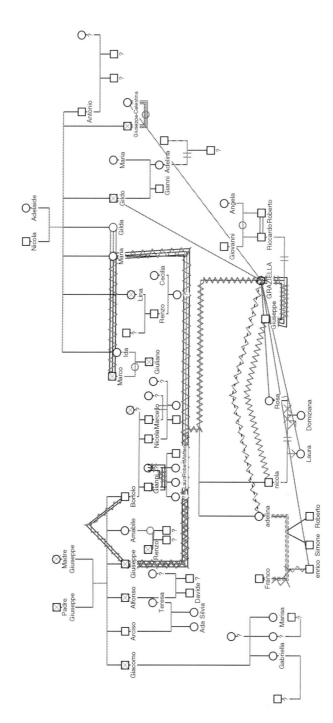

Fig. 5.2 Client's genogram (GenoPro 2007 v.20.0.6)

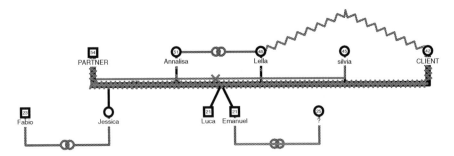

Fig. 5.3 Client's partner genogram for intimate relationships (GenoPro 2007 v.20.0.6)

dysfunctional and characterized by conflict, violence, and abuse. The client defined her relationship with her parents as "painful and disappointing," portrayed by continuous rebellion against the father's punitive authority during childhood and by sexual transgressions during adolescence and adulthood. The client's relationships with all her siblings (all older than her) were also abusive and conflictive, irrespective of the siblings' gender. The connections between the client and her extensive family of origin are distant and superficial.

Intimate Relationships

For this client, marriage at an early age represented the possibility of finally leaving the family. The sharp contrast between the families of origins of the clients two partners—her ex-husband and her current partner—emerged clearly from the genograms. The client's ex-husband, in fact, came from a family where relationships among all members were warm, close, supportive, and positive. The client reported that her ex-husband's relationship with his own brother was especially positive and intense, as she had "never experienced." Nevertheless, the client divorced her husband after 10 years of marriage to enter into a cohabiting, abusive, and sexually promiscuous relationship with her current partner, a 54-year-old man who has been divorced three times and has three children (ages 22, 21, and 21) with different partners (see Fig. 5.3).

The two ex-wives of the client's current partner ended up in a homosexual relationship, raising together the twin children the man had with his second wife. His first daughter and one of his twins have been able to build a stable heterosexual relationship, whereas the third son is a declared homosexual who lives alone. The client's current partner had aggressive and dysfunctional relationships with all his ex-wives, was not involved in the lives of his children, did not honor his economic responsibilities, and deeply involved the client in his financial and relational problems, somehow depending on her for support and care. The client and her male partner cohabited in an apartment owned by the client. They shared a passion for martial arts and also worked together during the evening at the gym owned by him—a martial art instructor.

Psychosocial Functioning

Many different types of loss appear to have impinged upon on the client's current situation. First, the loss of a meaningful, positive relationship with her father appeared to be significant. Her father was never caring or loving; rather he was overcontrolling, punitive, authoritarian, and unaffectionate. This relational model negatively influenced the client's ability to build affective and stable relationships with male partners and consequently led to a positive interpretation and tolerance of abusive, controlling, and violent behaviors. Second, the loss of her family also appeared to affect her current level of functioning. Specifically, the client reported that she never fit in or belonged while growing up, and eventually she was adopted by her maternal aunt. Taken together, these losses, perceived abandonment, abuse, and lack of support and caring all negatively affected the client's self-identity and self-esteem, increased her fears, and played an important role in all her intimate relationships. Moreover, her lack of a positive family model or even any idea of family strongly governed her decision not to have children of her own. However, despite numerous traumas, the client was able to build an alternative support system within her family of origin, at a second- and third-generation level, as well as a network of friends, colleagues, and trainees she could rely on for support and care. She valued relationships and possessed the ability to share joys and hurts and be emotionally available to others—but rarely to herself.

The client was functional in her friendships and relationships in the workplace. In those relationships and settings, she was able to balance her resources in a flexible way. However, in intimate and romantic relationships, she showed a tendency toward inappropriate companions with unrealistic expectations. Raised in a family characterized by negative emotionality and low levels of affection, she tended to hide or bury her emotions and to avoid them. As a consequence, those hidden emotions were often expressed as overt hostility, fear, anger, sorrow, and embarrassment—causing her feelings of deep emotional fragility yet also leading to a disinhibited, risky sexuality and impulsive acting-out that were often destructive. Her hurt feelings especially were always oriented toward the self, showing a tendency to be anxious, unsure, and inadequate: always in doubt and fully responsible for others.

The disequilibrium in the client's ability to set a safe psychological distance in intimate relationships was evidenced by inappropriate and often contradictory approach–avoidance behaviors, that is, seeking emotional and sexual closeness while being afraid of intimacy and psychological proximity. In her romantic relationships, she impulsively repeated the same dysfunctional patterns with little awareness, adopting a relational style that was manipulative, competitive, coactive, and reactive, characterized by continuous and reciprocal conflict and rejection, verbal attacks, physical violence, and other types of abuse. She was attracted to authoritarian, physically strong male figures. In addition, she tended to submit to, comply with, and identify these men as positive role models, while differentiating, opposing, and distancing herself from fragile, feminine female figures, whom she viewed negatively. Of particular relevance was the fact that she entered into a deadly DT with her current partner and his second wife, alternating among the roles of victim, rescuer, and persecutor. This ineffective behavior (i.e., rotating among roles in the deadly DT) was in response to her partner's roles and her own preferred behaviors and roles in reaction to his manipulative narrative or scripts. Nevertheless, she kept functioning adequately in other settings, was able to make courageous and autonomous choices to seek help, and was open to changing her life for the better.

Overall Assessment

Resources

A battery of tests based on RCT (Cusinato & L'Abate, 2011) was administered to the client during a 1-year treatment period. These tests revealed intellectual resources, willpower, and inner strength that in the end, with the support of the therapist, allowed the client to understand the crucial factors in her current abusive relationship and to focus on her own potential. The treatment promoted insight into her difficult childhood history and how it led to numerous unsuccessful and dysfunctional intimate relationships, as well as insight into the deadly DT game she was playing with her current partner and his previous wife.

Relational Competence Assessment

This client scored 38 on the Chabot Emotional Differentiation Scale (CEDS; Licht & Chabot, 2006), indicating a low intrapsychic differentiation. *Intrapsychic differentiation* is the capacity to distinguish between emotional and cognitive functioning, while differentiating on a continuum the automatic, uncontrolled emotional reaction from a controlled, flexible, calm, and independent behavior, guided by the ability to reflect and by principles and values. The client's score of 50 on the Intimacy Anxiety Scale (IAS; Descutner & Thelen, 1991) indicated a high fear of intimacy, which she also experienced in other relationships, although to a lesser degree, as confirmed by a score of 48 on the Anxiety About Transition Scale (AaTS; Marteau & Bekker, 1992). She was not satisfied with her life, as indicated by a score of 33 on the Satisfaction with Life Scale (SLC; Diener, Emmons, Larsen, & Griffin, 1985), and she showed some symptoms of depression, as indicated by a score of 56 on the Center for Epidemiologic Studies Depression Scale (CES-D; Radloff, 1977). However, a score of 66 on the Relational Awareness Scale and her scores on the Relational Answer Questionnaire (RAQ, Cusinato & L'Abate, 2011) in T points (Emotionality = 63; Rationality = 55; Action = 63; Awareness = 47; Context = 50) were adequate and reflected resources that could sustain her recovery and change despite her current and past stressful life events.

The Deadly DT

Identifying the client's starting position or role as victim on the deadly DT helped her recognize the aspects of herself she was denying. When the therapist illustrated

Fig. 5.4 Client's deadly DT:
starting position as victim

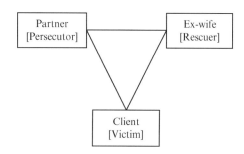

the three roles (i.e., points or positions on the deadly DT) with the client (victim) at the lower point, the current partner (persecutor) on the left point on the triangle, and the partner's ex-wife (rescuer) at the right point on the triangle, the two extremes, or shadow aspects, of the client's victimhood became explicit and clear. While living on or in the triangle, the client—serving in all three roles at times—was expressing her denied or repressed power. Guilt and shame were the driving forces for the perpetuation of the deadly DT. Judging some thought or feeling within herself as unacceptable, the client was unconsciously looking for individuals who had these same traits but at the same time hated them for it. The client's projection onto both her partner and his ex-wife was a propelling force for maintaining the triangle, ensuring continued victimization. All individuals involved were unconsciously repeating and validating their own childhood dramas by projecting their painful beliefs and judgments about themselves onto one another. These sorts of dysfunctional interactions were fostered by gender role confusion and sexual promiscuity.

Victim Role

The role of victim (i.e., shadow child) implies being vulnerable, needy, frail, powerless, and defective. Victims have accepted a definition of themselves as intrinsically damaged and incapable, projecting an attitude of being weak, fragile, or not smart enough. Their greatest fear is not being able to make it. That anxiety forces them to be hypervigilant and searching for someone stronger or more capable to take care of them, which leads to their denial of their problem-solving abilities and their potential for self-generated power. Feeling at the mercy of others, mistreated, intrinsically defective, or just wrong, they see themselves as broken and unfixable. However, this does not prevent them from feeling highly resentful toward those on whom they depend (Forrest, 2008).

The client in this case (as victim) often used guilt in an effort to manipulate her rescuer (partner's ex-wife) into taking care of and feeling sorry for her. In adopting the victim role and maintaining the deadly DT in relation to her male partner, she was confirming to him and herself that she could not make it on her own. She believed she was innately defective, unlovable, incapable, and in need of a rescuer—but simultaneously she was angry at her partner's ex-wife, who was putting her down for her inability to end the relationship with an abusive partner (as the ex-wife successfully did by obtaining a divorce). See Fig. 5.4.

Fig. 5.5 Client's deadly DT:
middle position as rescuer

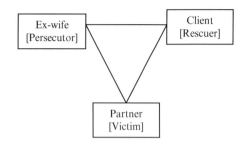

Rescuer Role

The role of rescuer (i.e., shadow mother) can be described as codependent, enabling, and overly protective. This role often develops from an unconscious need to feel valued. Rescuers usually grow up in families where their dependency needs are not acknowledged, in an environment where their needs are negated, so they tend to treat themselves with the same degree of negligence that they experienced as children. Without permission to take care of themselves, they suppress their needs and turn instead to taking care of others, believing their total value comes from how much they do for others, in an attempt to garner validation, feel important, or foster dependency and avoid abandonment (Forrest, 2008).

The client attempted to rescue her partner (victim) from the attacks of his second wife (persecutor), revolving mostly around issues of parental and masculine inadequacy as well as economic worthlessness. As rescuer, the client was reinforcing an unrealistic image of herself as strong while denying her own needs, in the process producing more shame and deeper denial surrounding those needs. When in the roles of caretaker and conflict mediator between her partner and his second ex-wife, the client denied her own power by setting inappropriate boundaries. She occupied the rescuer position, with her natural capacity for organizing as well as her wonderful nurturing ability. However, as rescuer she was denying herself the benefit of these abilities, by refusing to nurture or set priorities for herself and then finding herself obsessed about intervening in the life of her partner's ex-wife in unhealthy ways, taking responsibility for her partner's irresponsible choices and actions. These characteristics are commonly thought of as primarily feminine characteristics, so the rescuer can be seen as a distorted expression of the feminine aspect.

See Fig. 5.5.

Persecutor Role

The role of persecutor (i.e., shadow father) usually involves complete denial about one's blaming tactics. A persecutor argues that attacks are warranted and necessary for self-protection. This is a shame-based role most often taken on by someone who received overt mental or physical abuse during childhood. A persecutor may choose to emulate one or more primary childhood abusers, preferring to identify with those seen as having power and strength to become perpetrators. The persecutor protects

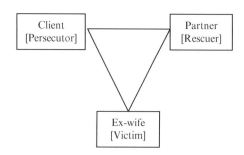

Fig. 5.6 Client's deadly DT: final position as persecutor

himself or herself using authoritarian, controlling, and punishing methods, seeking to overcome feelings of helplessness and shame by overpowering others using manipulation and brute force. Domination becomes the most prevalent style of interaction: bullying, preaching, threatening, stalking, blaming, lecturing, interrogating, and outright attacking. The persecutor always needs someone to blame in an attempt to deny her or her own vulnerability, because the persecutor's greatest fear is powerlessness. Because the persecutor judges and denies his or her own inadequacy, fear, and vulnerability, the persecutor needs some other place to project these disowned feelings, someone perceived as weak, to prove that his or her own destructively painful story about the world is true (Forrest, 2008).

When in the role of persecutor on the triangle, the client believed the world was dangerous and used fear and intimidation as tools to keep the partner's ex-wife in her place. That is, the client felt she was an innocent bystander in a dangerous world where others were always out to hurt her. Her only chance, therefore, was to strike first to survive, thereby keeping herself in perpetual defense–offense status. The persecutor has a deep-seated sense of justice and believes in the use of power and assertiveness, protection, guidance, and boundary setting—all innately positive abilities that are important in self-care. However, a persecutor exercises these abilities in twisted ways: not fully acknowledging and claiming these aspects of self but rather denying them as an unconscious, irresponsible, and distorted expression of the masculine aspect of self. This distortion was especially evident in the case of the client, where the pathologized feminine and masculine characteristics of both partners were confounded with gender and sexuality inadequacies and confusion. Violence—physical and psychological—was interpreted as an appropriate way to express power or as a necessary defense. Simultaneously, as persecutor the client was seeing herself again as only the innocent victim who had to protect herself by retaliating. She justified her hurtful behavior as getting back at her persecutor and suppressed her caring, nurturing qualities, instead solving problems through anger, abuse, and control. See Fig. 5.6.

Relational Competence (RC)-Ecomap

This Ecomap is an assessment tool, suitable for idiographic analysis in the clinic practice and nomothetic analysis in research, for representing and analyzing significant relationships with reference to models of relational competence theory

Table 5.1 Context of resources exchanged in intimate relationship (RC-Ecomap, Ratio of the Log-Linear Parameter Estimate)

Family	Work	Survival	Enjoyment
−7.152	2.695	1.559	**6.827**

Table 5.2 Type of resources exchanged in intimate relationship (RC-Ecomap, Ratio of the Log-Linear Parameter Estimate)

Money	Goods	Info	Services	Importance	Intimacy
−4.527	−5.064	3.047	−1.425	**10.627**	**5.396**

Table 5.3 Ratio between resources given and received in intimate relationship (RC-Ecomap, Ratio of the Log-Linear Parameter Estimate)

Given	Received
−0.047	0.047

(L'Abate, 2010). The map allows for an identification of the contexts of meaningful relationships and the resources exchanged in those relationships. Using RC-Ecomap (Colesso, 2011, 2012; Cusinato & Colesso, 2010), the therapist mapped the client's relationships in four different contexts (family, work, survival, and enjoyment) and investigated the type of resources (money, goods, information, services, sense of importance, and intimacy) she exchanged with intimate others. This mapping allowed the therapist to evaluate the client's relational competence while understanding both the strengths and weaknesses of her current relationships. Not surprisingly, results showed a significant negative investment in family and a significant positive investment in enjoyment, confirming that friends represented for the client an important point of reference, somehow compensating for and substituting family dysfunctional relations. See Table 5.1.

Moreover, the client preferred exchanging resources such as sense of importance and intimacy in relationships with others, further confirming her need for emotional connections and feelings of self-worth. See Table 5.2.

However, looking at the direction of the client's exchanges, the amount given and received is identical (Table 5.3), but the first is significantly negative, indicating that in the end she received more from those relationships than what she invested. Interactions were not significant.

Case Example: Conclusion

As consequence of triangle living, the client was suffering irrespective of her position on the triangle: all three roles led her to emotional, mental, and even physical pain. Efforts to avoid pain, by blaming or looking for someone to take care of her, only ended up generating greater pain and confusion. She became engaged in the deadly DT because of dysfunctional relationships with her parents and siblings and the lack of warmth and affection in her family of origin. She was chasing herself and different reflections and projections of self on others around the triangle, relegating herself to living in reaction to others rather than spontaneously and free through personal choice. She was following the rules and the agendas of others and her own unconscious dysfunctional beliefs. Unhealthy beliefs (scripts) about herself and the world, instilled in childhood, were rigid rules that the client needed to violate.

Given the findings of the comprehensive assessment, several treatment recommendations were indicated. First, it was important that the client talk and share feelings about the repeated sexual abuse she suffered in childhood and early adolescence. Her discounted and unacknowledged feelings became impulsive reactions: inner forces driving her behavior and setting her up for a continuous victim perspective. She grew up without permission to acknowledge or express feelings, for her family had decided early in life that her feelings were unacceptable. She continued to attach belief to painful stories about herself that were generating more negative feelings. Those denied and suppressed emotions became secret pockets of shame within her psyche. They only served to alienate her from others and sentence her to life on the triangle. She was at the mercy of her own misery because she did not know what to do with or about those feelings. Those feelings dissipated once the beliefs behind them were made conscious and addressed. In the end, the client reached greater understanding of herself and no longer had the need to suppress uncomfortable feelings and to escape pain using various avoidance tactics.

The client had engaged in triangulation because of drama, trauma, and painful feelings that were ruling her life, triggering guilt or fear. This circular process was also prompting her to be reactive and to maintain the triangulation process in an attempt to control or get rid of the painful feelings. In the role of rescuer, she was keeping herself from feeling bad and instead feeling better by fixing someone else's problem. This role gave her a false sense of being in control, which felt temporarily empowering. She then came to realize that this increased sense of power came at the expense of the other person in the triangle, thereby further fostering her sense of guilt. The client's denial came out of negative self-judgment; she could not accept her thoughts, behaviors, and feelings because they were too painful and unacceptable. She came to know and accept her personal truth and to recognize the manipulation, hidden agendas, and dishonesty of all players on or in the triangle, including herself, while regaining a sense of personal identity and respect.

When she finally was able to face the truth about herself and the others involved in the triangle and slowly came to recognize the deadly DT roles and dynamics with the support of the therapist, the client rediscovered her abilities and qualities, was able to set up appropriate boundaries, and distanced herself from pain and anger. She then learned to experience a fulfilling life through a conscious willingness to detriangle herself from the roles and the drama. She learned to free herself from the painful beliefs that kept her trapped on the triangle and to handle her uncomfortable feelings, such as guilt, without acting on them, while recognizing that her guilt was a response learned in a dysfunctional family whose dictums—now internalized beliefs—were generating only misery. In the end, she successfully ended the relationship and took legal action against her partner for bullying and stalking. She obtained a restraining order, and the partner was ordered by the court to leave her apartment.

Implications for Bullying Intervention: Practice and Research

Building supportive relationships in all social contexts, using a whole-community approach, represents the key to reducing bullying and creating safer environments not only in schools but also in the workplace as well as intimate relationships. The importance of prosocial behaviors and strategies to create healthy relationships needs to be highlighted (Sawyer et al., 2011). Conflict resolution skills also need to be taught, because some individuals resort to violence when threatened (James et al., 2011). Possible pathways to empowerment are not unidirectional. Increased opportunities to participate in community life—either at school, in the workplace, or at home—are empowering and increase trust in one's own capacities, which creates more opportunities and possible choices. A state of powerlessness, in contrast, facilitates learned helplessness, alienation, and avoidance as well as rage, anger, and decreased social responsibility and participation, while only preserving the status quo (Arcidiacono et al., 2007).

Parent education and teacher training programs may need to focus on developing more supportive and assertive family and classroom environments that foster negotiated cooperative relationships. These generational relationships should be the emphasis of preventive efforts to change both the family environment and the school and classroom environment. Developing strong, supportive parent–child and teacher–student relationships reduces bullying (Murray-Harvey & Slee 2010). However, as all types of power imbalance relationships are related to bullying, preventive interventions need to venture beyond family and school settings to include other normative environments, such as working and intimate relationships. Branch and Murray (2008) found that the impact of workplace bullying and other antisocial behaviors can be reduced by interventions that promote emotional intelligence and interpersonal skills as well as by restorative justice practices within organizations.

Bullying Assessments, Interventions, and Treatment Strategies

Many interventions directed toward ameliorating or reducing bullying have been proposed by researchers from different disciplines; however, their efficacy and effectiveness have not been fully established.

Seminal bullying researcher and scholar, Rigby (2010), proposed six basic intervention foci to inform bullying interventions in schools: (a) traditional disciplinary approach, (b) strengthening the victim, (c) mediation, (d) restorative practice, (e) support group method, and (f) method of shared concern. The *traditional disciplinary approach* recommends clear behavior standards and uses punishment (e.g., detention, loss of privileges, chores to be undertaken, and even suspension) to prevent and deter bullies from repeating their behavior. *Strengthening the victim* helps students to confront a bully assertively, that is, to stand firm and discourage the bullying behavior through calm and controlled language and to redress the balance of perceived power. *Mediation* assists the bully and the victim in resolving their differences and helps them find a peaceful win–win solution or compromise. *Restorative practice* encourages admission of bullying by the perpetrator and attempts to engender genuine remorse, helping the bully take steps to restore damaged relationships. The *support group method* gains the cooperation of the perpetrators by revealing to them the distress that has been experienced by the victim at a meeting in which students supportive of the victim are also present. Finally, Rigby (2010) suggested that the *method of shared concern* empowers the bully to assist in resolving the bully/victim problem through the use of individual and group meetings with the participants.

In addition to interventions focused on the individuals directly involved in bullying, valuable work on the role that bystanders play in the context of bullying has been reported by Salmivalli (1999, 2000), Pepler and Craig (2008, 2009), and Rigby and colleagues (Bauman, Rigby, & Hoppa, 2008; Rigby, & Bauman, 2010). Toward this end, Rigby and Bauman (2007) specifically addressed the issue of bystander-focused interventions (i.e., the third component of the victim, persecutor, and rescuer triangle reviewed earlier) given that school bullying may be reduced by prompting students who observe bullying to act in such a way as to discourage it.

Research has found that school bullies often glory in the presence of an audience, which provides then a theater. The watchers, in fact, either enjoy the spectacle or watch the bullying process in a disengaged manner (Rigby & Johnson, 2008). Bystanders good intentions, ranging from simple moral justifications to the desire for reciprocal benefit to feelings of empathy or close identification with the victim, can be used to help stop bullying by catalyzing discussions about bullying and rehearsing what they might say when they see bullying taking place.

Improving the tendency to support victims in bullying situations can be achieved through direct prosocial and behavioral interventions (active discouraging) or watching without joining in (passive discouraging). Moreover, as helping someone in a potentially difficult or dangerous situation requires a degree of confidence in one's ability to affect outcomes in a positive way, students' and teachers' self-efficacy can also be raised through specific training programs (Howard, Horne, & Joliff, 2001). Finally, as the most effective influence on children's bystander behavior is their friends' expectations, intervening on positive peer influence may reduce or ameliorate bullying. Although much more research is still needed in this area, bystander-focused interventions appear to be a promising strategy because most bullying takes place when bystanders are present, and when bystanders take action there is a high chance that the bullying will be reduced.

In order to establish the extent to which successful, efficacious, and effective bullying interventions exist, the measurement of the bullying processes in addition to the associated outcomes needs to be assessed critically. There are several measures that have been described in the literature that may be useful when attempting to better understand bullying behaviors and outcomes. Rigby and his colleagues have made numerous contributions to the literature on the development, validation, and refinement of bullying measures. Rigby and his colleagues have developed some of the most widely used self-report questionnaires: (a) *Peer Relations Assessment Questionnaire-Revised* (PRAQ-R; Rigby, 1997), (b) the http://www.

kenrigby.net/The%20Bullying%20Prevalence%20Questionnaire.pdf (BPQ; Rigby & Slee, 1993), (c) the http://www.kenrigby.net/Revised%20Pro-Victim.pdf (RPVS; Rigby & Slee, 1999), (d) the http://www.kenrigby.net/The%20Handling%20 Bullying%20Questionnaire.pdf (HBQ; Bauman et al., Bauman et al., 2008), and (e) the *Peer Relations Questionnaire* (PRQ; Rigby & Slee, 1995a,1995b). Different than some of the self-report measures mentioned above, the PRAQ-R (also mentioned above) was developed so that data could be derived from multiple informants.

An additional option that may inform assessment, treatment, and intervention strategies is the proposed bullying workbook (see Appendix E) derived from different sources in diverse countries around the world (Smith, Cowie, Olafsson, & Liefooghe, 2002) , in conjunction with L'Abate's deadly DT's framework (L'Abate, 2009) proposed in this book. The workbook is based on Rigby and colleagues' Bullying Questionnaires (see Rigby, 1997; Rigby & Slee, 1993, 1995a, 1995b) and glossary including various terms that refer to different categories of direct and indirect interpersonal aggression, imbalance of power, repetition, and frequency. The workbook is proposed as a comprehensive self-help intervention for education and training with individuals who present as victims, persecutors, and rescuers.

Conclusion

Bullying is a complex social phenomenon (Sawyer et al., 2011) that requires interventions at different levels to target improving the social climate at home, school, and workplace and to provide ways to encourage positive alternatives to negative power struggles (Bordon, Tessarolo, & Gianesini, 2011). Bullying needs to be understood and depicted as a triangle of power dynamics, a destructive deadly DT (L'Abate, 2009), rather than glorified, modeled, and otherwise ignored by adults. Within an ecological framework, bullying dynamics in a school setting are seen to extend beyond the children to include peers, teachers, the school, community, and parents (Sawyer et al., 2011). Research has mostly centered on the role of adults involved in children's lives, or the perspective of teachers, rather than the adults' direct involvement and responsibility. Family characteristics such as attachment and parenting styles (Gianesini, 2011) as well as parental behaviors may either contribute to bullying or moderate its impact, but the way in which key adult figures like teachers understand, recognize, and respond to bullying are critical factors to consider as well. Bullying behavior has its origin in parenting as well as in the school environment, and different developmental pathways to bullying and victimization have been put forward (Smith & Myron-Wilson, 1998).

Many theories and empirical research have provided valuable insight into the developmental aspect of bullying behavior. However, very few (Nation et al., 2008) have investigated the parallel processes of generational and relational power disadvantage that both youth and adults share in their relationships with parents, peers, teachers, colleagues, and significant others in family, school, social, and work settings. This lack of power can indeed manifest bullying behaviors across all relationship types and at different developmental stages, although it remains an indicator of a delay in psychosocial development and of difficulties in engaging in cooperative problem solving and decision making with others in relationships.

References

Andreou, E. (2004). Bully/victim problems and their association with Machiavellianism and self-efficacy in Greek primary school children. *British Journal of Educational Psychology, 74,* 297–309. doi:10.1348/000709904773839897.

Arcidiacono, C., Procentese, F., & Di Napoli, I. (2007). Youth, community belonging, planning and power. *Journal of Community & Applied Social Psychology, 17,* 280–295. doi:10.1002/casp.935.

Bauman, S., Rigby, K., & Hoppa, K. (2008). US teachers' and school counsellors' strategies for handling school bullying incidents. *Educational Psychology, 28,* 837–856.

Bordon, E., Tessarolo, M., & Gianesini, G. (2011). *The paradigms of a constructed reality: An overview of bullying through Italian newspapers.* In: 69th Annual International Council of Psychologists Conference, Washington, DC.

Bowers, L., Smith, P. K., & Binney, V. (1992). Cohesion and power in the families of children involved in bully/victim problems at school. *Journal of Family Therapy, 14,* 371–387. doi:10.1046/j.1992.00467.x.

Bowes, L., Maughan, B., Caspi, A., Moffitt, T. E., & Arseneault, L. (2010). Families promote emotional and behavioural resilience to bullying: Evidence of an environmental effect. *Journal of Child Psychology and Psychiatry, 51,* 809–817. doi:10.1111/j.1469-7610.2010.02216.x.

Branch, S., & Murray, J. (2008). *Building relationships and resilience in the workplace: Construction of a workplace bullying training program.* Paper presented at the Australia and New Zealand Academy of Management 22nd ANZAM Conference: Managing in the Pacific Century, University of Auckland, New Zealand.

Brendgen, M., Wanner, B., Vitaro, F., Bukowski, W. M., & Tremblay, R. E. (2007). Verbal abuse by the teacher during childhood and academic, behavioral, and emotional adjustment in young adulthood. *Journal of Educational Psychology, 99,* 26–38. doi:10.1037/0022-0663.99.1.26.

Colesso, W. (2011). *RC-Ecomap: A valid and reliable tool to assess intimate relationships.* Dissertation, University of Padua.

Colesso, W. (2012). Updating the RC-EcoMap: A multi-model, theory-derived instrument. In M. Cusinato & L. L'Abate (Eds.), *Advances in relational competence theory: With special attention to alexithymia.* New York: Nova Science.

Coloroso, B. (2005). A bully's bystanders are never innocent. *Educational Digest, 70*(8), 49–51.

Curtner-Smith, M. E. (2000). Mechanisms by which family processes contribute to school-age boys' bullying. *Child Study Journal, 30,* 169–186.

Cusinato, M., & Colesso, W. (2010). Studio delle relazioni significative con RC-Ecomap nella ricerca psicosociale [Study of significant relationships using RC-Ecomap in psychosocial research]. *Psicologia Sociale, 3,* 471–492. doi:10.1482/33188.

Cusinato, M., & L'Abate, L. (2011). *Advances in relational competence theory: With special attention to alexithymia.* New York: Nova Science.

Descutner, C. L., & Thelen, M. H. (1991). Development and validation of a fear-of- intimacy scale. *Psychological Assessment, 3*(2), 218–225.

Diener, E., Emmons, R. A., Larsen, R. J., & Griffin, S. (1985). The satisfaction with life scale. *Journal of Personality Assessment, 49,* 71–75.

Emerson, R. M. (1972). Exchange theory: Part 1. A psychological basis for social exchange. In J. Berger, M. Zelditch, & B. Anderson (Eds.), *Sociological theories in progress* (Vol. 2, pp. 38–57). Boston, MA: Houghton-Mifflin.

Eslea, M., & Smith, P. K. (2000). Pupil and parent attitudes towards bullying in primary schools. *European Journal of Psychology of Education, 15*, 207–219. doi:10.1007/BF03173175.

Finnegan, R. A., Hodges, E. V. E., & Perry, D. G. (1998). Victimization by peers: Associations with children's reports of mother-child interaction. *Journal of Personality and Social Psychology, 75*, 1076–1086. doi:10.1037/0022-3514.75.4.1076.

Flaspohler, P. D., Elfstrom, J. L., Vanderzee, K. L., Sink, H. E., & Birchmeier, Z. (2009). Stand by me: The effects of peer and teacher support in mitigating the impact of bullying on quality of life. *Psychology in the Schools, 46*, 636–649. doi:10.1002/pits.20404.

Forrest, L. (2008, June 26). The three faces of victim: An overview of the drama triangle. Retrieved from http://www.lynneforrest.com/html/the-faces-of-victim

Gianesini, G. (2000). *A multivariate approach to the dynamic of violence within intimate relationships: An application of theory of coercive power in exchange*. Unpublished master's thesis, University of Central Florida, Orlando, FL.

Gianesini, G. (2010). *Building relationships in the workplace. Organizational culture and psychological health*. Germany: VDM Verlag.

Gianesini, G. (2011). Alexithymia dimensions and perceived emotional parenting styles. In M. Cusinato & L. L'Abate (Eds.), *Advances in relational competence theory: With special attention to alexithymia*. New York: NOVA.

Giorgi, G., Ando, M., Arenas, A., Shoss, M. K., & Leon-Perez, J. M. (2013). Exploring personal and organizational determinants of workplace bullying and its prevalence in a Japanese sample. *Psychology of Violence*. Advance online publication. doi:10.1037/a0028049

Goldstein, S. E., Young, A., & Boyd, C. (2008). Relational aggression at school: Associations with school safety and social climate. *Journal of Youth and Adolescence, 37*, 641–654. doi:10.1007/s10964-007-9192-4.

Hoover, R. L. (2005). *A methodological study of family and personality variables associated with discrimination and bullying*. Dissertation, University of Cincinnati.

Howard, N. M., Horne, A. H., & Jolliff, D. (2001). Self-efficacy in a new training model for the prevention of bullying in schools. *Journal of Emotional Abuse, 2*, 181–191.

Jacobson, N. S. (1992). Behavioral couple therapy: A new beginning. *Behavior Therapy, 23*, 493–506. doi:10.1016/S0005-7894(05)80218-7.

James, D., Flynn, A., Lawlor, M., Courtney, P., Murphy, N., & Henry, B. (2011). A friend in deed? Can adolescent girls be taught to understand relational bullying? *Child Abuse Review, 20*, 439–454. doi:10.1002/car.1120.

Karpman, S. (1968). Fairy tales and script drama analysis. *Transactional Analysis Bulletin, 7*(26), 39–43.

Komiyama, K. (1986). A study of the background factors related to bullying among junior high school students. *Reports of the National Research Institute of Police Science, 27*, 38–53.

L'Abate, L. (2009). The drama triangle: An attempt to resurrect a neglected pathogenic model in family therapy theory and practice. *The American Journal of Family Therapy, 37*, 1–11. doi:10.1080/01926180701870163.

L'Abate, L. (2010). *Relational competence theory: Research and mental health applications*. New York: Springer.

Lawler, E. J., & Yoon, J. (1996). Commitment in exchange relations: Test of a theory of relational cohesion. *American Sociological Review, 61*, 89–108. doi:10.2307/2096408.

Leadbeater, B., & Hoglund, W. (2006). Changing the social contexts of peer victimization. *Journal of the Canadian Academy of Child and Adolescent Psychiatry, 15*, 21–26.

Leadbeater, B., Hoglund, W., & Woods, T. (2003). Changing contexts? The effects of a primary prevention program on classroom levels of peer relational and physical victimization. *Journal of Community Psychology, 31*, 397–418. doi:10.1002/jcop.10057.

Licht, C., & Chabot, D. (2006). The Chabot emotional differentiation scale: A theoretically and psychometrically sound instrument for measuring Bowen's aspect of differentiation. *Journal of Marital and Family Therapy, 31*, 167–180.

Marteau, T., & Bekker, H. (1992). The development of a six-item short-form of the state scale of the Spielberger State-Trait Anxiety Inventory (STAI). *British Journal of Clinical Psychology, 31*, 301–306.

Menesini, E., Camodeca, M., & Nocentini, A. (2010). Bullying among siblings: The role of personality and relational variables. *British Journal of Developmental Psychology, 28*, 921–939. doi:10.1348/026151009X479402.

Molm, L. D. (1997). Risk and power use: Constraints on the use of coercion in exchange. *American Sociological Review, 62*, 113–133. doi:10.2307/2657455.

Murray-Harvey, R., & Slee, P. T. (2010). School and home relationships and their impact on school bullying. *School Psychology International, 31*, 271–295. doi:10.1177/0143034310366206.

Nation, M., Vieno, A., Perkins, D. D., & Santinello, M. (2008). Bullying in school and adolescent sense of empowerment: An analysis of relationships with parents, friends, and teachers. *Journal of Community and Applied Social Psychology, 18*, 211–232. doi:10.1002/casp.921.

Nickerson, A. B., Mele, D., & Osborne-Oliver, K. M. (2010). Parent-child relationships and bullying. In S. R. Jimerson, S. M. Swearer, & D. L. Espelage (Eds.), *Handbook of bullying in schools: An international perspective* (pp. 187–197). New York: Routledge.

Nishina, A., Juvonen, J., & Witkow, M. R. (2005). Sticks and stones may break my bones, but names will make me feel sick: The psychosocial, somatic, and scholastic consequences of peer harassment. *Journal of Clinical Child and Adolescent Psychology, 34*, 37–48. doi:10.1207/s15374424jccp3401_4.

Pellegrini, A. D., & Long, J. D. (2002). A longitudinal study of bullying, dominance, and victimization during the transition from primary school through secondary school. *British Journal of Developmental Psychology, 20*, 259–280. doi:10.1348/026151002166442.

Pepler, D., & Craig, W. (Eds.). (2008). *Understanding and addressing bullying: An international perspective*. Bloomington, IN: AuthorHouse.

Pepler, D., & Craig, W. (2009). Peer dynamics in bullying: Considerations for social architecture in schools. In J. Lupart & A. McKeogh (Eds.), *Building capacity for diversity in Canadian schools* (pp. 285–303). Markham: Fitzhenry & Whiteside.

Pepler, D. J., Craig, W. M., Connolly, J. A., Yuile, A., McMaster, L., & Jiang, D. (2006). A developmental perspective on bullying. *Aggressive Behavior, 32*, 376–384. doi:10.1002/ab.20136.

Perkins, D. D., & Zimmerman, M. A. (1995). Empowerment theory, research, and application. *American Journal of Community Psychology, 23*, 569–579. doi:10.1007/BF02506982.

Radloff, L. S. (1977). The CES-D scale: A self report depression scale for research in the general population. *Applied Psychological Measurement, 1*, 385–401.

Rican, P., Klicperova, M., & Koucka, T. (1993). Families of bullies and their victims: A children's view. *Studia Psychologica, 35*, 261–265.

Rigby, K. (1997). *The Peer Relations Assessment Questionnaires (PRAQ)*. Point Lonsdale, VIC: The Professional Reading Guide.

Rigby, K. (2010). *Bullying interventions in schools: Six basic approaches*. Camberwell, VIC: Australian Council for Educational Research.

Rigby, K., & Bauman, S. (2007). What teachers think should be done about cases of bullying. *Professional Educator, 6*, 6.

Rigby, K., & Bauman, S. (2010). How school personnel tackle cases of bullying: A critical examination. In S. Jimerson, S. Swearer, & D. Espelage (Eds.), *The international handbook of school bullying* (pp. 455–468). New York: Routledge.

Rigby, L., & Johnson, B. (2008). Playground Heroes. *Greater Good Magazine*. Retrieved from http://www.kenrigby.net/playground-hero.pdf

Rigby, K., & Slee, P. T. (1993). Dimensions of interpersonal relation among Australian children and implications for psychological well-being. *Journal of Social Psychology, 133*, 33–42.

Rigby, K., & Slee, P. T. (1995a). *Manual for the Peer Relations Questionnaire (PRQ)*. Underdale: University of South Australia.

Rigby, K., & Slee, P. T. (1995b). *The Peer Relations Questionnaire*. Underdale: University of South Australia.

Rigby, K., & Slee, P. T. (1999). The pro-victim scale. In S. Sharp (Ed.), *Bullying behavior in schools* (pp. 31–33). Windsor, Berkshire: NFER-NELSON.

Roland, E., & Galloway, D. (2002). Classroom influences on bullying. *Educational Research, 44*, 299–312. doi:10.1080/0013188022000031597.

Rowe, K. J., & Rowe, K. S. (2002). What matters most: Evidence-based findings of key factors affecting the educational experiences and outcomes for girls and boys throughout their primary and secondary schooling. *eNews*. Retrieved from http://www.acer.edu.au/enews/2002/05

Salmivalli, C. (1999). Participant role approach to school bullying: Implications for interventions. *Journal of Adolescence, 22*, 453–459. doi:10.1006/jado.1999.0239.

Salmivalli, C. (2000). Bullying and the peer group: A review. *Aggression and Violent Behavior, 15*, 112–120.

Sawyer, J.-L., Mishna, F., Pepler, D., & Wiener, J. (2011). The missing voice: Parents' perspectives of bullying. *Children and Youth Services Review, 33*, 1795–1803. doi:10.1016/j.childyouth.2011.05.010.

Scholte, R. H., & van Aken, M. A. G. (2006). Peer relations in adolescence. In S. Jackson (Ed.), *Handbook of adolescent development* (pp. 175–199). New York: Psychology Press.

Schwartz, D., Dodge, K. A., Pettit, G. S., & Bates, J. E. (1997). The early socialization of aggressive victims of bullying. *Child Development, 68*, 665–675. doi:10.1111/j.1467-8624.1997.tb04228.x.

Smith, P. K., Cowie, H., Olafsson, R., & Liefooghe, A. (2002). Definitions of bullying: a comparison of terms used, and age and sex differences, in a 14-country international comparison. *Child Development, 73*, 1119–1133.

Smith, P. K., & Myron-Wilson, R. (1998). Parenting and school bullying. *Journal of Clinical and Child Psychology and Psychiatry, 3*, 405–417. doi:10.1177/1359104598033006.

Spriggs, A. L., Iannotti, R. J., Nansel, T. R., & Haynie, D. L. (2007). Adolescent bullying involvement and perceived family, peer and school relations: Commonalities and differences across race/ethnicity. *Journal of Adolescent Health, 41*, 283–293. doi:10.1016/j.jadohealth.2007.04.009.

Chapter 6
Stockholm Syndrome

Stockholm syndrome is defined as the bonding and role reversal that often occurs in the context of captor–hostage entrapment. The term was first introduced following a bank robbery that took place in Stockholm, Sweden, in 1973, in which four bank tellers were held captive for 6 days. The term was primarily used to describe the phenomenon of "reciprocal feelings of attachment" that developed between captor and hostages during the six-day ordeal (Ochberg, 2006, p. 145). More specifically, Ochberg's (2006) definition described (a) a victim's expression of positive affect toward his or her captor, which are reciprocated by the captor, and (b) the victim's expression of negative affect toward would-be rescuers. A victim's paradoxical expression of sympathy or protection for the captor characterizes a shift in role—from that of victim to one of rescuer of the perpetrator—whereas rescuers are repositioned as potential victimizers.

Numerous theoretical explanations for this type of bonding and role reversal have been offered (Jameson, 2010). Missing are explanations grounded in systems theory that (a) integrate both intrapersonal phenomena and interpersonal dynamics and (b) move beyond dyadic understandings to include "thirdness" (Raggatt, 2010, p. 400). This chapter therefore proposes a systemic account of the bonding and role reversal inherent in situations of traumatic entrapment—an account grounded in relational competence theory (RCT; L'Abate, Cusinato, Maino, Colesso, & Scilletta, 2010). This chapter integrates explanatory threads in the existing literature on Stockholm syndrome with the RCT constructs of distance and temporal regulation, as well as their representation in self-identity processes and interpersonal styles (Cusinato & L'Abate, 2008a, 2008b; L'Abate, 1983; L'Abate et al., 2010) and the deadly drama triangle (DT; Karpman, 1968, 2009; L'Abate, 2009; L'Abate et al., 2010).

Research and Conceptual Background

High-profile cases with significant media coverage often draw attention to Stockholm syndrome (Namnyak et al., 2008), and this includes the more recent case involving Jaycee Lee Dugard (Alleyne, 2009; Fitzpatrick, 2009). Yet little attention

L.M. Hooper et al., *Models of Psychopathology: Generational Processes and Relational Roles*, DOI 10.1007/978-1-4614-8081-5_6,
© Springer Science+Business Media New York 2014

over the years has been given to the empirical study of Stockholm syndrome (Namnyak et al., 2008). In addition, Jameson (2010) argued that Stockholm syndrome "has little basis in contemporary authorized psychological knowledge" (p. 339), and Namnyak and colleagues noted that Stockholm syndrome does not exist in any of the formal diagnostic classification systems, such as the *Diagnostic and Statistical Manual of Mental Disorders* (*DSM-IV-TR*; American Psychiatric Association [APA], 2000). Nevertheless, what little empirical research that does exist has generally supported academic theoretical depictions of the phenomenon (e.g., Auerbach, Kiesler, Strentz, Schmidt, & Serio, 1994; Graham et al., 1995), and findings have confirmed the presence of Stockholm syndrome in some hostages post-captivity (e.g., Favaro, Degortes, Colombo, & Santonastaso, 2000; Speckhard, Tarabrina, Krasnov, & Mufel, 2005a, 2005b; Wesselius & DeSarno, 1983).

Furthermore, the bonding and role reversal that are characteristic of kidnapping or hostage situations have been extended to situations involving child maltreatment (Goddard & Stanley, 1994; Jülich, 2005) and intimate partner violence (Graham et al., 1995; Grigsby & Hartman, 1997). Graham and colleagues posited four conditions thought to create a context conducive to the bonding and role reversal characteristic of Stockholm syndrome: (a) the victim's perception of a threat to survival, (b) the victim's perception of kindness from the perpetrator, (c) isolation from would-be rescuers, and (d) the victim's perception of an inability to escape. Stockholm syndrome has therefore received academic attention as symptomatology associated with various forms of traumatic entrapment and posttraumatic stress disorders (Cantor & Price, 2007; Graham et al., 1995; Pearn, 2000).

Interviewing victims is a common method of identifying Stockholm syndrome (Jameson, 2010), but Graham et al. (1995) also developed a 49-item self-report scale to assess for Stockholm syndrome. Graham et al. found evidence of a three-factor structure for Stockholm syndrome consisting of (a) core Stockholm syndrome, (b) psychological damage, and (c) love dependence. The first factor, core Stockholm syndrome, is defined by cognitive distortions such as self-blame and denial of the abuse; the second factor, psychological damage, is defined by scale items that assess self-esteem, depression, and loss of self. The third factor on Graham et al.'s scale, love dependence, consists of items such as "I am extremely attached to my partner" and "Without my partner, I have nothing to live for." As part of their construct validation of the Stockholm syndrome scale in samples of female college students, Graham et al. found that increased Stockholm syndrome scale scores correspond to increased scores on measures of psychological violence, physical violence, borderline personality disorder symptomatology, and psychological distress.

Auerbach et al. (1994) studied Stockholm syndrome by exploring participants' experiences of a simulated captor–hostage situation. The researchers found that better hostage adjustment occurs when hostages view the terrorist as friendly and less dominant and when the captor views the hostages as friendly. Auerbach et al. suggested that the findings supported a hypothesized transactional mechanism for Stockholm syndrome. That is, when more reciprocity is experienced along the control dimension of interpersonal behavior, and when more correspondence occurs along the affiliation dimension, persons under conditions of traumatic entrapment show better adjustment. Auerbach et al. also found that hostages who receive training in emotion-focused coping strategies, and specifically avoidant strategies, show more favorable adjustment than those who receive problem-focused coping training (see also Strentz & Auerbach, 1988). Auerbach et al. defined *emotion-focused coping* as emphasizing "detachment from the stressor while focusing on feelings inconsistent with stress," and they defined *problem-focused coping* as directing "attention outside self and use of active/assertive behavior" designed to change the circumstances, including the captor (p. 210).

Research with actual kidnapping victims has demonstrated an association between Stockholm syndrome and the length of time in captivity (Favaro et al., 2000). Favaro et al. found that an increased number of humiliating or depriving experiences is associated with evidence of Stockholm syndrome among victims. Furthermore, half of the victims ($n = 12$) in Favaro et al.'s sample developed a positive bond with their captors (Favaro et al., 2000), whereas Speckhard et al. (2005a) found evidence of Stockholm syndrome in 91 % ($n = 10$) of their sample of hostage victims.

Prominent Theories of Stockholm Syndrome

Two of the more prominent theoretical explanations for the bonding and role reversal that occur under conditions of traumatic entrapment include (a) neurobiological explanations that ground the bonding in evolutionary brain development and the automatic survival response of appeasement (Cantor & Price, 2007) and (b) psychodynamic explanations that posit the recreation of a symbiotic relationship between perpetrator and victim (Ochberg, 2006). Both theories situate traumatic bonding and role reversal within an interpersonal context along the dimensions of power/control and affiliation/affection (Auerbach et al., 1994). In addition, both theories attend to intrapersonal phenomena as part of the explanatory framework, in the form of emotional responses to traumatic entrapment, as well as basic human needs and motivations.

Cantor and Price (2007) drew conclusions about traumatic entrapment based on the study of mammalian responses to threatening situations. Given the four conditions thought to generate Stockholm syndrome (Graham et al., 1995), as well as the dominant–subordinate relational dynamic between perpetrator and victim, the only viable response to traumatic entrapment appears to be appeasement (Cantor & Price, 2007). Appeasement occurs at more primitive levels of information processing, as part of the older brain system; as a result, appeasement is more automatic, quick, and efficient (Cantor & Price, 2007). "Appeasement serves a de-escalating function" (Cantor & Price, 2007, p. 380), as the victim seeks affiliation and comfort from the perpetrator rather than from other victims. The perpetrator may perceive a victim's affiliative actions toward other victims as a threat, and the automatic response from a perpetrator in a position of power is more likely to be an aggressive attack (Cantor & Price, 2007). Although appeasement may be a more primary, instinctive relational response to traumatic entrapment, victims may also rationally respond by intentionally engaging in submissive, compliant, and placating behaviors. Role reversal thus occurs when the victim moves closer to the perpetrator and begins to position himself or herself in a cordial, if not amicable, relation to the perpetrator. The victim is drawn into a supportive and protective role to maintain order, particularly when the perpetrator responds favorably to the victim's appeasement.

Ochberg (2006) suggested that the bonding and role reversal that exemplify Stockholm syndrome are products of recreating a symbiotic relationship between perpetrator and victim, reminiscent of the early child–caregiver relationship, such that the victim becomes dependent upon the perpetrator for survival. The regressive, infantilizing experience of traumatic entrapment is thought to result in "a primitive gratitude for the gift of life, an emotion that eventually develops and differentiates into varieties of affection and love" (Ochberg, 2006, p. 145; see also Strentz, 1980). Symbiotic relationships imply that "both people derive benefit from the attachment" (Kerr & Bowen, 1988, p. 68), and in situations of traumatic entrapment, at the very least, the victim survives so long as the perpetrator maintains control. The intensity of the symbiosis is perhaps best understood in terms of gradations along the togetherness–separateness continuum (Kerr & Bowen, 1988), that is, fusion along the affiliation dimension of interpersonal functioning. Symbiosis may also be defined as the extreme end of the likeness continuum where the similarity–dissimilarity dialectic yields a position of extreme identification with the other as same as self (Cusinato & L'Abate, 2008a; L'Abate et al., 2010). In addition, symbiosis may be thought of in spatial terms, reflecting ambiguity and confusion as to where the self begins and ends in relation to the other, because self and other are thought to be intra- and interpersonally undifferentiated (Kerr & Bowen, 1988; L'Abate, 1983; L'Abate et al., 2010). Given the dominant–subordinate dynamic of traumatic entrapment, any expression by the victim of self as separate from the perpetrator may be viewed as a threat by the perpetrator, potentially resulting in further victimization to restore order along the control dimension of interpersonal relating. Role reversal occurs as the victim begins to view the perpetrator as the rescuer keeping him or her alive. As the victim shifts roles, outside would-be rescuers become potential perpetrators, because they represent a threat to the relative stability and safety of the symbiotic relationship.

A Systemic Expansion of Stockholm Syndrome Based on Relational Competence Theory

The complexity of Stockholm syndrome requires a theoretical framework that attends to both intra- and interpersonal processes and that does so in a way that accounts for the depth of distress, confusion, and pain associated with situations of traumatic entrapment (Speckhard et al., 2005b).

Two central organizational constructs of RCT with direct relevance to advancing a systemic understanding of Stockholm syndrome are (a) the ability to love and (b) the ability to self-regulate (L'Abate et al., 2010). Auerbach et al. (1994) suggested that a similar two-dimensional model, comprising affiliation and control, is necessary to understand the paradoxical bonding and role reversal of Stockholm syndrome. The *affiliation* dimension is a corollary of L'Abate et al.'s (2010) dimension of the ability to love, which refers to the "expressive, communal side of relationships, that is, closeness, requiring little if any action, except to be present, attuned, and available emotionally" (L'Abate et al., 2010, p. 98). As a result, the ability to love corresponds closely with Bakan's (1966) core motivation for human behavior: communion. The *communion* dimension refers to the pursuit of relational needs and goals, such as intimacy, support, friendship, and security (Bauer & McAdams, 2004; Diehl, Owen, & Youngblade, 2004; Kumashiro, Rusbult, & Finkel, 2008). Auerbach et al. (1994) conceptualized and assessed affiliation in terms of a continuum of friendliness to hostility.

In contrast to the affiliation dimension, Auerbach et al. (1994) conceptualized and assessed the dimension of *control* in terms of a hierarchical continuum of dominant–subordinate social positioning. The dimension of control appears to correspond to Bakan's (1966) core motivation of *agency*, the pursuit of personal goals and self-oriented needs, such as autonomy, competence, individual growth, and exploration (Bauer & McAdams, 2004; Diehl et al., 2004; Kumashiro et al., 2008). Control therefore refers to a self-focus that at one extreme—as is evident in traumatic entrapment—involves little regard for the other and his or her well-being (Cusinato & L'Abate, 2008b; L'Abate et al., 2010). Self-goals and self-expansion may be put above the welfare of others, resulting in efforts to manipulate, coerce, and dominate another person for personal gain; extreme selfishness is often associated with interpersonal violence (Cusinato & L'Abate, 2008b; L'Abate et al., 2010). The other extreme displayed by victims can be characterized as a focus on appeasement by placating and accommodating the other. In the situation of traumatic entrapment, this extreme stems from attempts to get basic self needs met, notably survival, albeit most often at a more automatic and implicit level of functioning (Cantor & Price, 2007). The selflessness (Cusinato & L'Abate, 2008b; L'Abate et al., 2010) displayed by such victims may be an automatic, reactive response or an intentional effort to cope with the life-threatening conditions of traumatic entrapment (Cantor & Price, 2007).

L'Abate et al. (2010) suggested that the ability to self-regulate may be "a superordinate process overseeing and overarching both communion and agency" (p. 104). L'Abate et al. framed communion and agency in terms of the relational dimensions of space and time, with *relational competence* defined as the ability to regulate both (a) the dimension of space or approach–avoidance tendencies and (b) the dimension of time or discharge–delay tendencies (L'Abate et al., 2010). Regulating space within a relationship involves balancing the degree of interpersonal closeness and distance, whereas regulating time involves balancing personal disinhibition and self-constraint. The dimensions of space and time also have a strong presence in the systemic and phenomenological theories of Bowen's family systems theory (BFST; Kerr & Bowen, 1988) and dialogical self theory (DST; Hermans, Kempen, & van Loon, 1992). The central construct of BFST is differentiation of self, defined as the ability to regulate both interpersonal closeness–distance impulses and emotional reactivity (Kerr & Bowen, 1988; Skowron & Dendy, 2004; Skowron, Holmes, & Sabatelli, 2003).

Differentiation is thus a term that describes the ability to self-regulate along the dimensions of communion and agency. Meanwhile, a central premise within DST is the understanding that individuals are in a continuous state of relational self-identity construction (see also L'Abate et al., 2010), with regard to external others in social interaction as well as to imagined others spatially arranged within the self (Hermans et al., 1992). Constructive internal dialogue between imagined others and parts of the self, activated during interpersonal relating, requires the ability to self-reflect on here-and-now emotions and cognitions (Hermans, 2003).

One of the strengths of RCT is therefore the attention given to observable interpersonal processes while also employing constructs that give attention to intra-personal phenomena such as the ability to self-regulate (L'Abate et al., 2010) and the interactive development tension between self-identity narratives and interpersonal styles (Cusinato & L'Abate, 2008a, 2008b; L'Abate, 1983; L'Abate et al., 2010). The deadly DT (Karpman, 1968, 2009; L'Abate, 2009; L'Abate et al., 2010) captures the "both–and" perspective of RCT's systemic orientation and introduces the concept of "thirdness" (Raggatt, 2010, p. 400).

Adding a Third to the Intra- and Interpersonal Dynamics of Stockholm Syndrome

The deadly DT (Karpman, 1968, 2009) comprises three fluid roles: victim, persecu-tor, and rescuer. Each role in the deadly DT is an extension of the inability to self-regulate and the tendency instead to engage in "a reactively repetitive and [potentially] vengefully abusive style" of relating (L'Abate et al., 2010, p. 213). According to Karpman (2009), the deadly DT exists simultaneously on interper-sonal and intrapersonal levels. The "Inner Self Drama Triangle" (Karpman, 2009, p. 112) involves a dynamic positioning within the self of both positive and negative aspects of agency dimension in each corner or point of the triangle. Karpman (2009) employed a dialogical metaphor to describe the inner positioning that occurs during the interpersonal role changes among triangle positions. Successful resolution of inner conflict in each corner of the triangle requires self-awareness of one's capacity to exercise agency and facilitate dialogue between contrasting voices. The *victim* position of the triangle, for example, involves an inner conflict between self-pity and self-acceptance (Karpman, 2009), and the victim might resolve the conflict by negotiating appeasing behaviors motivated by helplessness and those motivated by a resolve to alter circumstances. Successful resolution of the victim's inner con-flict requires self-awareness of his or her capacity to exercise agency and facilitate dialogue between the voices of self-pity and self-acceptance. Similarly, successful resolution of the tension in the *perpetrator* position of the triangle involves facilitat-ing dialogic exchange between the voices of self-sabotage and self-determination (Karpman, 2009), which might consist of navigating maleficent behaviors motivated by reckless disregard for both self and other and more calculated motiva-tions for power and control. Finally, the *rescuer* role within the triangle involves negotiating between the voices of self-protection and self-love (Karpman, 2009).

For example, self-protection might involve benevolent behaviors motivated by fulfilling self needs whereas self-love might refer to motivations of genuine compassion and concern for the other's welfare.

According to Karpman (2009), escaping the deadly DT's reactive and repetitive pattern of relating requires choosing to act upon the positive voices engaged in dialogic exchange within each of the corners. Furthermore, escaping the deadly DT involves (a) taking partial responsibility for playing the role of persecutor, (b) displaying some appreciation toward would-be rescuers, and (c) showing some sympathy toward the other as victim (Karpman, 2009). In other words, both self-awareness and intentionality are required to break the deadly DT cycle.

What seems apparent under conditions of traumatic entrapment is that the more reactive voice of self-pity, defined as "a self-sacrificial helplessness" (Karpman, 2009, p. 112), can actually be functional, because it increases the likelihood of survival. Action from a position of self-acceptance might involve intentional efforts toward appeasement and thereby similarly promote survival. Reactivity is generally associated with perpetuating the deadly DT; however, under conditions of traumatic entrapment, both reactive and intentional actions seem to promote positive adaptation in the form of paradoxical bonding and role changes. In other words, self-pity and self-acceptance—that is, the reactive and intentional perpetuation of the deadly DT—are both adaptive coping strategies under conditions of traumatic entrapment (see Jameson, 2010). Despite the negative consequences associated with traumatic entrapment (Graham et al., 1995; Speckhard et al., 2005a, 2005b), Stockholm syndrome appears to be a functional adaptation to life-threatening, fear-inducing situations (Strentz, 1980).

Stockholm Syndrome and Positive Bonds

When generated under conditions of traumatic entrapment, the adaptive positive bond and role reversals within the deadly DT can be further examined in light of additional triadic understandings of interpersonal and intrapersonal functioning. Raggatt (2007), for example, suggested three different forms of dialogical positioning: (a) the dimension of time, (b) intrapersonal dynamics, and (c) social positioning. The first form, *dimension of time*, is a dialogical positioning from the perspective of a continuous metastory that is compiled and constructed from the different positions within the multivoiced self. *Intrapersonal dynamics*, the second positioning, involves "sources of dynamic [inner] conflict" (Raggatt, 2007, p. 364):

> While we are morally attuned to the good and the bad, our strivings are also directed towards at least three other fundamental motivational goal states: affective—to maximize pleasure and minimize pain; agentic—to act in the world as if we were 'independent' beings, to assert ourselves; and communion—to find intimacy, attachment and connection with the social world. (Raggatt, 2007, p. 365)

The third position, *social positioning*, refers to institutional and political roles within the larger system that influence intra- and interpersonal dialogical exchange.

Of these three forms of dialogical positioning, the second form, intrapersonal dynamics, is consistent with the role given to regulating agency and communion in interpersonal behavior within RCT (L'Abate et al., 2010), the ability to move to a meta-reflecting position in order to self-regulate within DST (Hermans, 2003), and the capacity to navigate agency motivations within the deadly DT (Karpman, 2009). Meanwhile, social positioning opens up the intra- and interpersonal dialogical relating to the involvement of a third party, thereby framing human behavior as a function of triangling processes (Karpman, 1968, 2009; Kerr & Bowen, 1988; L'Abate, 2009; L'Abate et al., 2010).

Differentiated functioning refers to (a) nonreactive, intentional negotiating between multiple voices within the self and (b) balancing togetherness and separateness impulses and negotiating interpersonal space in relationships, that is, intra- and interpersonal self-regulation (Kerr & Bowen, 1988). L'Abate et al. (2010; L'Abate, 1983) defined the nonreactive, intentional negotiation of intrapersonal impulses and interpersonal space as relational competence, specifically conductivity. *Conductivity* refers to "caring and compassioned concern and commitment to creative change through confrontation and clarification of content and context" (L'Abate, 1983, p. 278). Poorly differentiated functioning consists of a lack of awareness of one's multiplicity of voices and self-in-context (Dimaggio, Hermans, & Lysaker, 2010), resulting in reactive–repetitive or apathetic–abusive interpersonal relating (L'Abate, 1983; L'Abate et al., 2010).

Under conditions of traumatic entrapment, the victim and perpetrator are initially forced into relating with each other because of the perpetrator's performance of an apathetic–abusive relational style, which corresponds to the voice of self-sabotage within deadly DT. At some point, both victim and perpetrator become engaged in a reactive–repetitive style of relating, as they maneuver about deadly DT (L'Abate, 1983; L'Abate et al., 2010). Differentiated functioning involves moving to a reflective position to facilitate dialogue between different voices. Self-reflection enables persons to become mindful of multiple voices, to engage in perspective-taking between parts of the self, and to facilitate dialogue between differing voices (Dimaggio et al., 2010). The ability to self-regulate as a metadimension (L'Abate et al., 2010) suggests that movement to a reflexive or metacognitive position is necessary for (a) balancing closeness and distance between self and other and between differing self-aspects and (b) balancing discharge and delay tendencies or under- and overregulated emotional reactivity.

Both space and time dimensions of human behavior become convoluted and commingled in the context of perpetrator–victim relating in traumatic entrapment. In terms of the space dimension, the perpetrator and victim are engaged in an extreme closeness, or symbiotic fusion. However, along the time dimension, the perpetrator is an extreme position of control, and the victim is in an extreme position of powerlessness, except perhaps for any agency exercised by the victim around intentional appeasement to survive the ordeal. Given that persons are constituted in part by the other's presence within the self and the internalization of the relationship with the other, self and experience are closely tied to the other person (Hermans, 2003; Hermans et al., 1992). Under conditions of traumatic entrapment, the victim's awareness of intersubjectivity (Jameson, 2010) or ontological relationality (Slife &

Wiggins, 2009) may be severely limited, yet the paradoxical positive bonding that can occur under these conditions is a direct outgrowth of the ontological reality of self as separate yet together, distinct yet connected (Volf, 1996).

The self is thus "an emergent construct that comes into being relationally" (L'Abate et al., 2010, p. 12). On one level, an individual is dependent upon the other for his or her very being, and self is therefore perpetually constructed within this ontological relational reality. Under conditions of traumatic entrapment, however, dependence on the perpetrator is not only an ontological reality but also an existential reality, because the victim's very survival depends on the perpetrator. Under conditions of traumatic entrapment, to be differentiated—that is, to display relational competence through a relational style of conductivity—demands that the victim is (a) aware of the ontological relational self and (b) capable of effectively negotiating communion and agency impulses and then intentionally acting upon that effective negotiation (L'Abate, 1983; L'Abate et al., 2010).

Given that trauma seems to result in restricted multiplicity within the self (Dimaggio et al., 2010), the self that seems to be constructed under traumatic entrapment is more solely characterized by dependence, submission, compliance, and gratitude for being kept alive. That is, according to RCT, it is a selfhood oriented toward selflessness (Cusinato & L'Abate, 2008b; L'Abate et al., 2010), defined by extreme concern for other at the expense of attending to the self's needs (L'Abate et al., 2010). According to Ochberg (2006), dependence, placation, and gratitude provide the basis for the positive bond between victim and perpetrator. Trauma can (a) disrupt the coherence of inner voices that narrate experience during self-identity construction (White, 2006) and (b) impose a selfless identity upon the victim (Cusinato & L'Abate, 2008b; L'Abate et al., 2010; Volf, 1996). A selfless identity is characterized by dependence, submission, and placation, rather than the ideal of a full identity (Cusinato & L'Abate, 2008b; L'Abate et al., 2010), which is constructed through and consists of initiative, intentionality, and agency.

Furthermore, alternative self-narratives corresponding to the different positions within the deadly DT can be constructed. From the victim role within the triangle, the "I," for example, may attend to the voice of self-pity (Karpman, 2009), recall memories of autonomy and choice making, and compare those to the severely restricted environment that is traumatic entrapment. The corresponding experience may be one of despair, hopelessness, and helplessness. However, the "I" may also voice self-acceptance from the victim position (Karpman, 2009) that demonstrates an awareness of the dependence and submission tied to immediate survival and therefore repositions the perpetrator as a rescuer holding the keys to survival. The corresponding experience may then be one of appeasement, gratitude, and identification with the perpetrator. An inner conflict may arise, accounting for incoherence and ambivalence. The inner conflict may be resolved through constructive dialogue between the voices of self-pity and self-acceptance, such that intentional appeasement is a chosen course of action. Alternatively, dialogue may not occur, and appeasement remains an automatic, reactive response to the fear and threat imposed upon the victim by the perpetrator. Whether intentional or reactive, however, appeasement seems to set the stage for experiencing a positive bond between perpetrator and victim.

Stockholm Syndrome and Role Reversal

Two possible mechanisms for the role reversal of Stockholm syndrome may be described based on the literature on relational triangles. Triangles are assumed to be the basic structure of group behavior, and their functioning is thought to be "rooted in an instinctual process [that] reflect automatic emotional reactiveness of human beings to one another" (Kerr & Bowen, 1988, p. 144). Traumatic entrapment is a triangle instigated by the perpetrator. Once the triangle is initiated, the interpersonal dynamics between the members of the triangle unfold according to instinctual processes "around attachment and the impact of anxiety on that attachment" (Kerr & Bowen, 1988, p. 145). When integrated with the core motivations for human behavior, triangles may be said to be the interpersonal working-out of the intrapersonal processes involved in negotiating the dialectic of communion and agency needs and goals. The need for safe and secure emotional attachments with others, intimacy, and connection (Kerr & Bowen, 1988; L'Abate et al., 2010) is one of the relational forces fueling the functioning within triangles. Relational anxiety results from unmet attachment needs and thwarted efforts to obtain togetherness goals, at an implicit and automatic level of experiencing, which can result in movement within the triangle to manage the anxiety.

Therefore, one mechanism of the inherent functioning in triangles is anxiety, specifically associated with the interpersonal dimension of communion (Bakan, 1966; L'Abate et al., 2010) or affiliation (Auerbach et al., 1994). Each individual's functioning within a triangle is a function of the level of anxiety experienced throughout the system (Kerr & Bowen, 1988). Role shifts within a triangle therefore seem tied to attempts to regulate felt anxiety. The roles of a triangle may be described as insiders and outsiders (Kerr & Bowen, 1988), with perpetrator and victim as the *insiders* and rescuers as the *outsiders* in the corresponding deadly DT under conditions of traumatic entrapment. In addition, the roles of anxiety generator, anxiety amplifier, and anxiety dampener may also be assumed (Kerr & Bowen, 1988), with direct correspondence to the respective deadly DT roles of captor (or perpetrator), rescuer, and victim. Kerr and Bowen (1988) further suggested that at lower levels of anxiety, the insiders of a triangle work to exclude the outsider, thereby dampening the felt anxiety; at more anxious levels, in contrast, the outsider is actively enlisted to dampen the anxiety (Kerr & Bowen, 1988). At the highest levels of anxiety, all individuals seek to move to an outsider position and escape or avoid the anxiety (Kerr & Bowen, 1988). However, under conditions of traumatic entrapment, neither recruiting the outsider to dampen the anxiety nor escaping the anxiety-provoking situation is an option (Cantor & Price, 2007), so the only remaining option is for the victim to collude with the perpetrator against outside rescuers.

Traumatic entrapment is an intense, fear-provoking situation characterized by threat and ambiguity experienced by the victim, yet the perpetrator similarly seems to experience anxiety (Cantor & Price, 2007). Anxiety is a visceral response to real or imagined threat (Kerr & Bowen, 1988). However, tying anxiety to the communion dimension requires conceptualizing anxiety on two levels: (a) immediate anxiety stemming from situation specific conditions and (b) existential anxiety stemming from the individual's developmental history. Basic human needs for intimacy, support, safety, and security are in jeopardy under conditions of traumatic entrapment, thereby activating a persistent, existential anxiety. Thus, moving from an outsider position of victim to an insider position of rescuer—such that both perpetrator and victim may now be deemed insiders—can be understood as a dynamic of the perpetrator's recruitment of the victim to take an insider position alongside the perpetrator against outside, would-be rescuers, thereby calming the anxiety felt by both the perpetrator and victim.

A second possible mechanism of the relational functioning within triangles involves the dimension of control (Auerbach et al., 1994; Zerin, 1988): specifically (a) maintaining a hierarchical dominant–subordinate structure and (b) exercising individual agency within the deadly DT. Deadly DTs (Karpman, 1968, 2009; L'Abate, 2009; L'Abate et al., 2010) consist of a hierarchy (Zerin, 1988), with both perpetrator and rescuer in positions of power and with the victim in a subordinate position. Role changes within the triangle may result from "an effort to reclaim the one-up position" or from "effort[s] by the participants to restructure the…hierarchy" (Zerin, 1988, p. 95). The dynamic of control has a long history in the study of interpersonal violence (Aosved & Long, 2006; Carlson & Jones, 2010; Langhinrichsen-Rohling, 2010), and it is thought to underlie most types of interpersonal violence—if not, contribute to all such types. The desire to exert power over another person through violent acts is thought to stem from the interaction between individual tendencies and a cultural context and social structure that nurture and support violence (Aosved & Long, 2006; Carlson & Jones, 2010). Individual tendencies, in the form of agency as a core motivation for human behavior, refer to the abilities to choose for, express, and expand oneself and to meet personal needs for autonomy, competence, achievement, and accomplishment. Exercising agency in the service of the self is an inherent need, yet the ability to choose for, express, and expand oneself can result in domineering and abusive behavior toward others (Cusinato & L'Abate, 2008b; L'Abate et al., 2010). Given that the rescuer is typically in a more powerful position relative to the victim (Zerin, 1988), the victim's movement to a role of rescuer may satisfy his or her agency needs through attaining a more powerful social position.

Furthermore, appeasement may be seen as a willful, rational act (Cantor & Price, 2007). As such, it suggests that the victim may be able to achieve a sense of power or control, and therefore some sense of need fulfillment, through exercising his or her capacity as an active agent. Various kinds of affiliation behaviors directed toward the perpetrator can be deemed acts of appeasement that defuse hostility and anxiety (Cantor & Price, 2007). The victim who responds to the perpetrator in a nonthreatening, compliant, and friendly manner may prolong survival and potentially adjust better (Auerbach et al., 1994). Appeasement therefore can be considered an adaptive strategy; if affiliation behaviors are reciprocated by the perpetrator, they can elicit greater compliance and placation. The victim's change to a role of rescuer within the triangle therefore stems from the desire to exercise some control over a powerless situation, thereby meeting agency needs.

Finally, the dynamics of triangles may be applied to dialogical self-construction that provides a synthesis of intra- and interpersonal explanations for both the positive bond and role reversal of Stockholm syndrome. Raggatt (2010) suggested that dialogical self-identity construction often involves symbolic third members, for example, a triangle comprising (a) "I" Position 1, (b) "I" Position 2, and (c) other. The other may be another person, real or imagined, or may be a significant event or some symbolic object (Raggatt, 2010). Third members mediate the relationship between the parts of the self and "divide the self, but at the same time they provide the grounds for integration" (Raggatt, 2010, p. 401). According to Raggatt, "without reflection through otherness, there can be no self" (p. 403). Under conditions of traumatic entrapment, the perpetrator becomes a symbolic other and interpretive force for the victim's inner dialogical relations. The perpetrator sets the interpretive frame for the self that is constructed in the context of the captor–hostage relating. Given the threat, fear, anxiety, and basic needs for survival, affiliation, and agency that are symbiotically dependent on the perpetrator, the self that becomes constructed under conditions of traumatic entrapment is a selfless identity (Cusinato & L'Abate, 2008b; L'Abate et al., 2010). Given that persons can and often do exhibit agency even under the direst of trauma circumstances (White, 2006), role shifting may be deemed an act that contributes to survival despite lacking conductive relational functioning (L'Abate, 1983; L'Abate et al., 2010).

Implications for Practice

Clinical work with victims of traumatic entrapment initially involves reconciling three controversial issues regarding Stockholm syndrome: (a) the lack of clarity and consensus concerning Stockholm syndrome as a diagnostic classification (Namnyak et al., 2008); (b) the absence of Stockholm syndrome as a construct in the mainstream psychology literature (Jameson, 2010), perhaps most notably the clinical literature; and (c) the apparent reluctance of hostages to seek help post-captivity (Speckhard et al., 2005b; Wesselius & DeSarno, 1983). The latter issue may be the result of continued use of avoidance strategies (Auerbach et al., 1994) that were employed effectively during the siege. Given the first two concerns, treatment with victims of traumatic entrapment necessarily seems to require (a) careful assessment of the deadly DT while the victim was held captive and (b) explicit attention to post-captivity symptomatology. Thus, although formal diagnostic classification and corresponding treatment models may be lacking, Stockholm syndrome may still be a useful clinical construct. When understood from the perspective of RCT, clinicians can attend to intra- and interpersonal triangling processes that occurred during captivity and thereby provide direction for post-captivity intervention with victims of traumatic entrapment.

Irrespective of a formal diagnosis, hostages do tend to experience a range of post-captivity responses that seem to respond well to mental health treatment. For example, Speckhard et al. (2005a) identified grief, anger, and guilt as typical emotional experiences after captivity. Perhaps the most notable emotional response was the difficulty expressed by victims over the paradoxical nature of their experience, such as "grief over the death of the terrorist" and guilt over having survived the ordeal (Speckhard et al., 2005a, p. 138). Because the bonding and role reversal typical of traumatic entrapment are inherently paradoxical, it makes sense that victims would experience ongoing difficulty with making sense of their experience. Effective treatment would therefore focus on resolving post-captivity experiences associated with the paradoxical positive bonding that occurred under the conditions of traumatic entrapment (Graham et al., 1995).

Furthermore, in light of the association between humiliation or deprivation and Stockholm syndrome (Favaro et al., 2000), symptomatology after captivity seems tied to the extent of humiliation and deprivation that occurred during captivity (Flynn, 1987; Goddard & Stanley, 1994). Symptomatology after captivity also seems tied to the individual's trauma history with victims who have "unresolved losses or traumatization" presenting with more complex symptomatology (Speckhard et al., 2005b, p. 19). Finally, victims also tend to present after captivity with heightened arousal levels (Graham et al., 1995) due to the behavioral and emotional dysregulation that occurred as a result of the intense threat and fear provoked during the entrapment. Triangling processes are the mechanism by which communion and agency needs, behavior, and emotion are regulated. Treatment therefore requires a focus on promoting increased self-regulation, because "an inner aversive state motivates victims to seek resolution of those contradictory feelings" (Graham et al., 1995, p. 18).

Effective resolution of the contradictory feelings and difficulties in making meaning after captivity seems, therefore, to involve constructing a self-full identity (Cusinato & L'Abate, 2008b; L'Abate et al., 2010). Much of the symptomatology after captivity is consistent with that associated with a selfless identity, specifically those symptoms related to mood and dissociative disorders (Cusinato & L'Abate, 2008b; L'Abate et al., 2010). Facilitation of self-full identity construction involves (a) enhancing agency and (b) promoting affect regulation. First, moving from a selfless to self-full identity appears primarily to involve a shift in the victim's sense of agency (Cusinato & L'Abate, 2008b; L'Abate et al., 2010), that is, his or her experience of self as capable, competent, and autonomous. Agency may be enhanced by attending to the victim's resilience during the ordeal and normalizing the bonding and role reversal as adaptive responses demanded by the life-threatening anxiety of the entrapment. Both implicit (reactive) and explicit (intentional) appeasement may be reframed as resilient actions symbolic of the victim's creativity, initiative, and agency (White, 2006). Clinicians may further enhance agency and draw forth a self-full identity through a collaborative relationship that actively recruits the client in treatment decision making (Adams-Westcott, Dafforn, & Sterne, 1993), seeks to make attributions that locate agency in the actions of the client, and achieves increased agency through externalizing conversations that personify and separate the symptoms from the identity of the client (Adams-Westcott et al., 1993; White & Epston, 1990).

Second, movement toward a self-full identity also seems to involve promoting affect regulation (Angus & Greenberg, 2011). Promoting affect regulation can also increase personal agency and facilitate meaning-making of experience, because affect regulation, agency, and meaning-making exist in systemic relation to each other. An attuned and empathic therapist may bring the contradictory emotions experienced after captivity into explicit dialogic exchange during therapy by facilitating the victim's voicing of different parts of the self (Angus & Greenberg, 2011; Dimaggio et al., 2010; Hermans, 2003; Hermans et al., 1992). For example, the victim may experience inner conflict over grief for victims and captors alike who died during the hostage situation, and grief for the victims may simultaneously conflict with guilt for having survived the ordeal. The therapist in this situation becomes the "thirdness" who mediates dialogic exchanges (Raggatt, 2010) by contextualizing, normalizing, and externalizing the client's responses. Clinical intervention might also involve exploring experiences (Angus & Greenberg, 2011; White & Epston, 1990) that stand in contrast to the negative affective experiences. The therapist might then ask the victim to include the contrasting experience in the dialogue with grief and guilt. For example, the client may be asked to attend to and reflect on an emerging voice of self as resilient, or a relational experience of communion with significant others; the client can then ask this emerging voice to make sense of guilt. The therapist may also then ask the client to act out or practice living out the alternative, contrasting voice in tangible ways (White & Epston, 1990).

Conclusion

Under conditions of traumatic entrapment, communion and agency motivations are regulated through triangling processes involving (a) internal dialogues between multiple voices of the victim, mediated through the captor as symbolic, third other and (b) interpersonal role shifts that reposition the victim and perpetrator as rescuers and thereby reposition the actual outside rescuers as victims. Victims are in a subordinate position, with their agency motivations and needs controlled by the perpetrator. Despite the powerlessness and dependency of the victim, agency needs seem to be achieved at implicit and explicit levels of functioning. Whether implicit or explicit appeasement prolongs survival, increases affiliation between victim and perpetrator, and restructures the hierarchy of the system. Moving from outside victim to inside rescuer fulfills agency needs by repositioning the victim in a more powerful social position and meets communion needs by soothing, affiliation-based anxiety as the victim and perpetrator aligned against would-be outside rescuers. The presence of the perpetrator as "thirdness" imposes a selfless identity, one of dependent subordinate, upon the victim. Internal dialogical exchanges between self-pity and self-acceptance may conflict with self-full identity remembered in the past or imagined in the future as the victim tries to make sense of and respond to the perpetrator. Appeasement is an adaptive coping strategy, but it also contributes to common post-captivity symptoms such as emotional dysregulation and difficulty. Clinical intervention focuses on enhancing agency and promoting affect regulation as ways to move the victim toward self-full identity.

References

Adams-Westcott, J., Dafforn, T. A., & Sterne, P. (1993). Escaping victim life stories and co-constructing personal agency. In S. G. Gilligan & R. Price (Eds.), *Therapeutic conversations* (pp. 258–271). New York: Norton.

Alleyne, R. (2009, August 28). Jaycee Lee Dugard may have succumbed to 'Stockholm syndrome.' *The Telegraph*. Retrieved from http://www.telegraph.co.uk/news/newstopics/jaycee-lee-dugard/6106991/Jaycee-Lee-Dugard-may-have-succumbed-to-Stockholm-Syndrome.html

American Psychiatric Association. (2000). *Diagnostic and statistical manual of mental health disorders* (4th ed., text rev.). Washington, DC: Author.

Angus, L., & Greenberg, L. (2011). *Working with narrative in emotion-focused therapy*. Washington, DC: American Psychological Association.

Aosved, A. C., & Long, P. J. (2006). Co-occurrence of rape myth acceptance, sexism, racism, homophobia, ageism, classism, and religious intolerance. *Sex Roles, 55*, 481–492. doi:10.1007/s11199-006-9101-4.

Auerbach, S. M., Kiesler, D. J., Strentz, T., Schmidt, J. A., & Serio, C. D. (1994). Interpersonal impacts and adjustment to the stress of simulated captivity: An empirical test of the Stockholm syndrome. *Journal of Social and Clinical Psychology, 13*, 207–221. doi:10.1521/jscp.1994.13.2.207.

Bakan, D. (1966). *The duality of human existence: Isolation and communion in Western man*. Boston, MA: Beacon.

Bauer, J. J., & McAdams, D. P. (2004). Growth goals, maturity, and well-being. *Developmental Psychology, 40*, 114–127. doi:10.1037/0012-1649.40.1.114.

Cantor, C., & Price, J. (2007). Traumatic entrapment, appeasement and complex post-traumatic stress disorder: Evolutionary perspectives of hostage reactions, domestic abuse and the Stockholm syndrome. *Australian and New Zealand Journal of Psychiatry, 41*, 377–384. doi:10.1080/00048670701261178.

Carlson, R. G., & Jones, K. D. (2010). Continuum of conflict and control: A conceptualization of intimate partner violence typologies. *Addictions and Offender Issues, 18*, 248–254. doi:10.1177/1066480710371795.

Cusinato, M., & L'Abate, L. (2008a). Likeness: A hidden ingredient in family therapy. *American Journal of Family Therapy, 36*, 116–125. doi:10.1080/01926180701189812.

Cusinato, M., & L'Abate, L. (2008b). Selfhood: A hidden ingredient in family therapy. *Journal of Family Psychotherapy, 19*, 320–329. doi:10.1080/08975350802475064.

Diehl, M., Owen, S. K., & Youngblade, L. M. (2004). Agency and communion attributes in adults' spontaneous self-representations. *International Journal of Behavioral Development, 28*, 1–15. doi:10.1080/01650250344000226.

Dimaggio, G., Hermans, H. J. M., & Lysaker, P. H. (2010). Health and adaptation in a multiple self: The role of absence of dialogue and poor metacognition in clinical populations. *Theory & Psychology, 20*, 379–399. doi:10.1177/0959354310363319.

Favaro, A., Degortes, D., Colombo, G., & Santonastaso, P. (2000). The effects of trauma among kidnap victims in Sardinia, Italy. *Psychological Medicine: A Journal of Research in Psychiatry and the Allied Sciences, 30*, 975–980. doi:10.1017/S0033291799001877.

Fitzpatrick, L. (2009). Stockholm syndrome. *Time, 174*(10), 19.

Flynn, E. E. (1987). Victims of terrorism: Dimensions of the victim experience. In P. Wilkinson & A. M. Stewart (Eds.), *Contemporary research on terrorism* (pp. 337–355). Aberdeen: Aberdeen University Press.

Goddard, C. R., & Stanley, J. R. (1994). Viewing the abusive parent and the abused child as captor and hostage: The application of hostage theory to the effects of child abuse. *Journal of Interpersonal Violence, 9*, 258–269. doi:10.1177/088626094009002008.

Graham, D. L. R., Rawlings, E. I., Ihms, K., Latimer, D., Foliano, J., Thompson, A., et al. (1995). A scale for identifying "Stockholm syndrome" reactions in young dating women: Factor structure, reliability, and validity. *Violence and Victims, 10*, 3–22.

Grigsby, N., & Hartman, B. (1997). The barriers model: An integrated strategy for intervention with battered women. *Psychotherapy, 34*, 485–497. doi:10.1037/h0087721.

Hermans, H. J. M. (2003). The construction and reconstruction of dialogical self. *Journal of Constructivist Psychology, 16*, 89–130. doi:10.1080/10720530390117902.

Hermans, H. J. M., Kempen, H. J., & van Loon, R. J. (1992). The dialogical self: Beyond individualism and rationalism. *American Psychologist, 47*, 23–33. doi:10.1037/0003-066X.47.1.23.

Jameson, C. (2010). The "short step" from love to hypnosis: A reconsideration of the Stockholm syndrome. *Journal for Cultural Research, 14*, 337–355. doi:10.1080/14797581003765309.

Jülich, S. (2005). Stockholm syndrome and child sexual abuse. *Journal of Child Sexual Abuse, 14*, 107–129. doi:10.1300/J070v14n03_06.

Karpman, S. B. (1968). Fairy tales and script drama analysis. *Transactional Analysis Bulletin, 7*, 39–43.

Karpman, S. B. (2009). Sex games people play: Intimacy blocks, games, and scripts. *Transactional Analysis Journal, 39*, 103–116.

Kerr, M. E., & Bowen, M. (1988). *Family evaluation*. New York: W. W. Norton.

Kumashiro, M., Rusbult, C. E., & Finkel, E. J. (2008). Navigating personal and relational concerns: The quest for equilibrium. *Journal of Personality and Social Psychology, 95*, 94–110. doi:10.1037/0022-3514.95.1.94.

L'Abate, L. (1983). Styles in intimate relationships: The A-R-C Model. *Personnel & Guidance Journal, 61*, 277–283. doi:10.1111/j.2164-4918.1983.tb00025.x.

L'Abate, L. (2009). The drama triangle: An attempt to resurrect a neglected pathogenic model in family therapy theory and practice. *The American Journal of Family Therapy, 37*, 1–11. doi:10.1080/01926180701870163.

L'Abate, L., Cusinato, M., Maino, E., Colesso, W., & Scilletta, C. (2010). *Relational competence theory: Research and mental health applications*. New York: Springer. doi:10.1007/978-1-4419-5665-1.

Langhinrichsen-Rohling, J. (2010). Controversies involving gender and intimate partner violence in the United States. *Sex Roles, 62*, 179–193. doi:10.1007/s11199-009-9628-2.

Namnyak, M., Tufton, N., Szekely, R., Toal, M., Worboys, S., & Sampson, E. L. (2008). 'Stockholm syndrome': Psychiatric diagnosis or urban myth? *Acta Psychiatrica Scandinavica, 117*, 4–11. doi:10.1111/j.1600-0447.2007.01112.x.

Ochberg, F. (2006). There is reason in action. In C. R. Figley (Ed.), *Mapping trauma and its wake: Autobiographic essays by pioneer trauma scholars* (pp. 137–151). New York: Routledge.

Pearn, J. (2000). Traumatic stress disorders: A classification with implications for prevention and management. *Military Medicine, 165*, 434–440.

Raggatt, P. T. F. (2007). Forms of positioning in the dialogical self: A system of classification and the strange case of Dame Edna Everage. *Theory & Psychology, 17*, 355–382. doi:10.1177/0959354307077288.

Raggatt, P. T. F. (2010). The dialogical self and thirdness: A semiotic approach to positioning using dialogical triads. *Theory & Psychology, 20*, 400–419. doi:10.1177/0959354310364878.

Skowron, E. A., & Dendy, A. K. (2004). Differentiation of self and attachment in adulthood: Relational correlates of effortful control. *Contemporary Family Therapy, 26*, 337–357. doi:10.1023/B:COFT.0000037919.63750.9d.

Skowron, E. A., Holmes, S. E., & Sabatelli, R. M. (2003). Deconstructing differentiation: Self-regulation, interdependent relating, and well-being in adulthood. *Contemporary Family Therapy, 25*, 111–129. doi:10.1023/A:1022514306491.

Slife, B. D., & Wiggins, B. J. (2009). Taking relationship seriously in psychotherapy: Radical relationality. *Journal of Contemporary Psychotherapy, 39*, 17–24. doi:10.1007/s10879-008-9100-6.

Speckhard, A., Tarabrina, N., Krasnov, V., & Mufel, N. (2005a). Stockholm effects and psychological responses to captivity in hostages held by suicide terrorists. *Traumatology, 11*, 121–140. doi:10.1177/153476560501100206.

Speckhard, A., Tarabrina, N., Krasnov, V., & Mufel, N. (2005b). Posttraumatic and acute stress responses in hostages held by suicide terrorists in the takeover of a Moscow theater. *Traumatology, 11*, 3–21. doi:10.1177/153476560501100102.

Strentz, T. (1980). The Stockholm syndrome: Law enforcement policy and ego defenses of the hostage.*AnnalsoftheNewYorkAcademyofSciences,347*,137–150.doi:10.1111/j.1749-6632.1980. tb21263.x.

Strentz, T., & Auerbach, S. M. (1988). Adjustment to the stress of simulated captivity: Effects of emotion-focused vs. problem-focused preparation on hostages differing in locus of control. *Journal of Personality and Social Psychology, 55,* 652–660. doi:10.1037/0022-3514.55.4.652.

Volf, M. (1996). *Exclusion and embrace: A theological exploration of identity, otherness, and reconciliation.* Nashville, TN: Abingdon Press.

Wesselius, C. L., & DeSarno, J. V. (1983). The anatomy of a hostage situation. *Behavioral Sciences and the Law, 1,* 33–45. doi:10.1002/bsl.2370010207.

White, M. (2006). Working with people who are suffering the consequences of multiple trauma: A narrative perspective. In D. Denborough (Ed.), *Trauma: Narrative responses to traumatic experience* (pp. 25–85). Adelaide: Dulwich Centre Publications.

White, M., & Epston, D. (1990). *Narrative means to therapeutic ends.* New York: Norton.

Zerin, M. (1988). An application of the drama triangle to family therapy. *Transactional Analysis Journal, 18,* 94–101.

Chapter 7
Psychopathology and Self-Regulation: Assessment, Case Conceptualization, and Intervention

The previous four chapters outlined four models of relational psychopathology: parentification, parental alienating behavior, bullying, and Stockholm syndrome. Each chapter applied relational competence theory (RCT), specifically the deadly drama triangle (DT), to a particular expression of intra- and interpersonal dysfunction. As discussed in Chap. 1, a model is defined not only by the application of an overarching theory but also by underlying dimensions that can be empirically examined. The dimension of self-regulation—along with its aftereffects and corollaries such as (a) the ability to negotiate approach–avoidance and discharge–delay tendencies, (b) the ability to regulate communion and agency motivations, or (c) the ability to intra- and interpersonally differentiate a self-full identity—appears to have relevance for all four models of psychopathology (Cusinato & L'Abate, 2008; L'Abate, Cusinato, Maino, Colesso, & Scilletta, 2010) presented in Chaps. 3–6. Indeed, L'Abate et al. (2010) defined *relational competence* as the ability to self-regulate, arguing that self-regulation may be "a superordinate process" (p. 104).

This chapter discusses the implications of practice behavior, assessment, case conceptualization, and intervention based on relational psychopathology as a manifestation of difficulties in self-regulation. Specifically, this chapter focuses on the clinical tasks of assessment, case conceptualization, and intervention from a systems perspective (Nutt & Stanton, 2011; Stanton & Welsh, 2011). Several principles of RCT and the deadly DT undergird this discussion. The first principle is that intra- and interpersonal dysfunction is inherently "reactively repetitive" (L'Abate et al., 2010, p. 213; see also Karpman, 1968, 2009). The second principle is that the self is "an emergent construct that comes into being relationally" (L'Abate et al., 2010, p. 12). Reactivity primarily implies a difficulty in intrapersonal self-regulation, whereas the notion of a relationally constituted self primarily suggests that difficulty with self-regulation is embedded in an interpersonal context. A lack of intrapersonal self-awareness and a lack of self-in-context awareness (Volf, 1996) characterize the four models of relational psychopathology. The third RCT principle, conductivity, stands in contrast to a lack of intra- and interpersonal self-regulation (L'Abate, 1983; L'Abate et al., 2010). *Conductivity* refers to the nonreactive, intentional negotiation of intrapersonal impulses and interpersonal space. Conductivity thus grounds healthy relational functioning in self-regulation.

The critical construct of self-regulation encompasses the notion of an observing self (Bishop et al., 2004). *Self-regulation* can be defined as the ability to self-reflect on internal states and behavior and then modify one's behavior to mirror preferred, prosocial ideals and goals (McCullough & Willoughby, 2009). Self-regulation is a broad construct that incorporates emotional and behavioral self-regulation and the related constructs of self-monitoring, self-soothing, and self-control (Wills, Pokhrel, Morehouse, & Fenster, 2011). RCT and the deadly DT extend this conceptualization of self-regulation to an observing self-in-context, or what Shapiro and Schwartz (1999) described as "intentional systemic mindfulness" (p. 128). Self-regulation and mindfulness are corollary constructs, with mindfulness perhaps best defined as "present-centered attention and acceptance of one's experience" (Coffey, Hartman, & Fredrickson, 2010, p. 248). The practice of mindfulness is therefore one means of increasing self-regulation. Mindfulness practice is representative of a class of contemplative practices that one can employ to improve self-regulatory functioning (Davidson et al., 2012).

Self-regulation difficulty, or self-dysregulation, is increasingly recognized as an underlying dimension of various forms of psychopathology (e.g., Dimaggio, Hermans, & Lysaker, 2010; Greenberg, 2002; Ross & Babcock, 2010; Widiger, Livesley, & Clark, 2009). Given the link between parentification, parental alienation, bullying, or Stockholm syndrome and pathological outcomes, self-regulation and self-dysregulation appear to have specific relevance to these constructs as well. For example, empirical evidence has suggested that parentification exerts a dysregulating influence on the parentified individual, resulting in deleterious consequences (Jankowski & Hooper, 2012). Similarly, studies of bullying have demonstrated empirical associations with self-regulation difficulties in both victims and perpetrators of bullying (Garner & Hinton, 2010). Parental alienation and Stockholm syndrome have drawn considerably less empirical attention than parentification and bullying. Nevertheless, the scant empirical evidence that does exist has indicated that parental alienation is associated indirectly with indicators of self-dysregulation for the individual who is experiencing parents' alienation strategies (Baker & Ben-Ami, 2011; Ben-Ami & Baker, 2012). Victimization resulting from traumatic entrapment is likewise associated with indicators of self-dysregulation (Graham et al., 1995).

Given the preliminary evidence, effective intervention may depend on the clinician's ability to assess and conceptualize self-regulation difficulties as a function of an individual's relational contexts. In addition, effective performance of the clinical tasks of assessment, case conceptualization, and intervention is informed by the clinician's awareness of self-in-relation and his or her ability to self-regulate both intrapersonally and interpersonally throughout the therapeutic process. This chapter explores specific ways clinicians might assess, conceptualize, and intervene in clients' self-regulatory functioning. But first, the next section describes a philosophical framework for conceptualizing the effective performance of these clinical tasks. The next section also describes the importance of the therapists' own ability to self-regulate when working with clients who present with a history of parentification, parental alienation, bullying, or Stockholm syndrome. In other words, self-regulation has relevance for both the client and the therapist—and consequently for the effectiveness of the therapist's clinical tasks and practice behaviors: assessment, case conceptualization, and intervention.

Philosophical Grounding of the Clinical Tasks

The notion that the self is "an emergent construct that comes into being relationally" (L'Abate et al., 2010, p. 12) applies as much to the therapist's functioning within the therapist–client system as it applies to the individuals in relationship within the client system. A central premise of systems theory—and of theories informed by systems theory, such as RCT—continues to be the notion of relationality. *Relationality* refers to the philosophical argument that understanding anything, whether another person or oneself, cannot occur apart from understanding its relation to something or in conjunction with someone else (Shults & Sandage, 2006).

Theorists distinguish between first-order and second-order conceptualizations and applications of systems theory (e.g., Hoffman, 1985, 1990, 1991). Similarly, there are weaker and stronger forms of relationality, with stronger expressions described as ontological relationality (Slife, 2004; Slife & Wiggins, 2009). Second-order systems theory can be described as a move toward ontological relationality. Relationality is predominantly a conceptualization of (a) persons as self-contained individuals and (b) relationships comprising self-contained individuals in reciprocal interaction with one another (Slife, 2004; Slife & Wiggins, 2009). In contrast, stronger expressions extend relationality to the constitution of the self and the individual's moment-by-moment experience within relational contexts. As a result, ontological relationality can be summarized by several identity statements: (a) "I am who I am, in part, because of who you are" (Slife, 2004, p. 166); (b) "we are who we are not because we are separate from the others who are next to us, but because we are both separate and connected, both distinct and related" (Volf, 1996, p. 66); and (c) "the self-organization of the 'I' in relation to itself and the orientation of the 'I' to others is already and always mediated by the 'not I'" (Shults & Sandage, 2006, p. 57). The self is therefore in a perpetual state of construction, evidenced through and emerging from social interaction with actual external others and imagined internal others in continuous dialogue with each other (Hermans, Kempen, & van Loon, 1992).

Some have labeled ideas about a relationally constituted self as a third-order systems perspective (Dallos & Urry, 1999). But whether it is labeled as third-order systems theory or ontological relationality, perhaps the most fundamental implication for the clinical tasks of assessment, case conceptualization, and intervention is the conceptualization of the therapist as a participant observer of the therapist–client system (i.e., therapeutic context; see Hoffman, 1985). From the perspective of ontological relationality, the therapist is both connected to and yet separate from her or his clients through a complex process of "[distinguishing] from the other and the internalization of the relationship to the other;…[a process of] 'differentiation' in which both the self and the other take part by negotiating their identities in interaction with one another" (Volf, 1996, p. 66). As a participant in the therapist–client system, the therapist must continuously reflect on her or his influence on the client subsystem, monitor her or his reactions to the unfolding clinical process, and demonstrate keen attention to the influence of the client subsystem and larger social context on the therapist's own relating in therapy.

Weaker expressions of relationality have received the most attention in systemic formulations of assessment, case conceptualization, and intervention as evidenced by (a) the reframing of presenting problems in terms of dysfunctional relational dynamics and intervening to directly alter the interpersonal behavior of clients (Nutt & Stanton, 2011) and by (b) the numerous formal assessments that are available for quantifying first-order constructs (Carr, 2000). Some have noted, however, that systemic practitioners rarely use formal, empirical assessments (Bray, 2009; Carr, 2000). In addition, Bailey (2012) observed that recommended best practices in assessment for systems practitioners differ little from the individual practice literature and that little about the recommended practices was distinctively systemic. When formal assessments are based on a first-order application of systems theory (Carr, 2000), on the case conceptualization that emerges, and therefore on intervention that follows, these formal assessments tend to focus on commonly described systems first-order constructs. For example, first-order constructs such as structure, boundaries, intergenerational coalitions, intergenerational transmission processes, and fusion, cutoff, and other relational patterns are important to the assessment process (Bowen, 1978). Because second-order systems have been so influential in the advancement of systemic practices, practitioners may misconstrue first-order constructs and their assessment as contrary to a second- or third-order systems orientation (Carr, 2000). However, Carr contended that formal assessment of first-order constructs is not incompatible or incongruent with clinical practice grounded in second-order systems ideas.

Assessment, case conceptualization, and intervention from an ontological relationality perspective are grounded theory efforts (Charmaz, 2000). Clinicians perform these clinical tasks either within a particular relational context, from the bottom up, or ideally—according to Slife and Wiggins (2009)—from "good practice, which cannot be abstracted from specific contexts, [and] must precede and develop good theory" (p. 19). A diagnosis and corresponding case conceptualization may be thought of as a theory. The metaphor for therapy as qualitative research therefore suggests that each clinical task is a unique, contextually embedded, grounded activity (Heath, 1993). Assessment, case conceptualization, and intervention then borrow from the qualitative research metaphor and are defined by (a) clinical utility, (b) fit with the therapist–client system experience within the current therapeutic conversations and interactions, (c) coherence, and (d) the consensus of all involved (Ivey, Scheel, & Jankowski, 1999).

Additionally, clinical tasks from an ontological relationality perspective emphasize self-awareness of the therapist. One increasingly common way of framing the therapist's self-awareness rests on the notion of self-multiplicity and consists of an inner dialogue between parts of the self (e.g., Anderson, 2007a, 2007b;

Anderson & Gehart, 2009; Hermans, 2004; Rober, 1999, 2005). An ontological relationality perspective enables one to navigate the complexity inherent in clinical practice. Toward this end, it is important for the therapist to be aware of moments when a particular part of his or her self may be monopolizing the dialogue and restricting therapeutic conversation. The result may be an assessment of the clients' functioning that simply confirms the therapist's preconceived understanding, rather than a synthesis of therapist and clients' contributions that is grounded in the lived experience of the clients. For example, a clinician might fail to hear how a parentified child experiences both satisfaction and dissatisfaction in the adultlike caretaking role and instead frame the child's experience and the systems' functioning as exclusively pathological. Practitioners might increase their self-reflective skills by employing a strong relationality: effectively facilitating inner dialogue between multiple self-aspects while engaging in collaborative, open dialogic exchange with clients. For example, a clinician might realize that his or her framing of parentification as pathological is based upon the "not I" (Shults & Sandage, 2006, p. 57) and therefore implies something, or is implied by something, that is absent (White, 2000, 2006). That is, the nonpathological alternative also exists, can be known, and can be attended to within the therapeutic conversation. In this example it might mean recognizing that the child experiences a sense of identity, purpose, and belonging as a result of the parentification processes within the family system (Telzer & Fuligni, 2009).

Systemic Assessment and Case Conceptualization

Systemic practitioners ideally attend to the individual level of analysis, in addition to the family and larger social contexts, during clinical assessment and case conceptualization (Stanton & Welsh, 2011). Systemic practitioners are also encouraged to make use of both formal individual assessments and formal systems-focused assessments of family functioning when conceptualizing presenting problems and establishing treatment direction (Nutt & Stanton, 2011; Stanton & Welsh). In doing so, systemic practitioners focus on intra- and interpersonal aspects of client functioning (Jankowski et al., 2011; Jankowski, Ivey, & Vaughn, 2012). Finally, systemic practitioners ideally synthesize information obtained from formal assessments with that obtained from informal assessments—the latter referring to more intuitively, subjectively, and conversationally derived clinical information (Jankowski et al., 2011). Systemic clinical assessment and case conceptualization reap "the benefits of narratives from multiple sources . . . [and] it may be useful to consider scores from assessment instruments and the implications of these scores, not as global knowledge but as specialized local knowledge arising from conversations" (Carr, 2000, p. 126). To synthesize multiple sources of information, Carr noted, it is helpful to frame each source as potentially useful to understanding the functioning of the client system. This process also requires the clinician to hold and synthesize multiple perspectives simultaneously and to be cautious about privileging one particular perspective over another.

Systemic assessment and case conceptualization are therefore multilayered with multiple perspectives, requiring the clinician to exercise metacognitive skill to attend to myriad internal and external voices during the course of a therapeutic dialogue with clients. Clinicians must negotiate between previously constructed understandings grounded in diverse clinical and personal experiences, while they also attend to clients' verbal and nonverbal communication in the moment of the therapeutic conversation. The clinician's diverse inner voices could consist of theoretical models, research on family functioning, family-of-origin experiences, previous clients, or anything else that is activated during therapeutic conversations. Distinctively systemic assessment and case conceptualization also form a multidimensional process. Clinicians must use seemingly disparate and contradictory sources of information while navigating internal and external dialogues. Within the same clinical session, a clinician may use information based on expert opinion or quantitative data (e.g., formal diagnostic assessments) and synthesize that information with interpretive data, such as subjective experiences of the therapeutic relationship or observations of client interaction—all while receiving ongoing implicit and explicit feedback from the client about the direction of therapy and the helpfulness of the therapeutic conversation. Furthermore, while negotiating client feedback, systemic clinicians can be seen moving along different positioning dimensions (Jankowski et al., 2011, 2012; Vaughn, 2004).

Vaughn (2004) identified three positioning dimensions in the practice of systemic assessment, case conceptualization, and intervention: (a) connection–separateness, (b) expert–nonexpert, and (c) participant–observer. As an example of the first dimension, connection–separateness, there may be times when a therapist needs to move closer to a particular system member, seek shared experiences, and identify with the client—and perhaps do so with different system members at different points within a therapy session. At other times a therapist may need to increase internal and interpersonal space in order to reflect on the therapeutic process. In the second dimension, expert–nonexpert, there may be times when the therapist negotiates between a hierarchical, expert positioning and a more open, exploratory positioning. For example, a therapist may consult a formal diagnostic assessment of one of the family system members as a basis for a particular question. Or she or he may ask a question from a position of curiosity and a sincere desire to understand a client's experience. Finally, in the third dimension, participant–observer, there may be times when the therapist includes himself or herself as a participant in the change process, for example, telling the clients, "we can do this." At other times the therapist may move to an observer position and try to influence a client to take responsibility for change. The latter position may involve utilizing silence to create room in the conversation for the client to wrestle with the implications of a question posed to him or her.

Formal Assessments

Therapists may find it useful to employ an empirical assessment as one source of information about the functioning of different system members. In this section of the chapter (i.e., discussion on formal assessments), we provide a brief overview of a few psychometrically sound empirical measures of self-regulation. A central premise of ontological relationality is the interdependence of system members, so systemic assessment involves capturing each system member's perspective in a "round-robin design" (Cook & Kenny, 2004, p. 361). A round-robin design allows each level of analysis to be taken into consideration when conceptualizing the case: individual, dyad, and family levels. Individuals can be asked to complete a formal assessment of their own self-regulatory functioning, as in the traditional individual-oriented assessment approach. However, a round-robin design also has clinicians assess other system members' regulatory functioning in the context of different dyadic combinations.

For example, if the family consists of a mother, a female adolescent child, and a younger male child, the eldest child may complete an assessment of the mother's self-regulatory functioning within the mother–daughter relationship, and the eldest child may also assess the mother's self-regulatory functioning as evidenced within the relationship to the younger child. Similarly, the mother and younger child would complete assessments of each family member's self-regulatory functioning within the different dyads. Dyadic scores can then be created by calculating the mean from each person's score in the relationship. For example, the mother–daughter dyad score could be created by calculating the average of the mother's assessment of the daughter's functioning in their relationship and also the daughter's assessment of the mother's functioning in their relationship. Last, a family-level score could be calculated by averaging all scores obtained through the round-robin design.

As Cook and Kenny (2004) noted, the round-robin design enables the clinician to target intervention more effectively, because the dysfunction might be occurring primarily within one dyad within the system and not within the family's functioning as a whole. This finding would not necessarily mean that the other system members are not included in therapy. Rather, other system members might be recruited to help intervene more effectively in the dyad by offering alternative perspectives, openly expressing their experience of the dyad, or perhaps being encouraged to align with or move closer to other system members. Even though the dyad may be given primary attention, the foundational premise regarding the four models of relational psychopathology is that of the deadly DT, that is, triangling processes, or a triadic formulation of dysfunction. The clinician should therefore assess and conceptualize individual and systemic functioning with the triangle as the fundamental unit of analysis in mind (Kerr & Bowen, 1988).

Numerous instruments exist for measuring the broad construct of self-regulation. One common means of measuring self-regulation involves assessing effortful control, which may be assessed at different stages of the lifecycle. *Effortful control* refers to the capacity to focus attention, prevent undesirable behaviors, and overcome avoidance tendencies. The Adult Temperament Questionnaire (ATQ; Evans & Rothbart, 2007; Rothbart, Ahadi, & Evans, 2000), the Early Adolescent Temperament Questionnaire—Revised (EATQ-R; Ellis & Rothbart, 2001; see also Capaldi & Rothbart, 1992), the Temperament in Middle Childhood Questionnaire (TMCQ; Simonds, Kieras, Rueda, & Rothbart, 2007), and the Children's Behavior Questionnaire (CBQ; Putnam & Rothbart, 2006) all involve self-report measures that can be employed in modified round-robin assessment depending on the age of the children. In practice, the wording of items has to be adjusted to accommodate dyadic assessment of functioning using self-report instruments. Infant and early childhood measures also exist in which parents report on the functioning of their child (Gartstein & Rothbart, 2003; Putnam, Gartstein, & Rothbart, 2006).

Alternatively, the Difficulties in Emotion Regulation Scale (DERS; Gratz & Roemer, 2004) can be used as an indicator of self-regulation. The DERS measures awareness, acceptance of emotions, and (like effortful control) the ability to overcome feeling states and act in preferred, prosocial ways. Closely related to the DERS is the Five Facet Mindfulness Questionnaire (FFMQ; Baer, Smith, Hopkins, Krietemeyer, & Toney, 2006). The FFMQ is a self-report measure divided into five aspects of mindfulness: nonreactivity, observing, acting with awareness, describing/ labeling, and nonjudging of experience. Finally, if the therapist or clinician is more interested in assessing self-regulation along both behavioral and emotional dimensions, and also along intra- and interpersonal domains of functioning, the Differentiation of Self Inventory—Revised (DSI-R; Skowron & Schmitt, 2003) can be used. The DSI-R assesses for Bowen's (Kerr & Bowen, 1988) construct of differentiation of self. Evidence for the construct validity of differentiation of self as measured by the DSI-R supports its use as a measure of an individual's capacity for intra- and interpersonal self-regulation (Hooper, Marotta, & Lanthier, 2008; Jankowski & Hooper, 2012).

The use of empirical assessments is ideally synthesized with information from other sources. Jankowski and Ivey (2001) identified three categories of factors commonly used by clinicians during systemic assessment and case conceptualization: (a) interactional factors, (b) therapist-specific factors, and (c) contextual factors. The first category, interactional factors, consists of the clinician's awareness of the relational processes taking place within the therapist–client system. For example, a therapist may reflect on his or her emotional experience during the therapeutic conversation or observe clients' behavior and then use that information to formulate a problem definition and direction for clinical intervention. The second category, therapist-specific factors, refers to self-aspects of the therapist that he or she brings into the therapeutic dialogue and uses to inform assessment and case conceptualization. For example, a therapist may draw on previous clinical experience with another family and compare knowledge emerging from the current therapeutic conversation with the prior clinical knowledge. Finally, a therapist may be cognizant of and integrate a third category: larger contextual factors within which the therapist–client system is embedded. For example, a therapist may connect in-session conversation about the presenting problem, as well as his or her observations of client functioning, to conditions of poverty or the family's experience of job loss or unemployment.

The genogram (Kerr & Bowen, 1988; McGoldrick, Gerson, & Shellenberger, 1999) can be used to supplement empirical assessment of the system and to visually organize the information gathered during the therapeutic conversation. The genogram is ideally suited to the tracking of triangling processes throughout the system (McGoldrick et al., 1999; Titelman, 2008). The genogram can therefore be adapted to assess each of the four models of psychopathology presented in this book. For example, the genogram can map parentification processes that might include contextual factors that contributed to and still maintain a child's performance of an adult role within the family. Contextual factors might include chronic illness in one of the parents, divorce, or substance addiction in the parental subsystem (Hooper, 2012). The clinician could also map interactional processes based on observations obtained through the therapy session or the clinical interview. Interactional processes might consist of conflict within the parental subsystem, intense emotional closeness between a child and one of the parents, or a pattern of disengagement in one of the parent–child dyads. Finally, constructing a genogram from the perspective of ontological relationality requires the clinician to include himself or herself in the interactional processes; it specifically requires that he or she be mindful of triangling processes. The clinician must guard against replicating a relational process in the therapist–client system. For example, the clinician might inadvertently reinforce a parental role for a child in a parentified system by privileging his or her knowledge of family dynamics or suggesting that he or she can exercise agency to change the system.

The deadly DT can also be drawn on the genogram. The genogram has application beyond family systems and can be applied to bullying outside the family or to traumatic entrapments such as captor–hostage situations. The roles of victim, perpetrator, and rescuer can be identified, and the role shifts characteristic of the deadly DT can be mapped. For example, a client who has been the victim of traumatic entrapment can describe the movement from the victim of the perpetrator to the rescuer of the perpetrator. Other relational dynamics typical of traumatic entrapment can be identified, including distancing, fusion, and over- and underfunctioning. For example, symbiosis, or fusion, has been used to describe the captor–hostage relationship, thereby distancing would-be rescuers and positioning them as outsiders in the triangle. Would-be rescuers may then be framed as perpetrators, placing the victim at risk by posing a threat to the relative stability of the captor–hostage relationship. Again, the clinician must be mindful of his or her role in the therapist–client system. If the clinician is not attentive to his or her role, he or she could unknowingly reinforce a victim role for a client by ignoring the ways the client exercised resiliency, hardiness, or even posttraumatic growth in his or her responses to traumatic entrapment (or similarly, to parentification, bullying, or parental alienation).

Intervention

Effective intervention depends on the extent to which the therapist displays conductivity. L'Abate (1983) defined conductivity as "caring and compassioned concern and commitment to creative change through confrontation and clarification of content and context" (p. 278). Conductivity thus requires (a) awareness of the ontological relational self and (b) intra- and interpersonal self-regulation (L'Abate, 1983; L'Abate et al., 2010). Three primary applications to clinical practice and intervention are supported by conductivity. First, the clinician becomes a relational means of self-regulation for the client, or what Feld (2007) has called mutual regulation.

Jackson, Mackenzie, and Hobfoll (2000) described relational means of self-regulation as "self-in-social-setting regulation" (p. 276); from a Bowen theory perspective, the construct of triangling describes relational processes that have a self-regulating function within systems (Lassiter, 2008; Titelman, 2008). In the second application to clinical practice and intervention, mutual regulation rests upon the clinician's capacity for self-regulation. In the third application, differentiation of self becomes a primary goal for each person within the therapist–client system.

Given that each of the four models of relational psychopathology involves reactively repetitive triangling processes that prevent effective emotional and behavioral self-regulation, effective intervention necessitates creating a reflective space for clients to be able to gain awareness of the triangling processes and begin to make changes by detriangling or differentiating self from the system. Detriangling is a Bowen theory construct that typically refers to the clinician's role in therapy and her or his capacity to avoid getting caught up in the relational anxiety of the client system (Kerr & Bowen, 1988). A third-order or ontological relationality application of this construct heightens the need for the clinician to self-regulate her or his emotions and behaviors in therapy and adjust her or his behavior so as not to reactively and repetitively play out the deadly DT. As a potential rescuer, the therapist risks being repositioned by clients as a perpetrator, thereby becoming so isolated and distanced as to be ineffectual. The possibility that disequilibrium may be brought to the system as clients make an effort to change may result in a reactive role shifting in the therapeutic process, whereby a victim is recruited by the perpetrator to align against the therapist, making the therapist the victim and thereby maintaining the relative stability of the client subsystem.

Whereas detriangling typically refers to the clinician's task within the therapist–client system, differentiation of self describes the clinical aim for the clients. Nevertheless, the constructs appear to have equal applicability to clinician and clients within the context of therapeutic work to alter the deadly DT. Differentiating self, like detriangling, refers to the individual's capacity for self-regulation in the face of relational anxiety. Detriangling tends to also focus on the interpersonal processes within the therapist–client system, whereas differentiation of self can refer to both intrapersonal and interpersonal processes. Alternatively the term *mindfulness* can be applied to detriangling, differentiation of self, and self-regulation because all four constructs seem to share the two underlying dimensions of mindfulness. First, noticing one's emotional states and interpersonal behavior underlies the constructs. Second, acceptance is also an aspect of both self-regulation (as defined by differentiation of self) and mindfulness. Nonreactive, nonjudgmental intra- and interpersonal openness to present experience—typical of acceptance (Bishop et al., 2004; Coffey et al., 2010)—is a characteristic of persons scoring higher on measures of differentiation of self (Kerr & Bowen, 1988). For example, highly differentiated individuals are capable of "listen[ing] without reacting...[showing] respect [for] the identity of another without becoming critical...free to enjoy relationships...tolerant and respectful of differences...[and] intense feelings are well tolerated and so he[or she] does not act automatically to alleviate them" (Kerr & Bowen, 1988, p. 107). Detriangling has specific application to relational processes occurring between system members and the processes occurring within the therapist–client system. Specifically, clinicians must practice noticing and acceptance in the context of multiply embedded relational triangles.

Clinicians who work directly with parents in situations involving parentification or parental alienation might also intervene by educating parents on child development and relational triangles. Differentiation of self is a normative developmental process grounded in an individual's agency needs, specifically the needs for increased autonomy, self-sufficiency, and the resulting interpersonal distance that often occurs as one ages. Triangling is also a normative systems dynamic that facilitates the regulating of self and others' emotions and behavior and interpersonal closeness and distance. Knowledge of child development and triangling can thus offer parents a normalizing experience. The clinician can help parents learn to effectively regulate the anxiety they experience when their children attempt to differentiate. During this therapeutic process, it may be helpful for the clinician to explore parents' developmental experiences and discuss ways in which they themselves attempted to differentiate from their own parents. Parenting is, to some degree, influenced by parents' own level of differentiation of self, so a child's differentiating process offers a chance for the parent to work on his or her own intrapersonal and interpersonal functioning. Effective work with parents therefore involves coaching them to use different strategies to engage emotionally with their child rather than engaging in reactive and repetitive triangling processes. For example, parents can practice open, nonreactive, expressive communication with their child in the presence of a detriangled clinician. It may also be helpful to explore the parent's own family-of-origin relationships and look for ways that the parent can alter his or her behavior in those relationships.

Evidence-Based Practices

The clinical importance of addressing self-regulation difficulties has drawn significant attention. Two evidence-based approaches have obtained empirical support as practices for resolving self-regulation difficulties: emotion-focused therapies and mindfulness practices. Emotion-focused therapies attend to and intervene directly in affect regulation processes and have demonstrated clinical effectiveness with a range of presenting concerns (e.g., Elliott, Watson, Goldman, & Greenberg, 2004; Greenberg, 2002; Greenberg & Goldman, 2008; Johnson, 1996, 2002). Mindfulness practices, and the broader conceptual category of contemplative practices, have similarly demonstrated effectiveness with a diversity of clinical difficulties (e.g., Allen et al., 2006; Baer, 2003; Carmody & Baer, 2008; Fjorback, Arendt, Ørnbøl, Fink, & Walach, 2011).

Emotion-focused interventions focus on (a) resolving negative emotions and (b) promoting positive affect and prosocial relating (Greenberg, Warwar, & Malcolm, 2010), whereas mindfulness and other contemplative practices seek to promote change by increasing the individual's moment-by-moment awareness of emotional experience and behavior. Both kinds of interventions increase awareness, which then allows the person to respond intentionally, not reactively, within social relationships. The goals of increasing awareness to reduce reactivity and then responding proactively align closely with Bowen's (Kerr & Bowen, 1988) ideas about intra- and interpersonal differentiation. Differentiation of self is therefore a construct with the potential to provide a basis for an integrated approach to clinical work that draws on Bowen's family systems theory as well as on emotion-focused and contemplative practices. An integrated approach offers the clinician an effective means for facilitating clients' self-soothing. This means might then be used as a basis for assisting the client to relate differently with significant others outside of the therapeutic context, thereby promoting differentiated functioning. Finally, an integrated approach also offers the clinician effective means of intervening directly in the clients' relationships and promoting increased self-regulation by coaching clients on how to respond differently to each other in the here and now of the session— again facilitating increased differentiation of self.

Conclusion

Each of the four models of psychopathology consists of a lack of intra- and interpersonal self-regulation, or a lack of awareness of one's multiplicity of voices and self-in-context (Dimaggio et al., 2010). Self-dysregulation therefore results in reactive–repetitive interpersonal relating (L'Abate, 1983; L'Abate et al., 2010). However, under some conditions—perhaps most notably the conditions of traumatic entrapment and parentification—the reactive–repetitive responding may promote positive adaptation. So although assessment and case conceptualization might focus on the underlying dimension of self-dysregulation, systemic assessment and case conceptualization ideally attend to the ways in which the apparent dysfunction might also be functional and engender positive outcomes. An individual who experiences traumatic entrapment might display constricted awareness of self and might have repetitively shifted roles during the ordeal. However, these responses might in fact have enhanced the individual's survival (Cantor & Price, 2007). As another example, a parentified child may take care of a parent and younger siblings—but this might also promote positive growth (Hooper et al., 2008). Systemic assessment, case conceptualization, and intervention are thus oriented toward strength or resilience (Nutt & Stanton, 2011), and "relationship patterns that exist in seriously dysfunctional families are conceptualized as exaggerated versions of the same processes that are present in all families. In this sense, a natural systems orientation is a non-pathologizing theoretical framework that allows family psychology to approach human functioning from a strengths perspective" (p. 94).

Triangling processes are normative (Kerr & Bowen, 1988), and the ability to self-regulate is grounded in the basic human needs for communion and agency (L'Abate et al., 2010). In fact, triangling processes have a stabilizing effect on systems, thereby serving a relational regulating function for system members

(Kerr & Bowen, 1988; Titelman, 2008). Nevertheless, triangling processes can result in psychopathology due to the inherent tendency for triangling to occur at an automatic, implicit, reactive level of intra- and interpersonal functioning. Proactive, intentional acting in the face of the anxiety that fuels triangling becomes the clinical goal, which can be variously defined as growth toward systemic mindfulness (Shapiro & Schwartz, 1999), differentiation of self (Kerr & Bowen, 1988) or—as L'Abate et al. (2010) described—toward the relationally competent style of conductivity. Clinicians might benefit from a perspective grounded in ontological relationality that frames their role as an active participant in the therapist–client system and their ability to self-regulate amidst triangling processes and thereby effectively intervene in intra- and interpersonal regulation processes within the therapist–client system.

References

Allen, N. B., Chambers, R., Knight, W., Blashki, G., Ciechomski, L., Hassed, C., et al. (2006). Mindfulness-based psychotherapies: A review of conceptual foundations, empirical evidence and practical considerations. *Australian and New Zealand Journal of Psychiatry, 40*, 285–294. doi:10.1111/j.1440-1614.2006.01794.x.

Anderson, H. (2007a). The heart and soul of collaborative therapy: The philosophical stance—"a way of being" in relationship and conversation. In H. Anderson & D. Gehart (Eds.), *Collaborative therapy: Relationships and conversations that make a difference* (pp. 43–59). New York: Routledge/Taylor & Francis Group.

Anderson, H. (2007b). A postmodern umbrella: Language and knowledge as relational and generative, and inherently transforming. In H. Anderson & D. Gehart (Eds.), *Collaborative therapy: Relationships and conversations that make a difference* (pp. 7–19). New York: Routledge/Taylor & Francis Group.

Anderson, H., & Gehart, D. (2009). *Collaborative practice: Relationships and conversations that make a difference*. London: Routledge.

Baer, R. A. (2003). Mindfulness training as a clinical intervention: A conceptual and empirical review. *Clinical Psychology: Science and Practice, 10*, 125–143.

Baer, R. A., Smith, G. T., Hopkins, J., Krietemeyer, J., & Toney, L. (2006). Using self-report assessment methods to explore facets of mindfulness. *Assessment, 13*, 27–45.

Bailey, D. C. (2012). Assessment in marriage and family therapy: A review of clinical updates for family therapists. *Marriage & Family Review, 48*, 311–338. doi:10.1080/01494929.2012.674479.

Baker, A. L., & Ben-Ami, N. (2011). To turn a child against a parent is to turn a child against himself: The direct and indirect effects of exposure to parental alienation strategies on self-esteem and well-being. *Journal of Divorce & Remarriage, 52*, 472–489. doi:10.1080/1050255 6.2011.609424.

Ben-Ami, N., & Baker, A. J. L. (2012). The long-term correlates of childhood exposure to parental alienation on adult self-sufficiency and well-being. *American Journal of Family Therapy, 40*, 169–183. doi:10.1080/01926187.2011.601206.

Bishop, S. R., Lau, M., Shapiro, S., Carlson, L., Anderson, N. D., Carmody, J., et al. (2004). Mindfulness: A proposed operational definition. *Clinical Psychology: Science and Practice, 11*, 230–241. doi:10.1093/clipsy.bph077.

Bowen, M. (1978). *Family therapy in clinical practice*. New York: Jason Aronson.

Bray, J. H. (2009). Couple and family assessment. In J. H. Bray & M. Stanton (Eds.), *The Wiley-Blackwell handbook of family psychology* (pp. 151–164). West Sussex: Wiley-Blackwell. doi:10.1002/9781444310238.ch10.

Cantor, C., & Price, J. (2007). Traumatic entrapment, appeasement and complex post-traumatic stress disorder: Evolutionary perspectives of hostage reactions, domestic abuse and the Stockholm syndrome. *Australian and New Zealand Journal of Psychiatry, 41*, 377–384. doi:10.1080/00048670701261178.

Capaldi, D. M., & Rothbart, M. K. (1992). Development and validation of an early adolescent temperament measure. *The Journal of Early Adolescence, 12*, 153–173. doi:10.1177/0272431 692012002002.

Carmody, J., & Baer, R. A. (2008). Relationships between mindfulness practice and levels of mindfulness, medical and psychological symptoms and well-being in a mindfulness-based stress reduction program. *Journal of Behavioral Medicine, 31*, 23–33. doi:10.1007/s10865-007-9130-7.

Carr, A. (2000). Empirical approaches to family assessment. *Journal of Family Therapy, 22*, 121–127. doi:10.1111/1467-6427.00137.

Charmaz, K. (2000). Grounded theory: Objectivist and constructivist methods. In N. K. Denzin & Y. S. Lincoln (Eds.), *Handbook of qualitative research* (2nd ed., pp. 509–535). Thousand Oaks, CA: Sage.

Coffey, K. A., Hartman, M., & Fredrickson, B. L. (2010). Deconstructing mindfulness and constructing mental health: Understanding mindfulness and its mechanisms of action. *Mindfulness, 1*, 235–253. doi:10.1007/s12671-010-0033-2.

Cook, W. L., & Kenny, D. A. (2004). Application of the social relations model to family assessment. *Journal of Family Psychology, 18*, 361–371. doi:10.1037/0893-3200.18.2.361.

Cusinato, M., & L'Abate, L. (2008). Selfhood: A hidden ingredient in family therapy. *Journal of Family Psychotherapy, 19*, 320–329. doi:10.1080/08975350802475064.

Dallos, R., & Urry, A. (1999). Abandoning our parents and grandparents: Does social construction mean the end of systemic family therapy? *Journal of Family Therapy, 21*, 161–186. doi:10.1111/1467-6427.00112.

Davidson, R. J., Dunne, J., Eccles, J. S., Engle, A., Greenberg, M., Jennings, P., et al. (2012). Contemplative practices and mental training: Prospects for American education. *Child Development Perspectives, 6*, 146–153. doi:10.1111/j.1750-8606.2012.00240.x.

Dimaggio, G., Hermans, H. J. M., & Lysaker, P. H. (2010). Health and adaptation in a multiple self: The role of absence of dialogue and poor metacognition in clinical populations. *Theory & Psychology, 20*, 379–399. doi:10.1177/0959354310363319.

Elliott, R., Watson, J. C., Goldman, R. N., & Greenberg, L. S. (2004). *Learning emotion-focused therapy: The process-experiential approach to change.* Washington, DC: American Psychological Association. doi:10.1037/10725-000.

Ellis, L. K., & Rothbart, M. K. (2001). *Revision of the early adolescent temperament questionnaire.* Poster presented at the 2001 Biennial Meeting of the Society for Research in Child Development, Minneapolis, MN.

Evans, D. E., & Rothbart, M. K. (2007). Development of a model for adult temperament. *Journal of Research in Personality, 41*, 868–888.

Feld, B. G. (2007). The therapeutic effect of triadic interactive regulation on couple therapy. *Group, 31*, 171–183.

Fjorback, L. O., Arendt, M. M., Ørnbøl, E. E., Fink, P. P., & Walach, H. H. (2011). Mindfulness-based stress reduction and mindfulness-based cognitive therapy—a systematic review of randomized controlled trials. *Acta Psychiatrica Scandinavica, 124*, 102–119. doi:10.1111/j.1600-0447.2011.01704.x.

Garner, P. W., & Hinton, T. S. (2010). Emotional display rules and emotional self-regulation: Associations with bullying and victimization in community-based after school programs. *Journal of Community and Applied Social Psychology, 20*, 480–496. doi:10.1002/casp.1057.

Gartstein, M. A., & Rothbart, M. K. (2003). Studying infant temperament via the revised infant behavior questionnaire. *Infant Behavior and Development, 26*, 64–86.

Graham, D. L. R., Rawlings, E. I., Ihms, K., Latimer, D., Foliano, J., Thompson, A., et al. (1995). A scale for identifying "Stockholm syndrome" reactions in young dating women: Factor structure, reliability, and validity. *Violence and Victims, 10*, 3–22.

Gratz, K. L., & Roemer, L. (2004). Multidimensional assessment of emotion regulation and dysregulation: Development, factor structure, and initial validation of the difficulties in emotion regulations scale. *Journal of Psychopathology and Behavioral Assessment, 26*, 41–54.

Greenberg, L. S. (2002). Integrating an emotion-focused approach to treatment into psychotherapy integration. *Journal of Psychotherapy Integration, 12*, 154–189. doi:10.1037//1053-0479.12.2.154.

Greenberg, L. S., & Goldman, R. N. (2008). *Emotion-focused couples therapy: The dynamics of emotion, love, and power.* Washington, DC: American Psychological Association. doi:10.1037/11750-000.

Greenberg, L., Warwar, S., & Malcolm, W. (2010). Emotion-focused couples therapy and the facilitation of forgiveness. *Journal of Marital and Family Therapy, 36*, 28–42. doi:10.1111/j.1752-0606.2009.00185.x.

Heath, A. (1993). Reading signs. In A. H. Rambo, A. Heath, & R. J. Chenail (Eds.), *Practicing therapy: Exercises for growing therapists* (pp. 89–153). New York: W. W. Norton.

Hermans, H. J. M. (2004). The innovation of self-narratives: A dialogical approach. In L. E. Angus & J. McLeod (Eds.), *The handbook of narrative and psychotherapy: Practice, theory, and research* (pp. 175–191). Thousand Oaks, CA: Sage.

Hermans, H. J. M., Kempen, H. J., & van Loon, R. J. (1992). The dialogical self: Beyond individualism and rationalism. *American Psychologist, 47*, 23–33. doi:10.1037/0003-066X.47.1.23.

Hoffman, L. (1985). Beyond power and control: Toward a "second order" family systems therapy. *Family Systems Medicine, 3*, 381–396. doi:10.1037/h0089674.

Hoffman, L. (1990). Constructing realities: An art of lenses. *Family Process, 29*, 1–12.

Hoffman, L. (1991). A reflexive stance for family therapy. *Journal of Strategic & Systemic Therapies, 10*, 4–17.

Hooper, L. M. (2012). Parentification. In R. J. R. Levesque (Ed.), *Encyclopedia of adolescence* (Vol. 4, pp. 2023–2031). New York: Springer.

Hooper, L. M., Marotta, S. A., & Lanthier, R. P. (2008). Predictors of growth and distress following parentification among college students. *Journal of Child and Family Studies, 17*, 693–705.

Ivey, D. C., Scheel, M. J., & Jankowski, P. J. (1999). A contextual perspective of clinical judgement in couples and family therapy: Is the bridge too far? *Journal of Family Therapy, 21*, 339–359. doi:10.1111/1467-6427.00124.

Jackson, T., Mackenzie, J., & Hobfoll, S. E. (2000). Communal aspects of self-regulation. In M. Boekaerts, P. R. Pintrich, & M. Zeidner (Eds.), *Handbook of self-regulation* (pp. 275–300). San Diego, CA: Academic. doi:10.1016/B978-012109890-2/50038-X.

Jankowski, P. J., & Hooper, L. M. (2012). Differentiation of self: A validation study of the Bowen theory construct. *Couple and Family Psychology: Research and Practice, 1*, 226–243. doi:10.1037/a0027469.

Jankowski, P. J., & Ivey, D. C. (2001). Problem definition in marital and family therapy: A qualitative study. *Contemporary Family Therapy, 23*, 419–439. doi:10.1023/A:1013001012043.

Jankowski, P. J., Ivey, D. C., & Vaughn, M. J. (2011, August). *Contextualizing clinical judgment: Advancing a model of problem formation.* Paper presented at the 119th Annual Convention of the American Psychological Association, Washington, DC.

Jankowski, P. J., Ivey, D. C., & Vaughn, M. J. (2012). Re-visioning a model of clinical judgment for systemic practitioners. *Journal of Systemic Therapies, 31*, 17–35.

Johnson, S. M. (1996). *The practice of emotionally focused marital therapy: Creating connection.* New York: Brunner/Mazel.

Johnson, S. M. (2002). *Emotionally focused couple therapy with trauma survivors: Strengthening attachment bonds.* New York: Guilford.

Karpman, S. B. (1968). Fairy tales and script drama analysis. *Transactional Analysis Bulletin, 7*, 39–43.

Karpman, S. B. (2009). Sex games people play: Intimacy blocks, games, and scripts. *Transactional Analysis Journal, 39*, 103–116.

Kerr, M. E., & Bowen, M. (1988). *Family evaluation.* New York: W. W. Norton.

L'Abate, L. (1983). Styles in intimate relationships: The A-R-C Model. *Personnel & Guidance Journal, 61*, 277–283. doi:10.1111/j.2164-4918.1983.tb00025.x.

L'Abate, L., Cusinato, M., Maino, E., Colesso, W., & Scilletta, C. (2010). *Relational competence theory: Research and mental health applications*. New York: Springer. doi:10.1007/978-1-4419-5665-1.

Lassiter, L. L. (2008). The regulatory function of the triangle. In P. Titelman (Ed.), *Triangles: Bowen family systems theory perspectives* (pp. 63–89). New York: Haworth.

McCullough, M. E., & Willoughby, B. L. (2009). Religion, self-regulation, and self-control: Associations, explanations, and implications. *Psychological Bulletin, 135*, 69–93.

McGoldrick, M., Gerson, R., & Shellenberger, S. (1999). *Genograms: Assessment and intervention* (2nd ed.). New York: W. W. Norton.

Nutt, R. L., & Stanton, M. (2011). Family psychology specialty practice. *Couple and Family Psychology: Research and Practice, 1*, 92–105. doi:10.1037/2160-4096.1.S.91.

Putnam, S. P., Gartstein, M. A., & Rothbart, M. K. (2006). Measurement of fine-grained aspects of toddler temperament: The early childhood behavior questionnaire. *Infant Behavior and Development, 29*, 386–401.

Putnam, S. P., & Rothbart, M. K. (2006). Development of short and very short forms of the children's behavior questionnaire. *Journal of Personality Assessment, 87*, 102–112.

Rober, P. (1999). The therapist's inner conversation in family therapy practice: Some ideas about the self of the therapist, therapeutic impasse, and the process of reflection. *Family Process, 38*, 209–228.

Rober, P. (2005). The therapist's self in dialogical family therapy: Some ideas about not-knowing and the therapist's inner conversation. *Family Process, 44*, 477–495. doi:10.1111/j.1545-5300.2005.00073.x.

Ross, J. M., & Babcock, J. C. (2010). Gender and intimate partner violence in the United States: Confronting the controversies. *Sex Roles, 62*, 194–200. doi:10.1007/s11199-009-9677-6.

Rothbart, M. K., Ahadi, S. A., & Evans, D. E. (2000). Temperament and personality: Origins and outcomes. *Journal of Personality and Social Psychology, 78*, 122–135.

Shapiro, S. L., & Schwartz, G. E. (1999). Intentional systemic mindfulness: An integrative model for self-regulations and health. *Advances in Mind-Body Medicine, 15*, 128–134.

Shults, F. L., & Sandage, S. J. (2006). *Transforming spirituality: Integrating theology and psychology*. Grand Rapids, MI: Baker Academic.

Simonds, J., Kieras, J. E., Rueda, M. R., & Rothbart, M. K. (2007). Effortful control, executive attention, and emotional regulation in 7-10 year-old children. *Cognitive Development, 22*, 474–488.

Skowron, E. A., & Schmitt, T. A. (2003). Assessing interpersonal fusion: Reliability and validity of a new DSI fusion with others subscale. *Journal of Marital and Family Therapy, 29*, 209–222. doi:10.1111/j.1752-0606.2003.tb01201.x.

Slife, B. D. (2004). Taking practice seriously: Toward a relational ontology. *Journal of Theoretical and Philosophical Psychology, 24*, 157–178. doi:10.1037/h0091239.

Slife, B. D., & Wiggins, B. J. (2009). Taking relationship seriously in psychotherapy: Radical relationality. *Journal of Contemporary Psychotherapy, 39*, 17–24. doi:10.1007/s10879-008-9100-6.

Stanton, M., & Welsh, R. (2011). *Specialty competencies in couple and family psychology*. New York: Oxford University Press.

Telzer, E. H., & Fuligni, A. J. (2009). Daily family assistance and the psychological well-being of adolescents from Latin American, Asian, and European backgrounds. *Developmental Psychology, 45*, 1177–1189. doi:10.1037/a0014728.

Titelman, P. (2008). The concept of the triangle in Bowen theory: An overview. In P. Titelman (Ed.), *Triangles: Bowen family systems theory perspectives* (pp. 3–61). New York: Haworth.

Vaughn, M. J. (2004). Creating "maneuvering room": A grounded theory of language and influence in marriage and family therapy. *Contemporary Family Therapy, 26*, 425–442. doi:10.1007/s10591-004-0645-6.

Volf, M. (1996). *Exclusion and embrace: A theological exploration of identity, otherness, and reconciliation*. Nashville, TN: Abingdon Press.

White, M. (2000). Re-engaging with history: The absent but implicit. In M. White (Ed.), *Reflections on narrative practice* (pp. 35–58). Adelaide: Dulwich Centre Publications.

White, M. (2006). Working with people who are suffering the consequences of multiple trauma: A narrative perspective. In D. Denborough (Ed.), *Trauma: Narrative responses to traumatic experience* (pp. 25–85). Adelaide: Dulwich Centre Publications.

Widiger, T. A., Livesley, W. J., & Clark, L. A. (2009). An integrative dimensional classification of personality disorder. *Psychological Assessment, 21*, 243–255. doi:10.1037/a0016606.

Wills, T. A., Pokhrel, P., Morehouse, E., & Fenster, B. (2011). Behavioral and emotional regulation and adolescent substance use problems: A test of moderation effects in a dual-process model. *Psychology of Addictive Behaviors, 25*, 279–292. doi:10.1037/a0022870.

Chapter 8
Conclusion: Future of Relational Psychopathology

In some ways, the field of relational psychopathology is in its infancy. The four psychopathology models reviewed in this book—parentification, parental alienation, bullying, and Stockholm syndrome—inform the discourse about the complexity of determining what constitutes normal versus pathological roles, interactions, and relationships, including borderline psychopathology. The accumulated literature makes clear that many roles and relationships and their associated interactions fall somewhere on a continuum ranging from normality to psychopathology, although some of the models presented in this book have more empirical support than others. The extent of any link between severe psychopathology and the four psychopathology models discussed in this book remains less clear. More specifically, unequivocal empirical evidence does not yet exist for the presence of the roles, relationships, and processes described here in the etiology of severe psychopathology.

Some of the literature reviewed in this book (see Chaps. 3–6) links these models to psychological distress and disorders and to reduced physical health and functioning (Baker & Ben-Ami, 2011; Cantor & Price, 2007; Hooper, DeCoster, White-Chapman, & Voltz, 2011; Hooper, Doehler, Jankowski, & Tomek, 2012). However, not all the research on these connections has pointed to deleterious and pernicious outcomes (Ben-Ami & Baker, 2012; Hooper, 2012; Hooper, Marotta, & Lanthier, 2008). Therefore, we must conclude that the absence of a plethora of empirical literature for some of the models underscores the need to conceptualize these models—including their antecedents and aftereffects—as preliminary and varied, that is, not as leading only to general pathological outcomes, only to positive outcomes, or only to severe pathology.

In addition to the preliminary associations between these models and select factors—associations that have been amassed in the literature and described in this book—researchers and scholars are encouraged to examine pathways that uncover predictors, moderators, and mediators of these associations. Such future investigations have the potential to inform the development and testing of preventions, interventions, and treatments for relational distress. It could be that certain factors buffer or exacerbate outcomes like psychological distress, severe psychopathology,

L.M. Hooper et al., *Models of Psychopathology: Generational Processes and Relational Roles*, DOI 10.1007/978-1-4614-8081-5_8,
© Springer Science+Business Media New York 2014

resilience, and posttraumatic growth. Examples of such buffering or exacerbating factors include the length of time one is embedded in the context where the relationship emerges or the type of relational context in which parentification, parental alienation, bullying, or Stockholm syndrome takes place. Early childhood and current attachment styles could be an interesting construct to study in investigations that focus on factors that moderate the outcomes of these models. In addition to the criticality of context and relational factors in the emergence of psychopathology or wellness, it is also likely that cerebral, genetic, and physiological factors influence that emergence, although future research is needed to disentangle explanatory and causal models. The accuracy and complexity of defining and diagnosing psychopathology related to the four models is evidenced in their absence from the revised version of the current *Diagnostic and Statistical Manual of Mental Disorders* (4th ed., text rev.; *DSM-IV-TR*; American Psychiatric Association, 2000). Although the final version of the fifth edition (*DSM-V*) has not yet been published, it appears that parentification, parental alienation, bullying, and Stockholm syndrome will all be excluded from the proposed new edition.

Other challenges associated with conceptualizing, diagnosing, and treating relational psychopathology are evident in the nature of the models reviewed in this book. These models are different and, by definition, do not lend themselves to the commonly used linear and categorical classifications of psychopathology (Baldwin, Cole, & Baldwin, 1982; Garrison & Earls, 1987; Gelfand & Peterson, 1985; Hudson & Rapee, 2005). In fact, many clinicians and mental health providers are likely to question or reject the validity of these models, because they are in some ways inconsistent with how mental health providers have long considered and responded to psychological distress, dysfunctional behaviors, and psychopathology. Nonetheless, from the possible normative antecedents of these four psychopathologies, their commonalities defy linear attempts at classification and raise significant questions about whether past efforts to cluster and classify mental health symptoms represented an ill-fated attempt to understand mental illnesses without some clarity about their possible etiological origins in normative processes (Gelfand & Peterson, 1985; Haynes, 1992; Lahey, Moffitt, & Caspi, 2003; Sheets & Craighead, 2007; Skodol, 2012; Widiger, 2007). The information introduced in this book regarding the deadly drama triangle (DT; Karpman, 1968, 2009; L'Abate, 2009), relational competence theory (RCT), and the four psychopathology models offers researchers and scholars an alternative way to think about pathology going forward.

In the future, the deadly DT can be used as an important assessment tool for researchers, clinicians, and scholars in several ways (Karpman, 2009; L'Abate, 2009). The deadly DT can aid mental health providers in conceptualizing, diagnosing, and treating relational pathology. For example, the deadly DT as evidenced in parentification, parental alienation, bullying, and Stockholm syndrome helps clarify how conventional, linear thinking and individual approaches may not be reliable, valid, or applicable. In addition, the deadly DT helps elucidate how psychopathology can emerge from both functional and dysfunctional roles and relationships. These models not only raise questions about the applicability of intrapsychic psychiatric diagnoses that have been the norm since their inception, but the models also raise questions about how to intervene with people involved in deadly DTs. For example, these psychopathology models have shown how insidious triangles are (Kerr & Bowen, 1988; Titelman, 2008) and the extent to which they may have longer-lasting aftereffects than do linear emotional, mental, physical, or sexual abuse or poverty. Without a proper diagnosis—if one is warranted—treatment is often based on a single individual approach. Such an approach is problematic and ineffective if the individual returns to the same pathogenic triangular situation with significant others (intimates) or captors—in the case of Stockholm syndrome—who have been involved in the origin of the relational disorder.

Importantly, without awareness of the deleterious relational context (e.g., deadly DTs), how can clinicians and mental health providers address factors that are completely outside the individual's awareness, as well as that of significant others or intimates, as discussed in this book? Toward this end, Biglan, Flay, Embry, and Sandler (2012) underscored how an individual-focused approach may be ineffective:

> Without a drastic shift away from a focus on individual problems, to a focus on the prevalence of nurturing environments, progress in reducing mental, emotional, and behavioral disorders will continue at a glacial pace... If practice agencies continue to fund interventions that target only individual disorders, then it will be similarly difficult to discover efficient methods of preventing and treating problems. (p. 267)

Therefore, the importance of considering familial, relational, contextual, and environmental factors in the study and treatment of psychopathology cannot be overstated.

Even though the family system—including the parent system (Baldwin et al., 1982)—has been recognized as the natural context for psychopathology (Hudson & Rapee, 2005; L'Abate, 2006; Schneewind & Ruppert, 1998), another system or factor has been underrecognized and understudied, and it must be taken into consideration, namely, sibling position and the sibling system (Hooper et al., 2011; Kerr & Bowen, 1988; Toman, 1979). It would be valuable to explore the interactions among sibling position, various models of RCT, and the deadly DT, as outlined in Chap. 2. Even though sibling position has long been proffered in the clinical literature as being associated with diverse outcomes, it is less clear whether there is an empirical relation between sibling position and the outcomes of the four psychopathology models presented in this book. No sufficient empirical evidence exists about the validity or implications of sibling position with regard to pathological roles, interactions, and relationships. Future studies could explore sibling position as a possible moderator or predictor of outcomes related to the four models. When the validity of sibling position is sufficiently validated or invalidated, it will be possible to draw some preliminary conclusions about a possible interaction between sibling positions and models of psychopathology included in this book.

Parallels exist between researchers' and clinicians' perceptions about personality disorders and the four models presented in this book. These four models span the range between functionality and dysfunctionality, similar to the long-held view regarding personality disorders. Conceptually, most research about personality disorders and psychopathology has likely been representative of a myopic view, put forward models that place personality in a rigid box, and fail to clarify the criticality of self in relationship with significant others outside of that box (Barlow, 1993; Clarkin & Lenzenweger, 1996; Costa & Widiger, 1994; Livesley, 1995, 2001; Millon, 1981; Millon, Blaney, & Davis, 1999; Sheets & Craighead, 2007; Skodol, 2012; Widiger, 2007; Widiger, Livesley, & Clark, 2009). Moreover, the mention of family or even intimate relationships of any kind in past references on personality disorders is minimal if not absent, supporting the position that this has been an unexplored (if not bypassed) area in past conceptualizing about these disorders. Livesley, Jang, Jackson, & Vernon (1993), for instance, makes no mention of the family in early works, and later Livesley (2001) mentions the family minimally in updated works. Clarkin and Lenzenweger (1996) mentioned only "family therapy" but fail to expound on the criticality of the family. What is even more indicative of the monadic orientation of past psychological thinking about personality disorders is found in an otherwise excellent treatise about "models of causality in psychopathology" put forward by Haynes (1992), where no mention of the family was made.

By using only the personality construct, most researchers and theoreticians seem unable to advance and think specifically about human relationships in their own right. These relationships are worthy of separate conceptual and empirical evaluations and interventions, as explained in Chap. 2.

Furthermore, L'Abate (in press) has argued that the family and personality constructs are no longer tenable, either theoretically, empirically, or practically. Intimate relationships, identities, and roles are more appropriate and verifiable constructs than family qua family and personality qua personality. Indeed, as a new discovery, asserting the importance of the relationship between self-identity and intimacy (Skodol, 2012) allows for innovative research, not yet in the mainstream of current psychological thinking and consonant with most models of RCT, as summarized in Chap. 2 (L'Abate, in press). It is tempting to suggest that even within severe psychopathology there coexist personality disorders, as seen in many dual diagnoses or comorbidity. Even present-day attempts to reduce categories to dimensions, as discussed in Chap. 2, are not sufficient to deal with recent developments that attempt to add a relational component to static personality traits and psychiatric categories (Clay, 2012; Ewen, 1993; Feist & Feist, 2002; Klein, Kupfer, & Shea, 1993; Krueger & Tackett, 2006; L'Abate, 2006; Matthews, Deary, & Whiteman, 2003; McCrae & Costa, 1990; Page, 1983; Patterson, 1990; Skodol, 2012; Wrightsman, 1994a, 1994b).

As most of the chapters of this book attest, the links among the select roles, relationships, and dyadic and triadic interaction patterns evidenced between psychopathology and each of the four models—namely, parentification, parental alienation, bullying, and Stockholm syndrome—are complex and multifactorial. We hope that this book will help researchers and clinicians avoid conceptualizing the antecedents and outcomes of these models myopically. Perhaps the greatest challenge is disentangling when, for whom, and under what conditions these roles and relationships foretell psychopathology and likewise disentangling when, for whom, and under what conditions these roles and relationships foretell resiliency and growth. The second greatest challenge may lie in developing and testing interventions and treatments that meet the diverse needs of individuals and families who have experienced parentification, parental alienation, bullying, or Stockholm syndrome. Relational competence theory and the deadly drama triangle may offer researchers and clinicians a beginning point from which to conceptualize and develop innovative interventions and treatments.

References

American Psychiatric Association. (2000). *Diagnostic and statistical manual of mental health disorders* (4th ed., text rev.). Washington, DC: Author.

Baker, A. L., & Ben-Ami, N. (2011). To turn a child against a parent is to turn a child against himself: The direct and indirect effects of exposure to parental alienation strategies on self-esteem and well-being. *Journal of Divorce & Remarriage, 52*, 472–489. doi:10.1080/1050255 6.2011.609424.

Baldwin, A. L., Cole, R. E., & Baldwin, C. P. (1982). Parental pathology, family interaction, and the competence of the child in school. *Monographs of the Society for Research in Child Development, No. 197.*

Barlow, D. H. (Ed.). (1993). *Clinical handbook of psychological disorders.* New York: Guilford.

Ben-Ami, N., & Baker, A. J. L. (2012). The long-term correlates of childhood exposure to parental alienation on adult self-sufficiency and well-being. *American Journal of Family Therapy, 40*, 169–183. doi:10.1080/01926187.2011.601206.

Biglan, A., Flay, B. R., Embry, D. D., & Sandler, I. N. (2012). The critical role of nurturing environments for promoting human well-being. *American Psychologist, 67*, 257–271.

Cantor, C., & Price, J. (2007). Traumatic entrapment, appeasement and complex post-traumatic stress disorder: Evolutionary perspectives of hostage reactions, domestic abuse and the Stockholm syndrome. *Australian and New Zealand Journal of Psychiatry, 41*, 377–384. doi:10.1080/00048670701261178.

Clarkin, J. F., & Lenzenweger, M. E. (Eds.). (1996). *Major theories of personality disorders.* New York: Guilford.

Clay, R. A. (2012, February). Improving disorder classification, worldwide. *Monitor on Psychology*, 40–44.

Costa, O. T., & Widiger, T. A. (Eds.). (1994). *Personality disorders and the five-factor model of personality.* Washington, DC: American Psychological Association.

Ewen, R. B. (1993). *An introduction to theories of personality.* Hillsdale, NJ: Erlbaum.

Feist, J., & Feist, G. J. (2002). *Theories of personality.* Boston, MA: McGraw-Hill.

Garrison, W. T., & Earls, F. J. (1987). *Temperament and child psychopathology.* Thousand Oaks, CA: Sage.

Gelfand, D. M., & Peterson, L. (1985). *Child development and psychopathology.* Beverly Hills, CA: Sage.

Haynes, S. N. (1992). *Models of causality and psychopathology: Toward dynamic, synthetic, and nonlinear models of behavior disorders.* New York: Macmillan.

Hooper, L. M. (2012). Parentification. In R. J. R. Levesque (Ed.), *Encyclopedia of adolescence* (Vol. 4, pp. 2023–2031). New York: Springer.

Hooper, L. M., DeCoster, J., White-Chapman, N., & Voltz, M. L. (2011). Characterizing the magnitude of the relation between self-reported childhood parentification and adult psychopathology: A meta-analysis. *Journal of Clinical Psychology, 67*, 1028–1043. doi:10.1002/jclp.20807.

Hooper, L. M., Doehler, K., Jankowski, P. J., & Tomek, S. E. (2012). Patterns of self-reported alcohol use, depressive symptoms, and body mass index in a family sample: The buffering effects of parentification. *The Family Journal: Counseling and Therapy for Couples and Families, 20*, 164–178. doi:10.1177/1066480711435320.

Hooper, L. M., Marotta, S. A., & Lanthier, R. P. (2008). Predictors of growth and distress following parentification among college students. *Journal of Child and Family Studies, 17*, 693–705.

Hudson, J. L., & Rapee, R. N. (Eds.). (2005). *Psychopathology and the family*. Boston, MA: Elsevier.

Karpman, S. B. (1968). Fairy tales and script drama analysis. *Transactional Analysis Bulletin, 7*, 39–43.

Karpman, S. B. (2009). Sex games people play: Intimacy blocks, games, and scripts. *Transactional Analysis Journal, 39*, 103–116.

Kerr, M. E., & Bowen, M. (1988). *Family evaluation*. New York: W. W. Norton.

Klein, M. J., Kupfer, D. J., & Shea, M. T. (Eds.). (1993). *Personality and depression: A current view*. New York: Guilford.

Krueger, R. E., & Tackett, J. L. (Eds.). (2006). *Personality and psychopathology*. New York: Guilford.

L'Abate, L. (2006). Toward a relational theory for psychiatric classification. *American Journal of Family Therapy, 34*, 1–15.

L'Abate, L. (2009). The drama triangle: An attempt to resurrect a neglected pathogenic model in family therapy theory and practice. *The American Journal of Family Therapy, 37*, 1–11. doi:10.1080/01926180701870163.

L'Abate, L. (in press). *Emerging constructs in family and personality psychology*. New York: Springer-Science.

Lahey, B. B., Moffitt, T. T., & Caspi, A. (Eds.). (2003). *Causes of conduct disorder and juvenile delinquency*. New York: Guilford.

Livesley, W. J. (Ed.). (1995). *Personality disorders*. New York: Guilford.

Livesley, W. J. (Ed.). (2001). *Handbook of personality disorders: Theory, research, and treatment*. New York: Guilford.

Livesley, W. J., Jang, K. L., Jackson, D. N., & Vernon, P. A. (1993). Genetic and environmental contributions to dimensions of personality disorder. *The American Journal of Psychiatry, 150*, 1826–1831.

Matthews, G., Deary, I. J., & Whiteman, M. (2003). *Personality traits* (2nd ed). Cambridge, Cambridge University Press.

McCrae, R. R., & Costa, P. T., Jr. (1990). *Personality in adulthood*. New York: Guilford.

Millon, T. (1981). *Disorders of personality: DSM-III: Axis II*. New York: Wiley.

Millon, T., Blaney, P. H., & Davis, R. D. (Eds.). (1999). *Oxford textbooks of psychopathology*. New York: Oxford University Press.

Page, M. M. (Ed.). (1983). *Nebraska symposium on motivation: Personality—Current theory and research*. Lincoln, NE: Nebraska University Press.

Patterson, G. R. (Ed.). (1990). *Depression and aggression in family interaction*. Hillsdale, NJ: Erlbaum.

Schneewind, K. A., & Ruppert, S. (1998). *Personality and family development: An intergenerational, longitudinal comparison*. Mahwah, NJ: Erlbaum.

Sheets, E., & Craighead, W. E. (2007). Toward an empirically based classification of personality pathology. *Clinical Psychology: Science and Practice, 14*, 77–93.

Skodol, A. E. (2012). Personality disorders in DSM-5. *Annual Review of Clinical Psychology, 8*, 317–344.

Titelman, P. (2008). The concept of the triangle in Bowen theory: An overview. In P. Titelman (Ed.), *Triangles: Bowen family systems theory perspectives* (pp. 3–61). New York: Haworth.

Toman, W. (1979). *Family therapy and sibling position*. Northvale, NJ: Aronson.

Widiger, T. A. (2007). An empirically-based classification of personality pathology: Where do we go from here? *Clinical Psychology: Science and Practice, 14*, 94–97.

Widiger, T. A., Livesley, W. J., & Clark, L. A. (2009). An integrative dimensional classification of personality disorder. *Psychological Assessment, 21*, 243–255. doi:10.1037/a0016606.

Wrightsman, L. S. (1994a). *Adult personality development: Applications*. Thousand Oaks, CA: Sage.

Wrightsman, L. S. (1994b). *Adult personality development: Theories and concepts*. Thousand Oaks, CA: Sage.

Introduction to Appendices

Mental Health Services in the Twenty-First Century: The Benefits of Using Workbooks in Evaluation and Treatment Planning

The purpose of the appendices that follow is to provide useful exercises and workbooks for patients and providers that can inform and supplement mental health care for individuals, couples, and families with a history of relational and generational psychopathology as described in the chapters of this book. The utility of self-exploration writing exercises, similar to those found in Appendices A through F, has been described extensively by L'Abate (see L'Abate, 2013a). L'Abate argued that scientific principles in mental health treatments and interventions (e.g., health promotion, self-help, sickness prevention, psychotherapy, and rehabilitation) imply a continuous evaluation aimed at choosing the most appropriate approach followed by a consideration of the extent to which the approach is efficacious and effective. Most importantly, as L'Abate suggested, no psychological intervention should occur without pre- and post-evaluation, including some follow-up after the termination of mental health services. Although exploratory in nature, the six workbooks that appear in this book can be used to inform pre- and post-evaluation, treatment planning, and follow-up. These assessments can be done by the patient either as a stand-alone activity (self-evaluation) or with the provider's assistance during therapeutic sessions. The seminal issue to consider is what type of assessments and what kind of interventions should occur.

Psychological Evaluations and Interventions: Art or Science?

Mental health interventions must be based on replicable, standardized evaluation procedures and must rely on structured programs—preferably but not always in writing—rather than following an artistic, immediate, and mostly reactive approach.

L.M. Hooper et al., *Models of Psychopathology: Generational Processes and Relational Roles*, DOI 10.1007/978-1-4614-8081-5,
© Springer Science+Business Media New York 2014

Such evaluations recommended by L'Abate (see L'Abate, 2013c) can and should occur before providers begin working with patients and before providers establish a treatment plan. Importantly, these assessments can be done using a range of methods: face to face; in a virtual interaction (e.g., Skype or FaceTime); or via offline communication media (mail, facsimile, and phone). Irrespective of the method, these assessments should follow a sequential stepped-care approach as reviewed by L'Abate (2013a, 2013b). This flexibility in methods of conducting assessments enables providers to be efficient and culturally responsive, and it allows providers to use the range of methods available in the twenty-first century. It is simply not practical or possible in this century to maintain the one-on-one (or one professional–one patient) framework in face-to-face, talk-based healthcare encounters. Some scholars have contended that this approach is an outdated paradigm that cannot fulfill the increasing mental health needs of our diverse patient population (L'Abate, 2012a).

The importance of diverse approaches, such as the ones that support the workbooks in the appendices of this book, cannot be overstated. As long as therapists continue to rely completely and routinely on talk, rather than incorporating written as well as nonverbal approaches—such as self-evaluation (Cummings & O'Donohue, 2012; Harwood & L'Abate, 2010), health promotion (L'Abate, 2005, 2007), and sickness prevention—there will be limited empirical literature on whether and how much mental health providers are as efficient and effective as they could be. For example, it is plausible that the same therapeutic outcomes could be evidenced with writing and other nonverbal and pre- and post-therapeutic evaluation methods as compared to traditional therapy models. In addition, these methods could be beneficial and less expensive than talk-based psychotherapy. To survive, flourish, and culturally tailor evaluation and treatments relevant for this century, mental health professionals will need to rely more on replicable, cost-effective approaches that can be validated through research as well as through practice. This may mean relying more on distance writing and computer-assisted evaluations, assessments, and interventions (De Giacomo, L'Abate, Pennebaker, & Rumbaugh, 2010; L'Abate, 2011b, 2012c; L'Abate & Sweeney, 2011). Advances in the use of homework and workbook assignments (Kazantzis & L'Abate, 2007; L'Abate, 2011a), in technology (L'Abate & Kaiser, 2011) and in self-help methods (Harwood & L'Abate, 2010) all indicate that providers of any theoretical or therapeutic orientation have no reason not to rely on the range of well-validated choices that are available before they initiate talk-based, face-to-face, one-on-one counseling and psychotherapy (L'Abate, 2013c). Importantly, and as previously mentioned, these methods can enhance evaluation and treatment planning.

Evaluations and Treatment Planning: Programmed Writing and New Methods

Before employing an evaluation method, providers must consider numerous issues. First, they must contend with and select from many, sometime competing, evaluations and interventions: (a) talk-based versus writing-based; (b) structured versus unstructured; and (c) theory-grounded versus unrelated to theory (Sweeney & L'Abate, 2011).

Second, providers will have to choose between either (a) mimicking online their traditional face-to-face ways of conducting assessments and evaluations and delivering psychological interventions face to face or (b) infusing new, innovative, and technology-informed structured approaches (L'Abate, 2013a, 2013b, 2013c).

As a third issue to consider, providers will have to determine the extent to which new interventions that are conceptually and empirically based—as presented in the exploratory workbooks that appear in Appendices A–F—can be developed and used efficiently and effectively. Currently these workbooks have been presented as interactive exercises (L'Abate, 2011c) based on generational and relational processes (Cusinato & L'Abate, 2012).

The process used to develop interactive exercises and checklists—similar to the ones evinced in the Appendices—can be easily replicated (see L'Abate, 2011c). The process includes five steps: (1) surveys or checklists can be transformed to an interactive exercise by the simple conversion of asking participants to define (with or without a dictionary) each item (i.e., items on the survey or checklist); (2) participants can be directed to provide two personal examples for each item on the checklist, a nomothetic step; (3) participants can be directed to rank items according to how important they are to them, an idiographic step; (4) the results derived from the ranking process can be used to determine which items are important to the participant (or patient) and can inform a treatment plan; and (5) results derived from the ranking process can be used to determine the developmental origin, intensity, frequency, rate, and personal and relational outcomes of a select construct or process (e.g., parentification and personality disturbances).

Further validation of a checklist would involve at least four additional steps: (a) creating as many experimental items found in the literature, (b) administering the checklist to participants, (c) dropping nondifferentiating items and keeping those that show some differentiating properties in validity and reliability, and finally (d) administering checklists to find how each can differentiate one model from the others. Once a checklist is validated, it will be possible to (a) examine the extent to which it correlates in an expected way with other checklists, (b) expand it into an interactive exercise to evaluate its outcome compared with those of the other workbooks, and (c) make it available in a Web-based or otherwise computer-assisted version or practice.

In summary, the purpose of checklists is to (a) objectify each model, (b) differentiate one model from other models, and (c) convert each checklist into workbooks that could be administered for self-help, promotional, preventive, evaluation, assessment, and therapeutic purposes. The simple procedure described above allows scholars to convert, transform, and expand any checklist into a dynamic, interactive exercise to be administered to promote mental health, prevent mental illness, deal with crisis intervention, and provide psychotherapy. In addition to workbooks, other methods have been proposed to inform evaluation and treatment planning.

Supplementing Workbooks in Evaluation and Treatment Planning: Telehealth

Ever since the development of methods of communication, physicians and mental health providers have been using a range of frameworks to collect and exchange health-related information. The emergence of new shared media, such as virtual reality, is changing the ways in which providers and patients relate, communicate, interact, and live. The integration of telehealth or electronic health (e-health) technologies have given rise to the most prevalent and discussed methods of communication in mental health services. Many e-health practices have improved the quality of health care, demonstrated substantial cost savings, and contributed to state-of-the-art evaluation, treatment planning, and healthcare services (Riva, 2000).

The preliminary infusion and use of these technologies are dramatically changing provider–patient relationships, expectations, and behaviors. Consequently, some current, long-used evaluation and treatment models implemented by providers will have to adjust. For example, healthcare providers will need to make changes to their practices, to provide culturally competent and sensitive health care that relies on alternative methods of virtual interaction rather than traditional face-to-face methods such as paper-and-pencil surveys and in-person diagnostic interviews (Yellowlees & Nafiz, 2010). Many scholars, researchers, and providers have suggested that telehealth and telemedicine may facilitate more culturally responsive health care, particularly in rural communities.

Telehealth and telemedicine—referring to the use of telecommunications to provide health information and care across a distance—have emerged as a potentially effective way to provide general and specialty healthcare services. Providing mental health services via videoconferencing, Internet, or other technologies has become an increasingly routine component of mental health service delivery throughout the world. In a review of the literature, Richardson et al. (2009) described the extent to which the field of telemental health (including evaluation and treatment methods) has advanced the research agenda with implications for telemental healthcare delivery for special clinical populations. Richardson and colleagues suggested that the accumulated results have demonstrated that telemental health services are well received by patients, improve health outcomes, and are cost-effective. Moreover, they asserted that in randomized controlled studies, telemental health has demonstrated equivalent efficacy compared to face-to-face care in a variety of clinical settings and with specific patient populations. The research agenda and practice implications for telemental health have not been yet fully translated. The consequences for future research and practice are discussed further below.

Health providers in all disciplines must become visionaries in addressing education, training, and healthcare delivery in the next decade. The effects of technological, economic, social, and demographic changes in the United States will have a direct impact on healthcare needs and the healthcare profession (Miller & Gallicchio, 2007). Integrating new communications technologies will engender both benefits and challenges in healthcare providers' assessment and treatment planning processes. The new millennium brings the potential for an integrated and collaborative clinical, research, and educational environment to promote the most efficacious and effective patient care. The focus of this collaborative environment must address the critical elements of globalization, empowerment, technology, and leadership from a holistic perspective that is capable of bridging disciplinary, technological, and cultural gaps and transforming multiple healthcare systems and contexts.

Issues such as a lack of readiness in technology and providers' resistance to using available technology have all played a role in the slow adoption of technology in the healthcare field. Yet many researchers have found that adopting and fully using telehealth services to provide the highest-quality, most cost-effective services to individuals in need are paramount for primary care and mental health systems. In addition to providing a holistic approach to treatment, developing clinical interventions that are state-of-the-art and ecologically valid with measurable outcomes and developing an expert workforce with telehealth technologies is paramount. In addition have the capability to offer higher quality, effective services at lower costs than traditionally face-to-face services are necessary. This in turn will enable e-health providers to establish a competitive advantage in the behavioral healthcare market place, so important in today's economy (Hsieh, Gauthier, & Lin, 2011).

The Future of Evaluation, Treatment Planning, and Psychotherapy: Implications of Technology

Face-to-face talk psychotherapy can no longer assume the hegemonic leadership in behavioral health care (see Cummings & O'Donohue, 2012). Recent technological advances will take over many evaluative and therapeutic practices that were unavailable in the last century (L'Abate & Kaiser, 2012). Thus, mental health professionals must come up with more cost-effective and efficacious ways to help people in need based on a scientific framework, rather than an artistic paradigm, and may need to rely on distance writing rather than verbal communications between themselves and patients (L'Abate, 2013c). For example, video teleconferencing has also been used to deliver mental health treatment to geographically remote, underserved populations.

We are at a critical point in long-term use of telehealth technology. Many patients report it is less threatening and easier to be open and communicate via telehealth technology. Providing patient care via telemedicine and telepsychiatry is today limited only by insurance reimbursements. As more insurance companies start to reimburse for telepsychiatry treatments at the same rate as they do for face-to-face, in-person visits, the emerging medical field will grow exponentially.

Aiding in the expansion of telehealth is the fact that the number of adults in the United States who own tablet devices has nearly doubled between December 2011 and early January 2012; the same surge has also been seen with regard to dedicated e-book readers. By 2017, the number of wearable, wireless health and fitness devices will hit 169.5 million. There can be no doubt that mobile health will become much more significant and have important implications for evaluation, interventions, and treatment planning.

Finally, when we consider the impact of these profound changes on clinical practice and patient care, we must also consider the role of professional training. In addition to the ethical and cultural issues required for working with various technology methods, many things can go wrong with distance evaluation, assessment, telepractice, billing, and emergency backup (DeAngelis, 2012a, 2012b). Addressing clinical issues and equipment functionality can be complex; as with any new specialty area, competencies need to be formally developed. Despite the emergence of telemental health, paper-and-pencil workbooks continue to be useful in the evaluation and treatment planning process.

References

Cummings, N. A., & O'Donohue, W. D. (Eds.), *Restoring psychotherapy as the first line of intervention in behavioral care*. Dryden, NY: Ithaca Press.

Cusinato, M., & L'Abate, L. (Eds.). (2012). *Advances in relational competence theory: With special attention to alexithymia*. New York: Nova Science.

DeAngelis, T. (2012a, March). Practicing distance therapy, legally and ethically. *Monitor on Psychology, 43*, 52–53.

DeAngelis, T. (2012b, March). A second life for practice? *Monitor on Psychology, 43*, 48–51.

De Giacomo, P., L'Abate, L., Pennebaker, J. M., & Rumbaugh, D. M. (2010). From A to D: Amplifications and practices of Pennebaker's analogic to digital model in health promotion, prevention, and psychotherapy. *Clinical Psychology & Psychotherapy, 17*, 355–362.

Harwood, T. M., & L'Abate, L. (2010). *Self-help in mental health: A critical review*. New York: Springer-Science.

Hooper, L. M., Doehler, K., Wallace, S. A., & Hannah, N. J. (2011). The Parentification Inventory: Development, validation, and cross-validation. *The American Journal of Family Therapy, 39*, 226–241. doi:10.1080/01926187.2010.531652

Hsieh, C., Gauthier, M., & Lin, B. (2011). Information systems/information technology for competitive advantage: The case in behavioral healthcare service. International Journal of Electronic Healthcare, 6, 213–228.

Kazantzis, N., & L'Abate, L. (Eds.). (2007). *Handbook of homework assignments in psychotherapy and prevention*. New York: Springer-Science.

L'Abate, L. (2005). *Personality in intimate relationships: Socialization and psychopathology*. New York: Springer-Science.

L'Abate, L. (Ed.). (2007). *Low-cost approaches in physical and mental health: Theory, research, and practice*. New York: Springer-Science.

L'Abate, L. (2011a). *Hurt feelings: Theory and research in intimate relationships*. New York: Cambridge University Press.

L'Abate, L. (2011b). Psychotherapy consists of homework assignments: A radical iconoclastic conviction. In H. Rosenthal (Ed.), *Favorite counseling and therapy homework techniques: Classic anniversary edition* (pp. 219–229). New York: Routledge.

L'Abate, L. (2011c). *Sourcebook of interactive practice exercises in mental health*. New York: Springer-Science.

L'Abate, L. (2013a). *Clinical psychology and psychotherapy as a science: An iconoclastic perspective*. New York: Springer-Science.

L'Abate, L. (2013b). Recommended online computer-assisted treatments. In G. P. Koocher, J. C. Norcross, & B. A. Greene (Eds.), *Psychologists' desk reference* (3rd ed.). New York: Oxford University Press.

L'Abate, L. (2013c). *Research on pre-para-post-therapeutic activities in mental health: Prevention, promotion, psychotherapy and rehabilitation.* New York: Nova Science.

L'Abate, L., & Kaiser, D. L. (Eds.). (2012). *Handbook of technology in psychology, psychiatry, and neurology: Theory, research, and practice.* New York: Nova Science.

L'Abate, L., & Sweeney, L. G. (Eds.). (2011). *Research on writing approaches in mental health.* Bingley: Emerald Publishing Group Limited.

L'Abate, L., van Eigen, A., & Rigamonti, S. (2011). Relational and cross-cultural perspectives on non-violent externalizing personality disordered women: Introduction to research. *American Journal of Family Therapy, 39,* 325–347.

Miller, T. W., & Gallicchio, V. S. (2007). Allied health professionals with 2020 vision. *Journal of Allied Health, 36,* 236–240.

Richardson, L. K., Frueh, C. B., Grubaugh, A, L., Egede, L., Elhai, J. D., & Frueh, C. (2009). Current directions in videoconferencing tele-mental health research. *Clinical Psychology: Science and Practice, 16,* 323–338.

Riva, G. (2000). From telehealth to e-health: Internet and distributed virtual reality in health care. *CyberPsychology & Behavior, 3,* 989–998.

Sweeney, L. G., & L'Abate, L. (2011). The role of writing in mental health research. In L. L'Abate & L. G. Sweeney (Eds.), *Research on writing approaches in mental health* (pp. 3–21). Bingley, UK: Emerald Publishing Group Limited.

Yellowlees, P., & Nafiz, N. (2010). The psychiatrist-patient relationship of the future: Anytime, anywhere. *Harvard Review of Psychiatry, 18,* 96–102.

Appendix A
Workbook About the Deadly Drama Triangle

Purpose of This Workbook

The purpose of this workbook and its four interactive exercises is to help you become aware of a deadly drama triangle (DT) that affects anyone who is involved in a deadly DT. In addition, these activities will allow for an increased knowledge about the often experienced negative effects of deadly DTs.

Audience for This Workbook

These exercises are designed to be used by any adult wanting to better understand how triangles emerge in relationships and to conduct a self-assessment related to the deadly DT. These exercises can be used in private or in conjunction with work individuals may be doing with a therapist or other professional helper.

Practice Exercise No. 1

Name:_____ Age:_____ Gender:_____ Date: _____

Instructions

The table below lists different roles that many people play, corresponding to the three major roles of the deadly DT: **persecutor**, **rescuer**, and **victim**. You may want to consult a dictionary to find the definitions of these three major roles first. Then choose any three roles from each column and define how that particular role is carried out in your life. Give two examples of how you experience each role in your life.

L.M. Hooper et al., *Models of Psychopathology: Generational Processes and Relational Roles*, DOI 10.1007/978-1-4614-8081-5,
© Springer Science+Business Media New York 2014

Persecutor	Rescuer	Victim
Judge	Therapist	Criminal
Parent	Know-it-all or "I know better"	Defendant
Juror	Expert	Invalid
Policeman	"Big daddy"	Child
Patriot	Tycoon	Drug addict
Detective	Peacemaker	Servant
Preacher	Red Cross volunteer	Martyr
Executioner	Saint	Sinner
Inquisitor	Superman	Culprit
Oppressor	Superwoman	"Poor little me"
Inspector general	Wholesaler	Innocent
Interrogator	Angel	Oppressed

Persecutor Roles

Write each role you selected from the Persecutor list. Then add its definition, and provide two examples you have experienced in your daily life.

1. _____

Definition: _____

_____

_____

_____

Example a: _____

_____

_____

_____

Example b: _____

_____

_____

_____

2. _____

Definition: _____

_____

_____

_____

Example a: _____

_____

_____

_____

Example b: _____

_____

_____

_____

3. _____

Definition: _____

_____

_____

_____

Example a:_____

_____

_____

_____

Example b: _____

_____

_____

_____

Please explain why you have selected these three Persecutor roles and not others.

_____

_____

_____

_____

_____

Rescuer Roles

Write each role you selected from the Rescuer list. Then add its definition, and provide two examples you have experienced in your daily life.

1. _____

Definition: _____

_____

_____

_____

Example a: _____

_____

_____

_____

Example b: _____

_____

_____

_____

2. _____

Definition: _____

_____

_____

_____

Example a: _____

_____

_____

_____

Example b: _____

_____

_____

_____

3. _____

Definition: _____

_____

_____

_____

Example a: _____

_____

_____

_____

Example b: _____

_____

_____

_____

Please explain why you have selected these three Rescuer roles and not others.

_____

_____

_____

_____

_____

Victim Roles

Write each role you selected from the Victim list. Then add its definition, and provide two examples you have experienced in your daily life.

1. _____

Definition: _____

_____

_____

_____

Example a: _____

_____

_____

_____

Example b: _____

_____

_____

_____

2. _____

Definition: _____

_____

_____

_____

Example a: _____

_____

_____

_____

Example b: _____

_____

_____

_____

3. _____

Definition: _____

_____

_____

_____

Example a: _____

_____

_____

_____

Example b: _____

_____

_____

_____

Please explain why you have selected these three Victim roles and not others.

_____
_____
_____
_____
_____

Please explain how you feel about this exercise. Was it useful? Why or why not? Try to answer openly and honestly.

_____
_____
_____
_____
_____
_____
_____

Practice Exercise No. 2

Name:_____ Age:_____ Gender:_____ Date: _____

Instructions

Rank the types of each role in the deadly DT. To the left of the roles in each column, write the numbers 1 through 12, where 1 is the role that has the *most relevance* for you, and 12 is the role that has the *least relevance* for you.

Persecutor	Rescuer	Victim
_____ Judge	_____ Therapist	_____ Criminal
_____ Parent	_____ Know-it-all or "I know better"	_____ Defendant
_____ Juror	_____ Expert	_____ Invalid
_____ Policeman	_____ "Big daddy"	_____ Child
_____ Patriot	_____ Tycoon	_____ Drug addict
_____ Detective	_____ Peacemaker	_____ Servant
_____ Preacher	_____ Red Cross volunteer	_____ Martyr
_____ Executioner	_____ Saint	_____ Sinner
_____ Inquisitor	_____ Superman	_____ Culprit
_____ Oppressor	_____ Superwoman	_____ "Poor little me"
_____ Inspector general	_____ Wholesaler	_____ Innocent
_____ Interrogator	_____ Angel	_____ Oppressed

Please explain how you feel about this exercise. Was it useful? Why or why not? Try to answer openly and honestly.

_____
_____
_____
_____
_____
_____
_____

Practice Exercise No. 3

Name: _____ Age: _____ Gender: _____ Date: _____

Instructions

Describe examples of the deadly DT in each of the following categories.

a. Fiction

_____
_____
_____
_____
_____
_____
_____

b. Finances

_____
_____
_____
_____
_____
_____
_____

c. Politics

_____
_____
_____
_____
_____
_____
_____

d. Religion

_____
_____
_____
_____
_____
_____
_____

e. Wars

_____
_____
_____
_____
_____
_____
_____

f. Any other cultural or social area where the deadly DT may be presen

_____
_____
_____
_____
_____
_____
_____

Please explain how you feel about this exercise. Was it useful? Why or why not? Try
to answer openly and honestly.

_____
_____
_____
_____
_____
_____
_____

Practice Exercise No. 4

Name: _____ Age: _____ Gender: _____ Date: _____

Instructions

Try to remember three situations in which you either observed a deadly DT or were
personally involved in a deadly DT. Use the space provided to write about each situation. If you cannot think of any real-life examples, then you may make them up.

Situation 1

_____
_____
_____
_____
_____
_____
_____
_____

Situation 2

_____
_____
_____
_____
_____
_____
_____
_____

Situation 3

_____
_____
_____
_____
_____
_____
_____
_____

Please explain how you feel about this exercise. Was it useful? Why or why not? Try to answer openly and honestly.

_____
_____
_____
_____
_____
_____

How do you feel about this workbook on deadly DTs? Please use the space below to explain whether you like or dislike it. Identify which exercise you like best and which exercise you like least. You may find it helpful to rank the four exercises, giving a 1 to the exercise you liked best and a 4 to the one you liked least. If you did not like this workbook or any of its exercises, feel free to say so and explain the reason(s) behind your response.

Appendix B
Workbook for Individuals with Personality Disturbances (Disorders)

Purpose of This Workbook

Use this workbook to learn more about behaviors and interactions in your life that may be self-defeating or unrewarding. For a more complete opinion, ask your professional helper—such as your family therapist, psychologist, or counselor—to complete this workbook as well. As an alternative, you, your professional helper, or close friends may administer the original checklist on which this workbook is based (see resource entry). You may also find it helpful to involve others in your self-assessment. For example, you might ask relatives and friends who know you better than you may know yourself to complete this workbook given their knowledge of and relationship with you. After you receive their answers, compare them with your own responses to consider what behaviors apply to you the most.

Audience for This Workbook

These exercises are designed to be used by adults wanting to better understand their personality and characteristics and how they relate to others. These exercises can be used in private or in conjunction with work individuals may be doing with a therapist or other professional helper.

Resource for This Workbook

L'Abate, L., van Eigen, A., & Rigamonti, S. (2011). A relational and cross-cultural perspective on non-violent externalizing personality disordered women. *The American Journal of Family Therapy, 39,* 325–347.

L.M. Hooper et al., *Models of Psychopathology: Generational Processes and Relational Roles*, DOI 10.1007/978-1-4614-8081-5,
© Springer Science+Business Media New York 2014

Background Information

Name: _____ Age: _____ Gender: _____Date: _____

Education: _____ Occupation: _____

Number of children (gender and age): _____

Marital Status: Single _____Married _____Separated _____ Divorced _____
How many times? ____

Possible Diagnosis (If Any)

Please circle the cluster in which you may belong, including the "no diagnosis" cluster.

1. Cluster B: Antisocial, borderline, histrionic, narcissistic, and psychopathic behaviors
2. Cluster C: Anxious, avoidant, compulsive, depressive, fearful, and obsessive behaviors
3. No diagnosis: These diagnoses do not apply to me

Practice Exercise No. 1

Name: _____ Age: _____ Gender: _____ Date: _____

Instructions

Please define each behavior listed below. You may want to consult a dictionary if any are unfamiliar to you. Then give two examples of each behavior from your own life.

1. Having no guilt

Definition: _____

_____

_____

_____

Example a: _____

_____

_____

_____

Example b: _____

_____

_____

_____

2. Having no remorse

Definition: _____

_____

_____

_____

Example a: _____

_____

_____

_____

Example b: _____

_____

_____

_____

3. Having no shame

Definition: _____

_____

_____

_____

Example a: _____

_____

_____

_____

Example b: _____

_____

_____

_____

4. Experiencing addiction

Definition: _____

_____

_____

_____

Example a: _____

_____

_____

_____

Example b: _____

_____

_____

_____

5. Being aware of errors in others, especially partner(s)

Definition: _____

_____

_____

_____

Example a: _____

_____

_____

_____

Example b: _____

_____

_____

_____

6. Blaming others for your behavior

Definition: _____

_____

_____

_____

Example a: _____

_____

_____

_____

Example b: _____

_____

_____

_____

7. Cheating

Definition: _____

_____

_____

_____

Example a: _____

_____

_____

_____

Example b: _____

_____

_____

_____

8. Being deceitful

Definition: _____

_____

_____

_____

Example a: _____

_____

_____

_____

Example b: _____

_____

_____

_____

9. Engaging in either/or black-or-white thinking

Definition: _____

_____

_____

_____

Example a: _____

_____

_____

_____

Example b: _____

_____

_____

_____

10. Having difficulty controlling impulses

Definition: _____

_____

_____

_____

Example a: _____

_____

_____

_____

Example b: _____

_____

_____

_____

11. Being disorganized

Definition: _____

_____

_____

_____

Example a: _____

_____

_____

_____

Example b: _____

_____

_____

_____

12. Being egocentric

Definition: _____

_____

_____

_____

Example a: _____

_____

_____

_____

Example b: _____

_____

_____

_____

13. Making excuses to justify behavior

Definition: _____

_____

_____

_____

Example a: _____

_____

_____

_____

Example b: _____

_____

_____

_____

14. Externalizing

Definition: _____

_____

_____

_____

Example a: _____

_____

_____

_____

Example b: _____

_____

_____

_____

15. Demonstrating fears, foibles, and phobias

Definition: _____

_____

_____

_____

Example a: _____

_____

_____

_____

Example b: _____

_____

_____

_____

16. Being glib

Definition: _____

_____

_____

_____

Example a: _____

_____

_____

_____

Example b: _____

_____

_____

_____

17. Holding irrational beliefs

Definition: _____

_____

_____

_____

Example a: _____

_____

_____

_____

Example b: _____

_____

_____

_____

18. Pursuing hidden agendas

Definition: _____

_____

_____

_____

Example a: _____

_____

_____

_____

Example b: _____

_____

_____

_____

19. Not reciprocating

Definition: _____

_____

_____

_____

Example a: _____

_____

_____

_____

Example b: _____

_____

_____

_____

20. Being late (to appointments and other commitments)

Definition: _____

_____

_____

_____

Example a: _____

_____

_____

_____

Example b: _____

_____

_____

_____

21. Lying

Definition: _____

_____

_____

_____

Example a: _____

_____

_____

_____

Example b: _____

_____

_____

_____

22. Making big deals out of small things

Definition: _____

_____

_____

_____

Example a: _____

_____

_____

_____

Example b: _____

_____

_____

_____

23. Being manipulative

Definition: _____

_____

_____

_____

Example a: _____

_____

_____

_____

Example b: _____

_____

_____

_____

24. Being blind to or unaware of your own errors

Definition: _____

_____

_____

_____

Example a: _____

_____

_____

_____

Example b: _____

_____

_____

_____

25. Making perfectionist demands of partner(s) or others

Definition: _____

_____

_____

_____

Example a: _____

_____

_____

_____

Example b: _____

_____

_____

_____

26. Demonstrating poor impulse control

Definition: _____

_____

_____

_____

Example a: _____

_____

_____

_____

Example b: _____

_____

_____

_____

27. Demonstrating poor or selective housekeeping

Definition: _____

_____

_____

_____

Example a: _____

_____

_____

_____

Example b: _____

_____

_____

_____

28. Procrastinating

Definition: _____

_____

_____

_____

Example a: _____

_____

_____

_____

Example b: _____

_____

_____

_____

29. Projecting your own behaviors onto partner(s) or others

Definition: _____

_____

_____

_____

Example a: _____

_____

_____

_____

Example b: _____

_____

_____

_____

30. Reacting quickly to any perceived criticism or threat

Definition: _____

_____

_____

_____

Example a: _____

_____

_____

_____

Example b: _____

_____

_____

_____

31. Being sexually promiscuous

Definition: _____

_____

_____

_____

Example a: _____

_____

_____

_____

Example b: _____

_____

_____

_____

32. Being seductive

Definition: _____

_____

_____

_____

Example a: _____

_____

_____

_____

Example b: _____

_____

_____

_____

33. Having no plans for the future

Definition: _____

_____

_____

_____

Example a: _____

_____

_____

_____

Example b: _____

_____

_____

_____

34. Having a lack of regard for time

Definition: _____

_____

_____

_____

Example a: _____

_____

_____

_____

Example b: _____

_____

_____

_____

35. Being unaware of your own mistakes but highly aware of mistakes others make

Definition: _____

_____

_____

_____

Example a: _____

_____

_____

_____

Example b: _____

_____

_____

_____

36. Being undependable

Definition: _____

_____

_____

_____

Example a: _____

_____

_____

_____

Example b: _____

_____

_____

_____

37. Having unfounded concerns about your body

Definition: _____

_____

_____

_____

Example a: _____

_____

_____

_____

Example b: _____

_____

_____

_____

38. Having unrealistic expectations of partner(s) or intimate others

Definition: _____

_____

_____

_____

Example a: _____

_____

_____

_____

Example b: _____

_____

_____

_____

39. Being unreliable

Definition: _____

_____

_____

_____

Example a: _____

_____

_____

_____

Example b: _____

_____

_____

_____

40. Feeling unwarranted pessimism

Definition: _____

_____

_____

_____

Example a: _____

_____

_____

_____

Example b: _____

_____

_____

_____

41. Using finances recklessly

Definition: _____

_____

_____

_____

Example a: _____

_____

_____

_____

Example b: _____

_____

_____

_____

42. Any other self-defeating and non-rewarding behavior not listed above

What is it? _____

_____

_____

_____

Definition: _____

_____

_____

_____

Example a: _____

_____

_____

_____

Example b: _____

_____

_____

_____

Practice Exercise No. 2

Name: _____ Age: _____ Gender: _____ Date: _____

Purpose

Use this exercise to learn which behaviors you defined in the previous exercise are more important to you than other behaviors.

Instructions

Write 1 next to the most important behavior that you would like to change and improve. Write 2 next to the behavior that is second in importance to you and that you would like to change for the better. Write 3 next to the third most important behavior that you would like to improve. Continue (4, 5, 6, and so on) until you have ranked all the behaviors that are important to you and that you would like to improve.

Behavior	Importance
a. Having no guilt	
b. Having no remorse	
c. Having no shame	
d. Experiencing addiction	
e. Being aware of errors in others, especially partner(s)	
f. Blaming others for your behavior	
g. Cheating	
h. Being deceitful	
i. Engaging in either/or black-or-white thinking	
j. Having difficulty controlling impulses	
k. Being disorganized	
l. Being egocentric	
m. Making excuses to justify behavior	
n. Externalizing	
o. Demonstrating fears, foibles, and phobias	
p. Being glib	
q. Holding irrational beliefs	
r. Pursuing hidden agendas	
s. Not reciprocating	
t. Being late (to appointments and other commitments)	
u. Lying	
v. Making big deals out of small things	
w. Being manipulative	
x. Being blind to or unaware of your own errors	
y. Making perfectionist demands of partner(s) or others	
z. Demonstrating poor impulse control	
aa. Demonstrating poor or selective housekeeping	
bb. Procrastinating	

(continued)

(continued)

Behavior	Importance
cc. Projecting your own behaviors onto partner(s) or others	
dd. Reacting quickly to any perceived criticism or threat	
ee. Being sexually promiscuous	
ff. Being seductive	
gg. Having no plans for the future	
hh. Having a lack of regard for time	
ii. Being unaware of your own mistakes but highly aware of mistakes others make	
jj. Being undependable	
kk. Having unfounded concerns about your body	
ll. Having unrealistic expectations of partner(s) or intimate others	
mm. Being unreliable	
nn. Feeling unwarranted pessimism	
oo. Using finances recklessly	
pp. Your own behavior (write in)	

Practice Exercise No. 3

Name: _____ Age: _____ Gender: _____ Date: _____

Instructions

Use this exercise to understand in greater detail the behavior that you ranked as being most important to you and most in need of improvement. Please write that behavior below.

Behavior: _____

1. How is this behavior present in your life? Please explain in detail.

   _____
   _____
   _____

2. How often do you behave this way?
   a. Practically every day _____
   b. Once a week _____
   c. Couple of times a month _____
   d. Once a month _____
   e. Once every six months _____
   f. Once a year _____
   g. Once every few years _____

3. Describe the timing and frequency of this behavior in greater detail.

_____

_____

_____

_____

_____

4. How did this behavior come about? Do you remember when it started? Check which answer fits best.
   a. When I was a child (younger than 5 years of age) _____
   b. When I was in elementary school _____
   c. When I was in middle school _____
   d. When I was in high school _____
   e. After high school _____
   f. Any other time _____

5. What was going on when this behavior started? Explain the context or surrounding events in greater detail.

_____

_____

_____

_____

_____

6. Was this behavior acceptable or unacceptable? Why was it acceptable or unacceptable? Explain.

_____

_____

_____

_____

_____

7. Give three specific examples of how this behavior affects your life.

   Example a: _____

   _____

   _____

   Example b: _____

   _____

   _____

   Example c: _____

   _____

   _____

8. Give three specific examples of how this behavior affects your loved ones.

   Example a: _____

_____

_____

Example b: _____

_____

_____

Example c: _____

_____

_____

Application Exercise: This exercise can help you understand and achieve greater control over the behaviors you identified. **If you can start it, you can stop it.** For the next week, repeat the behavior at specific times (for instance, at 8 a.m., 12 noon, or 7 p.m.) on at least three days. Write down what happened in detail. For each repetition of this behavior, answer the following four questions in writing:
a. How did you start it?
b. What followed?
c. How did it end?
d. What did this behavior accomplish?

Time 1 (day started _____ time started _____)

a. _____
b. _____
c. _____
d. _____

Time 2 (day started _____ time started _____)

a. _____
b. _____
c. _____
d. _____

Time 3 (day started _____ time started _____)

a. _____
b. _____
c. _____
d. _____

Which of the following shows how you feel about this exercise?
a. Completely useless_____
b. Somewhat useless _____
c. So-so_____
d. Somewhat useful _____
e. Extremely useful _____

In the space provided, explain how you feel about this exercise. Was it useful? Why or why not? Try to answer openly and honestly.

_____

_____

_____

_____

Follow-Up Exercise

Name: _____ Age: _____ Gender: _____ Date: _____

Purpose
Use this exercise to review whether this workbook was helpful to you.

1. Select the answer that fits how you feel about this workbook.
   a. I did not like using this workbook at all. _____
   b. I did not like this workbook at all, but I am glad I got to use it. _____
   c. I am delighted I got a chance to use this workbook. _____
   d. I am not only delighted about using this workbook, but I wish all people with my experiences had a chance to use it. _____

2. How helpful was it to use this workbook? Check the answer that applies to you.
   a. Not helpful at all _____
   b. Somewhat helpful _____
   c. Helpful _____
   d. Very helpful _____

3. Which exercise did you like best? Write down the exercise number, and explain why you liked it best.

_____

_____

_____

_____

_____

4. Which exercise did you like least? Write down the exercise number, and explain
   . why you liked it least.

_____

_____

_____

_____

_____

Appendix C
Workbook About Parentification

Purpose of This Workbook

Use this workbook to learn more about your experiences of being parentified in your family of origin (i.e., your family when you were growing up). In addition to increasing your awareness of your experiences with family caregiving, this workbook is designed to help you better understand how the roles and responsibilities assigned to you as a child can affect your roles, responsibilities, and relationships as an adult.

Audience for This Workbook

These exercises are designed to be used by any adolescent, emerging adult, or adult wanting to better understand how parentification affects current roles and relationships. These exercises can be used in private or in conjunction with work individuals may be doing with a therapist or other professional helper.

Resources for This Workbook

Hooper, L. M. (2009). *Parentification inventory.* Available from L. M. Hooper, Department of Educational Studies in Psychology, Research Methodology, and Counseling, University of Alabama, Tuscaloosa, AL 35487.

L.M. Hooper et al., *Models of Psychopathology: Generational Processes and Relational Roles*, DOI 10.1007/978-1-4614-8081-5,
© Springer Science+Business Media New York 2014

Practice Exercise No. 1

Name: _____ Age: _____ Gender: _____ Date: _____

Instructions

In the exercises in this workbook, you will be asked to answer many questions related to parentification and what it means to you. In addition, you will be asked to describe the details of the parentification process (related events, when, and how long) and how parentification may have affected you.

Keep in mind that there are no right or wrong answers, and no judgment will be passed on your responses. If you do not like or disagree with a statement or do not want to answer a question, please feel free instead to explain what you feel or think about it, with examples to support your disagreement.

1. What does the term *parentified child* mean to you? Explain the term in your own words.

   _____
   _____
   _____
   _____
   _____

2. Now that you have defined *parentification*, in what age range do you believe someone can be a parentified child?

   _____

3. Describe how old you were when you experienced *parentification*.

   _____

4. How often do (or did) you experience *parentification*, as you defined it in question 1 above?
   a. Practically every day _____
   b. Once a week _____
   c. Couple of times a month _____
   d. Once a month _____
   e. Once every six months _____
   f. Once a year _____
   g. Once every few years _____

5. Describe the timing and frequency of your experiences of parentification in greater detail.

   _____
   _____
   _____
   _____
   _____

6. Do you remember when your experience of parentification started? Check which answer fits best.
   a. When I was a child (younger than 5 years of age) _____
   b. When I was in elementary school _____
   c. When I was in middle school _____
   d. When I was in high school _____
   e. After high school _____
   f. Any other time _____

7. Describe the context and events surrounding your parentification in greater detail.

   _____
   _____
   _____
   _____
   _____

8. At what age did your experience of parentification end?

   _____

9. Did you find it acceptable or unacceptable to be parentified? Why?

   _____
   _____
   _____
   _____
   _____

10. Did you find it beneficial or burdensome to be parentified? Why?

    _____
    _____
    _____
    _____
    _____

11. Give three specific examples of how being parentified affects your life now, if at all.

    Example a: _____
    _____
    Example b: _____
    _____
    Example c: _____
    _____

12. Give three specific examples of how your being parentified affects your loved ones.

Example a: _____

_____

Example b: _____

_____

Example c: _____

_____

13. The following table lists some ways to describe common experiences of the roles and responsibilities that are usually expected of individuals who are parentified in their family of origin. Read them carefully, and then rank them according to how they reflect your experiences. That is, assign the number 1 to the role and responsibility that applies to you the most. Then continue ranking until you have ranked all the items in order of their relevance to your experiences. If any roles or responsibilities were not part of your experiences, write "NA" instead of a number.

Note: **In the following list,** parent **can also refer to other adult caregivers in your family**

Roles and responsibilities	Relevance/importance
a. Being expected to comfort my sibling(s) when they were sad or having other problems	
b. Being entrusted with secrets that my parents shared about other family members	
c. Contributing to the family's finances	
d. Having time to be happy or sad even though I had to care for family members	
e. Helping my parent(s) make important decisions	
f. Being responsible for making sure my siblings went to bed every night	
g. Feeling appreciated by my family	
h. Engaging in family roles and responsibilities that were similar to those expected of others my age in my neighborhood	
i. Having time for play or homework even though I had family responsibilities	
j. Working and contributing to the family finances	
k. Being responsible for helping my sibling(s) complete homework	
l. Being the first person to whom family members usually turned when there was a family disagreement	
m. Being the primary person to discipline my sibling(s)	
n. Often helping to solve problems between my parent(s)	
o. Enjoying being given adult responsibilities in the family	

(continued)

(continued)

Roles and responsibilities	Relevance/importance
p. Being expected to comfort my parent(s) during emotional difficulties	
q. Being in charge of doing the family's laundry most of the time	
r. Serving as the referee for family conflicts	
s. Being the person with whom family members shared secrets	
t. Feeling like our family was a team and worked well together	
u. Being asked to do the grocery shopping more often than any other family members	
v. Serving in the role of translator for family members	
w. Other roles and responsibilities not described	
(write in):	
x. Other roles and responsibilities not described	
y. (Write in):	

14. Why did you rank these roles and responsibilities the way you did?

_____
_____
_____
_____
_____
_____

15. In the space provided, explain how you feel about this exercise. Was it useful? Why or why not? Try to answer openly and honestly.

_____
_____
_____
_____
_____
_____

Practice Exercise No. 2

Name: _____ Age: _____ Gender: _____ Date: _____

Purpose

Use this exercise to understand in greater detail the parentified role or responsibility you found to be most relevant to your own experiences—that is, the role or responsibility you assigned a 1 in the first exercise. Please write the role or responsibility below.

Role/responsibility: _____

1. How does this role or responsibility apply to you? Please explain in detail.

   _____
   _____
   _____
   _____
   _____

2. How often do (or did) you engage in this role or responsibility?
   a. Practically every day_____
   b. Once a week_____
   c. Couple of times a month_____
   d. Once a month_____
   e. Once every six months_____
   f. Once a year_____
   g. Once every few years_____

3. Please explain the timing and frequency of the behavior further.

   _____
   _____
   _____
   _____
   _____

4. How was this role or responsibility assigned to you?

   _____

5. Do you remember when this role or responsibility started? Check which answer
   fits best.
   a. When I was a child (younger than 5 years of age) _____
   b. When I was in elementary school _____
   c. When I was in middle school _____
   d. When I was in high school _____
   e. After high school _____
   f. Any other time _____

6. Describe the context and events surrounding your parentification in greater
   detail.

   _____
   _____
   _____
   _____
   _____

7. Was this role or responsibility acceptable or unacceptable? Why?

_____

_____

_____

_____

_____

8. Give three specific examples of how this role or responsibility affects (or affected) you.

Example a: _____

_____

_____

Example b: _____

_____

_____

Example c: _____

_____

_____

9. Give three specific examples of how this role or responsibility affects (or affected) your loved ones.

Example a: _____

_____

_____

Example b: _____

_____

_____

Example c: _____

_____

_____

10. In the space provided, explain how you feel about this exercise. Was it useful? Why or why not? Try to answer openly and honestly.

_____

_____

_____

_____

Follow-Up Exercise

Name: _____ Age: _____ Gender: _____ Date: _____

Purpose

Use this exercise to review whether this workbook was helpful to you.

5. Select the answer that fits how you feel about this workbook.
   a. I did not like using this workbook at all. _____
   b. I did not like this workbook at all, but I am glad I got to use it. _____
   c. I am delighted I got a chance to use this workbook. _____
   d. I am not only delighted about using this workbook, but I wish all people with my experiences had a chance to use it. _____

6. How helpful was it to use this workbook? Check the answer that applies to you.
   a. Not helpful at all _____
   b. Somewhat helpful _____
   c. Helpful _____
   d. Very helpful _____

7. Which exercise did you like best? Write down the exercise number, and explain why you liked it best.

   _____

   _____

   _____

   _____

   _____

8. Which exercise did you like least? Write down the exercise number, and explain why you liked it least.

   _____

   _____

   _____

   _____

   _____

Appendix D
Workbook About Parental Alienation Behavior

Purpose of This Workbook

The purpose of this workbook is to help you understand and reduce negative, alienating behaviors that may affect you and your family. If you have experienced alienation from a spouse or co-parent, this workbook is for you. Parental alienation behavior means that one parent excessively and sometimes wrongly criticizes the other parent (both as a person and as a parent) in an attempt to alienate their children against the other parent. This alienation may occur through alliances, coalitions, collusions, favoritisms, and overprotection of one child at the expense of other children, regardless of the alienated parent's opinions and wishes. As you complete the exercises, please answer the questions as freely as possible.

Audience for This Workbook

This workbook is for individuals who have experienced alienation behaviors from a partner or spouse. This workbook is relevant to anyone who has been alienated. These exercises can be used in private or in conjunction with work individuals may be doing with a therapist or other professional helper.

Resources for This Workbook

Hartson, J., & Payne, B. (2006). *Creating effective parenting plans: A developmental approach for lawyers and divorce professionals*. Chicago, IL: American Bar Association.

L.M. Hooper et al., *Models of Psychopathology: Generational Processes and Relational Roles*, DOI 10.1007/978-1-4614-8081-5,
© Springer Science+Business Media New York 2014

Practice Exercise No. 1

Name: _____ Age: _____ Gender: _____ Date: _____

Instructions

Use this exercise to learn about behaviors related to parental alienation that may be relevant to you as a person, as a partner, and as a parent or guardian. You will have an opportunity to provide your thoughts about parental alienation. Please answer openly and honestly.

Keep in mind that there are no right or wrong answers, and no judgment will be passed on your responses. If you do not like or disagree with a statement or do not want to answer a question, please feel free instead to explain what you feel or think about it, with examples to support your disagreement.

1. How would you define *parental alienation*?
   a. One parent's accusations of inadequacy, abuse, abandonment, and neglect on the part of the other parent
   b. Abduction without explanation
   c. Blackmail to obtain money by using the children as pawns
   d. Other—please explain: _____
   _____
   _____
   _____

   e. All of the above _____

If you answered *E*, "all of the above," please rank choices *A* through *D* from most relevant (1) to least relevant (5).

   a. _____
   b. _____
   c. _____
   d. _____

Please explain why you ranked the choices the way you did.
   _____
   _____
   _____
   _____
   _____

2. With which category (or role) do you *most* identify?
   a. Victim of parental alienation—parent _____
   b. Victim of parental alienation—child _____

    c. Victim of parental alienation—divorced spouse _____

    d. Victim of international abduction—parent _____

    e. Victim of international abduction—child _____

    f. All of the above _____

    g. None of the above _____

If you answered *F*, "all of the above," please rank choices *A* through *E* from most important (1) to least important (6).

    h. _____

    i. _____

    j. _____

    k. _____

    l. _____

Please explain why you ranked the choices the way you did.

_____

_____

_____

_____

_____

3. Has your life been affected by parental alienation, international abduction, or both?
    a. Yes, by parental alienation _____
    b. Yes, by international abduction _____
    c. Yes, by parental alienation and international abduction _____
    d. No, by none of the above _____

4. Explain in detail how your life has been affected by parental alienation behaviors, if at all.

_____

_____

_____

_____

_____

5. Describe your experiences, if any, with parental alienating behaviors by others.

_____

_____

_____

_____

_____

_____

_____

6. Review the experiences you described in question 5. When did most of these parental alienation behaviors occur?

   a. During marriage or living together _____

   b. After separation or divorce _____

   c. Other time _____

Explain your answer in detail.

_____

_____

_____

_____

_____

7. Add any other comments related to parental alienation behaviors.

_____

_____

_____

_____

_____

_____

8. Please explain how you feel about this exercise. Was it useful? Why or why not? Try to answer openly and honestly.

_____

_____

_____

_____

_____

_____

Practice Exercise No. 2

Name: _____Age: _____Gender: _____Date: _____

Purpose

Use this exercise to become aware of the possible negative effects of parental alienation behaviors on you and your family. As a reminder, this exercise is for parents who have experienced parental alienation behaviors from a spouse or partner.

Instructions

Please answer the questions to the best of your knowledge.

1. Does your child appear preoccupied with making negative comments or criticizing one parent unjustly or in an exaggerated way?
   a. Always (almost every day) _____
   b. Most of the time (about every other day) _____
   c. Sometimes (at least once a week) _____
   d. Occasionally (about once a month) _____
   e. Never _____

   Explain your answer in greater detail. If you answered E, "Never," you may proceed to the next question.

   _____
   _____
   _____
   _____

2. Does your child appear to strongly dislike or even hate one parent and express this feeling without embarrassment or guilt?
   a. Always (almost every day) _____
   b. Most of the time (about every other day) _____
   c. Sometimes (at least once a week) _____
   d. Occasionally (about once a month) _____
   e. Never _____

   Explain your answer in greater detail. If you answered E, "Never," you may proceed to the next question.

   _____
   _____
   _____
   _____

3. Does your child have a black-or-white either/or perspective (such as viewing one parent as wonderful and strongly disliking the other)?
   a. Always (almost every day) _____
   b. Most of the time (about every other day) _____
   c. Sometimes (at least once a week) _____
   d. Occasionally (about once a month) _____
   e. Never _____

   Explain your answer in greater detail. If you answered E, "Never," you may proceed to the next question.

   _____
   _____
   _____
   _____

4. Does your child express fear about the disliked or hated parent without stating specific events or while relating events that would not normally result in this level of anxiety or fear?
   a. Always (almost every day) _____
   b. Most of the time (about every other day) _____
   c. Sometimes (at least once a week) _____
   d. Occasionally (about once a month) _____
   e. Never _____

   Explain your answer in greater detail. If you answered *E*, "Never," you may proceed to the next question.

   _____
   _____
   _____
   _____

5. Is there significant anger between you and the other parent?
   a. Always (almost every day) _____
   b. Most of the time (about every other day) _____
   c. Sometimes (at least once a week) _____
   d. Occasionally (about once a month) _____
   e. Never _____

   Explain your answer in greater detail. If you answered *E*, "Never," you may proceed to the next question.

   _____
   _____
   _____
   _____

6. Does your child demonstrate behaviors that suggest an overly strong attachment to a favored parent?
   a. Always (almost every day) _____
   b. Most of the time (about every other day) _____
   c. Sometimes (at least once a week) _____
   d. Occasionally (about once a month) _____
   e. Never _____

   Explain your answer in greater detail. If you answered *E*, "Never," you may proceed to the next question.

   _____
   _____
   _____
   _____

7. Does the favored parent express the idea that the children would be better off not seeing the targeted parent?
   a. Always (almost every day) _____
   b. Most of the time (about every other day) _____
   c. Sometimes (at least once a week) _____
   d. Occasionally (about once a month) _____
   e. Never _____

   Explain your answer in greater detail. If you answered E, "Never," you may proceed to the next question.

   _____
   _____
   _____
   _____

8. Does the favored parent seem opposed to getting help to improve your joint parenting relationship?
   a. Always (almost every day) _____
   b. Most of the time (about every other day) _____
   c. Sometimes (at least once a week) _____
   d. Occasionally (about once a month) _____
   e. Never _____

   Explain your answer in greater detail. If you answered E, "Never," you may proceed to the next question.

   _____
   _____
   _____
   _____

9. Does the favored parent have a history of a need to control, a sense of entitlement, or manipulative or verbally abusive behavior?
   a. Always (almost every day) _____
   b. Most of the time (about every other day) _____
   c. Sometimes (at least once a week) _____
   d. Occasionally (about once a month) _____
   e. Never _____

   Explain your answer in greater detail. If you answered E, "Never," you may proceed to the next question.

   _____
   _____
   _____
   _____

10. Now rank questions 1 through 9 according to how important they are to you. Write a 1 next to the most important question and a 9 next to the least important.

Question	Importance
1	
2	
3	
4	
5	
6	
7	
8	
9	

11. Explain why you ranked the questions in the way you did.

_____
_____
_____
_____
_____
_____

12. Please explain how you feel about this exercise. Was it useful? Why or why not? Try to answer openly and honestly.

_____
_____
_____
_____
_____
_____

Follow-Up Exercise

Name: _____ Age: _____ Gender: _____ Date: _____

Purpose

Use this exercise to review whether this workbook was helpful to you.

9. Select the answer that fits how you feel about this workbook.
   a. I did not like using this workbook at all. _____
   b. I did not like this workbook at all, but I am glad I got to use it. _____

    c. I am delighted I got a chance to use this workbook. _____

    d. I am not only delighted about using this workbook, but I wish all people with my experiences had a chance to use it. _____

10. How helpful was it to use this workbook? Check the answer that applies to you.

    a. Not helpful at all _____

    b. Somewhat helpful _____

    c. Helpful _____

    d. Very helpful _____

11. Which exercise did you like best? Write down the exercise number, and explain why you liked it best.

_____

_____

_____

_____

_____

12. Which exercise did you like least? Write down the exercise number, and explain why you liked it least.

_____

_____

_____

_____

_____

Appendix E
Workbook About Bullying

Purpose of This Workbook

The purpose of this workbook is to help you become more aware of and sensitive to how destructive bullying is to yourself and others. Exercises in this workbook focus on helping you understand what reasons account for why you engage in bullying behavior and what you can do to stop bullying others.

Audience for This Workbook

This workbook is relevant to individuals who have engaged in bullying (i.e., bullied other people). These five exercises can be used in private or in conjunction with work individuals may be doing with a therapist or other professional helper.

Resources for This Workbook

Rigby, K. (1997). *The Peer Relations Assessment Questionnaires (PRAQ).* Point Lonsdale, VIC: The Professional Reading Guide.
Rigby, K., & Slee, P. T. (1993). Dimensions of interpersonal relation among Australian children and implications for psychological well-being. *Journal of Social Psychology, 133*, 33–42.
Rigby, K., & Slee, P. T. (1995a). *Manual for the Peer Relations Questionnaire (PRQ).* Underdale: University of South Australia.
Rigby, K., & Slee, P. T. (1995b). *The Peer Relations Questionnaire.* Underdale: University of South Australia.

Practice Exercise No. 1

Name: _____ Age: _____ Gender: _____ Date: _____

Purpose

The purpose of this exercise is for you to learn more about different types of bullying. Please answer the questions as freely as possible.

1. Bullying may be defined and expressed in many different ways. Read the types of bullying described below, and give two concrete examples of how you have seen each type of bullying in the real world.

   a. **Exerting Authority:** Having power or control over someone else.

   Example a: _____

   _____

   _____

   Example b: _____

   _____

   _____

   b. **Cyberstalking:** Repeatedly sending messages that are highly intimidating or include threats of harm; engaging in other online activities that make a person afraid for his or her safety.

   Example a: _____

   _____

   _____

   Example b: _____

   _____

   _____

   c. **Denigrating:** Putting down someone (either offline or online); saying, sending, or posting cruel gossip or rumors about a person to damage his or her reputation or relationships.

   Example a: _____

   _____

   _____

   Example b: _____

   _____

   _____

   d. **Excluding:** Intentionally excluding someone from an offline or online group.

   Example a: _____

   _____

   _____

Example b: _____

_____

_____

e. **Flaming:** Engaging in online fights using electronic messages, often with angry, demeaning, or vulgar language.

Example a: _____

_____

_____

Example b: _____

_____

_____

f. **Harassing:** Repeatedly sending offensive, rude, insulting, or unwanted messages.

Example a: _____

_____

_____

Example b: _____

_____

_____

g. **Hitting:** Assaulting somebody with kicks, punches, or shoves.

Example a: _____

_____

_____

Example b: _____

_____

_____

h. **Impersonating:** Posing as another person to send messages (online or offline) to make that person look bad, get that person in trouble or danger, or damage that person's reputation or friendships; may include breaking into someone's online account.

Example a: _____

_____

_____

Example b: _____

_____

_____

i. **Outing and Tricking:** Sharing someone's secrets or embarrassing information, offline or online; tricking someone into revealing secrets or embarrassing information and then sharing it with others.

Example a: _____

_____

_____

Example b: _____

_____

_____

j. **Trolling:** Posting provocative messages about sensitive topics to create conflict, upset people, and bait others into fighting.

Example a: _____

_____

_____

Example b: _____

_____

_____

k. **Other:** _____

Definition: _____

_____

_____

Example a: _____

_____

_____

Example b: _____

_____

_____

l. **Other:** _____

Definition: _____

_____

_____

Example a: _____

_____

_____

Example b: _____

_____

_____

2. Review the types of bullying in the previous list, and rank them according to the
types of bullying you have engaged in and enjoyed. Write a 1 next to the type of
bullying you like or engage in the most, and write a 12 next to the type you like
or engage in the least.

Type	Rank
a. Exerting authority	
b. Cyberstalking	
c. Denigrating	
d. Excluding	
e. Flaming	
f. Harassing	
g. Hitting	
h. Impersonating	
i. Outing and tricking	
j. Trolling	
k. Other: _____	
l. Other: _____	

3. Please explain why you ranked the types of bullying the way you did.

_____

_____

_____

_____

_____

_____

Practice Exercise No. 2

Name: _____ Age: _____ Gender: _____ Date: _____

Purpose

Use this exercise to learn more about why you might be bullying others.

Instructions

The following table lists possible reasons for bullying. Read these reasons carefully. Then use the second column to rank these reasons according to which reasons most apply or appeal to you, with 1 being the reason you like best, 2 being the reason you like second best, and so on. Write "NA" next to any reasons that do not apply or appeal to you at all.

Reasons	Appeals or applies to me
a. Enjoying the feeling of being powerful and in control	
b. Seeking to dominate or manipulate peers	
c. Wanting to be popular with others who envy my power	
d. Being physically larger and stronger than my peers	
e. Being impulsive	

(continued)

(continued)

Reasons	Appeals or applies to me
f. Loving to win at everything; hating to lose at anything	
g. Experiencing satisfaction or pleasure from another person's fear, discomfort, or pain	
h. Being concerned about others disrespecting me—respect means fear	
i. Having little or no empathy for others	
j. Having little or no compassion for others	
k. Being unable or unwilling to see things from another person's perspective (to "walk in someone else's shoes")	
l. Being willing to use and abuse other people to get what I want	
m. Defending my actions by insisting that others deserved it, asked for it, or provoked me—conflict is always someone else's fault	
n. Being good at hiding negative behaviors or doing them where people in authority can't notice	
o. Getting excited when conflicts arise between others	
p. Staying cool during conflicts in which I am directly involved	
q. Blaming other people for my problems	
r. Refusing to accept responsibility for my negative behaviors	
s. Lying in an attempt to stay out of trouble	
t. Expecting to be misunderstood, disrespected, and picked on—I attack before I can be attacked	
u. Interpreting ambiguous or innocent acts as purposeful and hostile; using these acts as excuses to strike out at others verbally or physically	
v. Testing authority figures by committing minor offenses, then waiting to see what will be done about them	
w. Disregarding or breaking school, home, or work rules	
x. Being generally defiant or antagonistic toward others	
y. Seeking or craving attention—negative attention is just as good as positive attention	
z. Attracting unusual negative attention from others; being corrected or disciplined more often than others	
aa. Being street-smart	
bb. Having a strong sense of self-importance, while denying the importance of others	
cc. Being mainly concerned with my own pleasure and well-being and not the pleasure and well-being of others	
dd. Being antisocial or lacking social skills	
ee. Having difficulty fitting into groups	
ff. Having a close network of a few friends who follow along with whatever I want to do	
gg. Having problems at school, work, or home and lacking coping skills other than anger and aggression	

1. Please explain why you ranked your reasons for bullying the way you did.

_____

_____

_____

_____

_____

2. Please explain how you feel about this exercise. Was it useful? Why or why not? Try to answer openly and honestly.

_____

_____

_____

_____

_____

Practice Exercise No. 3

Name: _____ Age: _____ Gender: _____ Date: _____

Purpose

The purpose of this exercise is to learn more about your specific experiences with bullying and any impact that bullying may have had on you.

1. Please give two concrete examples for each item.

   a. **I get called names by others.**

   Example a: _____

   _____

   _____

   Example b: _____

   _____

   _____

   b. **I give other people a hard time.**

   Example a: _____

   _____

   _____

   Example b: _____

   _____

   _____

   c. **I act up in class, at work, or at home.**

   Example a: _____

   _____

   _____

   Example b: _____

   _____

   _____

d. **I feel I can't trust others.**

Example a: _____

_____

_____

Example b: _____

_____

_____

e. **I get picked on by others.**

Example a: _____

_____

_____

Example b: _____

_____

_____

f. **I am part of a group that goes around teasing or annoying others.**

Example a: _____

_____

_____

Example b: _____

_____

_____

g. **I like to help people who are being harassed.**

Example a: _____

_____

_____

Example b: _____

_____

_____

h. **I like to make others scared of me.**

Example a: _____

_____

_____

Example b: _____

_____

_____

i. **Others leave me out of things on purpose.**

Example a: _____

_____

_____

Example b: _____
_____
_____

j. **I get into conflicts at school, work, or home.**

Example a: _____
_____
_____

Example b: _____
_____
_____

k. **I like to show others that I'm the boss.**

Example a: _____
_____
_____

Example b: _____
_____
_____

l. **I enjoy upsetting someone I can easily beat.**

Example a: _____
_____
_____

Example b: _____
_____
_____

m. **I like to get into a conflict or fight with someone I can easily beat.**

Example a: _____
_____
_____

Example b: _____
_____
_____

n. **Others make fun of me.**

Example a: _____
_____
_____

Example b: _____
_____
_____

o. **I get hit or pushed around by others.**

Example a: _____

_____

_____

Example b: _____

_____

_____

Practice Exercise No. 4

Name: _____ Age: _____ Gender: _____ Date: _____

Purpose

Individuals report many reasons for engaging in bullying behaviors. The purpose of this exercise is to examine factors that may influence your beliefs about bullying in general and why, in your opinion, bullying takes place in many different settings, such as school, work, or home.

1. Please give two concrete examples for each statement below. Provide examples that support your beliefs about each statement or that explain how you came to have this belief. If you do not agree with the statement, write "NA" on the line following the statement.

    a. **I believe that anyone who gets picked on a lot usually deserves it.**

    Example a: _____

    _____

    _____

    Example b: _____

    _____

    _____

2. **I believe a bully is a real coward.**

    Example a: _____

    _____

    _____

    Example b: _____

    _____

    _____

3. **I believe no one should complain about being bullied.**

    Example a: _____

    _____

    _____

Example b: _____
_____
_____

4. **I believe it's funny to see people get upset when they are teased or annoyed.**

Example a: _____
_____
_____

Example b: _____
_____
_____

5. **I believe that people who hurt others weaker than themselves should be told off.**

Example a: _____
_____
_____

Example b: _____
_____
_____

6. **People who are passive make me sick.**

Example a: _____
_____
_____

Example b: _____
_____
_____

7. **I believe you should not pick on someone who is weaker than you.**

Example a: _____
_____
_____

Example b: _____
_____
_____

8. **I believe nobody likes a wimp.**

Example a: _____
_____
_____

Example b: _____
_____
_____

9. **I like it when someone is picked on without reason.**

   Example a: _____

   _____

   _____

   Example b: _____

   _____

   _____

10. **Other (write the statement here):**

   Example a: _____

   _____

   _____

   Example b: _____

   _____

   _____

2. Review these beliefs about bullying, and rank them according to how much you agree they are good reasons to bully someone. Write a 1 next to the most important reason to engage in bullying behavior, a 2 next to the second most important reason to engage in bullying behavior, and so on. Write "NA" next to any reason that does not apply to you.

Reasons	Importance
a.	
b.	
c.	
d.	
e.	
f.	
g.	
h.	
i.	
j.	

3. Please explain why you ranked these reasons for bullying others in the way you did.

   _____

   _____

   _____

4. Please explain how you feel about this exercise. Was it useful? Why or why not? Try to answer openly and honestly.

   _____

   _____

   _____

   _____

Practice Exercise No. 5

Name:_____Age:_____Gender:_____Date:_____

Purpose

Use this exercise to understand in greater detail your beliefs about bullying others and the most important reason for bullying others that you identified in the previous exercise. By providing more information about your reason for bullying in this exercise, you may identify possible areas in need of improvement. In the space below, please record the reason for bullying that you ranked as most important.

Reason for bullying:_____
_____
_____

1. How does this reason apply to you? Please explain in detail.

    _____
    _____
    _____
    _____
    _____

2. How often do you behave this way?
    a. Practically every day _____
    b. Once a week _____
    c. Couple of times a month _____
    d. Once a month _____
    e. Once every six months _____
    f. Once a year _____
    g. Once every few years _____

3. Explain the timing and frequency of this behavior in greater detail.

    _____
    _____
    _____
    _____
    _____

4. Do you remember when you began to engage in bullying for this reason? Check which answer fits best.
    a. When I was a child (younger than 5 years of age) _____
    b. When I was in elementary school _____
    c. When I was in middle school _____
    d. When I was in high school _____

    e. After high school _____

    f. Any other time _____

5. Describe the context and events surrounding the reason for beginning this behavior in greater detail.

    _____

    _____

    _____

    _____

    _____

6. Was this reason acceptable or unacceptable? Why?

    _____

    _____

    _____

    _____

    _____

7. Give three specific examples of how these reasons for bullying affects or applies to you.

    Example a: _____

    _____

    _____

    Example b: _____

    _____

    _____

    Example c: _____

    _____

    _____

8. Give three specific examples of how these reasons for bullying affects or applies to your loved ones.

    Example a: _____

    _____

    _____

    Example b: _____

    _____

    _____

    Example c: _____

    _____

    _____

Application Exercise: The purpose of these exercises was to help you understand and achieve greater control over your reason for bullying. **If you can start it, you can stop it.** For the next week, repeat the behavior at specific times (for instance, at 8 a.m., 12 noon, or 7 p.m.) on at least three days. Write down what happened in detail. For each repetition of this behavior, answer the following four questions in writing:

a. How did you start it?
b. What followed?
c. How did it end?
d. What did this behavior accomplish?

Time 1 (day started _____ time started _____)

a. _____
b. _____
c. _____
d. _____

Time 2 (day started _____ time started _____)

a. _____
b. _____
c. _____
d. _____

Time 3 (day started _____ time started _____)

a. _____
b. _____
c. _____
d. _____

Which of the following shows how you feel about this exercise?

a. Completely useless _____
b. Somewhat useless _____
c. So-so _____
d. Somewhat useful _____
e. Extremely useful _____

In the space provided, explain how you feel about this exercise. Was it useful? Why or why not? Try to answer openly and honestly.

_____
_____
_____
_____
_____
_____

Appendix F
Workbook About Stockholm Syndrome

Purpose of This Workbook

The purpose of this workbook is to help you clarify behaviors, relationships, and reactions often experienced after being taken hostage or kept prisoner by someone else—sometimes in an intimate relationship, but often in non-intimate relationships.

Audience for This Workbook

These exercises are designed to help individuals who have experienced Stockholm syndrome better understand the later effects of Stockholm syndrome. It also can be used to conduct self-assessments related to the aftereffects or relational consequences of experiencing Stockholm syndrome. Even though women may be more likely to be the victims of Stockholm syndrome, it is also possible (although less likely) for men to become involved in such situation. These exercises can be used in private or in conjunction with work individuals may be doing with a therapist or other professional helper.

Resources for This Workbook

Graham, D. L. R., Rawlings, I. E., Ihms, K., Latimer, D., Foliano, J., Thompson, A., et al. (1995). A scale for identifying 'Stockholm Syndrome' reactions in young dating women: Factor structure, reliability, and validity. *Violence and Victims, 10*, 3–22.

Note: This workbook is based on the research and scales of Graham and colleagues. Please note that the scale that informs this workbook was originally constructed and validated with and for women. However, the items in this workbook were rewritten to be gender-neutral.

L.M. Hooper et al., *Models of Psychopathology: Generational Processes and Relational Roles*, DOI 10.1007/978-1-4614-8081-5,
© Springer Science+Business Media New York 2014

Practice Exercise No. 1

Name: _____ Age: _____ Gender: _____ Date: _____

Instructions

In the various exercises of this workbook, you will be asked to respond to many statements related to whether a given relationship may be damaging or detrimental for you. This relationship could be voluntary, meaning it is a relationship you have chosen; or it may be involuntary, a relationship forced upon you against your will.

Keep in mind that there are no right or wrong answers, and no judgment will be passed on your responses. If you do not like or disagree with a statement, please feel free instead to explain what you feel or think about it, with examples to support your disagreement.

Statements

For each statement below, please explain more specifically what that statement means to you. Then give two concrete examples of how that statement applies to your relationship with your partner(s), significant others, or friend(s).

Note: You do not need to rank any items during this first exercise.

1. **My partner's love and protection are more important than any hurt he or she might cause me.**

   Explanation: _____
   _____
   _____

   Example a: _____
   _____
   _____

   Example b: _____
   _____
   _____

   Rank: _____

2. **I need my partner's nurturing and protection to survive.**

   Explanation: _____
   _____
   _____

   Example a: _____
   _____
   _____

Example b: _____

_____

Rank: _____

3. **The problem is not that my partner is just an angry person; it is that I provoke him or her.**

Explanation: _____

_____

Example a: _____

_____

Example b: _____

_____

Rank: _____

4. **I need my partner's love to survive.**

Explanation: _____

_____

Example a: _____

_____

Example b: _____

_____

Rank: _____

5. **I am extremely attached to my partner.**

Explanation: _____

_____

Example a: _____

_____

Example b: _____

_____

Rank: _____

6. **My partner is like a god or goddess.**

Explanation: _____

_____

_____

Example a: _____

_____

_____

Example b: _____

_____

_____

Rank: _____

7. **My partner would not get so angry at me if others had not been mean to him or her.**

Explanation: _____

_____

_____

Example a: _____

_____

_____

Example b: _____

_____

_____

Rank: _____

8. **Something about me makes my partner unable to control his or her anger.**

Explanation: _____

_____

_____

Example a: _____

_____

_____

Example b: _____

_____

_____

Rank: _____

9. **When I start to get close to people, something bad happens.**

Explanation: _____

_____

_____

Example a: _____

_____

_____

Example b: _____

_____

_____

Rank: _____

10. **Other people see only my partner's negative side. They don't see all the small kindnesses he or she does for me that make me love my partner.**

Explanation: _____

_____

_____

Example a: _____

_____

_____

Example b: _____

_____

_____

Rank: _____

11. **I do not want others to know how angry my partner gets at me.**

Explanation: _____

_____

_____

Example a: _____

_____

_____

Example b: _____

_____

_____

Rank: _____

12. **I both love and fear my partner.**

Explanation: _____

_____

_____

Example a: _____

_____

_____

Example b: _____
_____
_____

Rank: _____

13. **I dislike it when others tell me my partner is not good for me.**

Explanation: _____
_____
_____

Example a: _____
_____
_____

Example b: _____
_____
_____

Rank: _____

14. **I know my partner is not a violent person; he or she just loses control.**

Explanation: _____
_____
_____

Example a: _____
_____
_____

Example b: _____
_____
_____

Rank: _____

15. **Without my partner, I have nothing to live for.**

Explanation: _____
_____
_____

Example a: _____
_____
_____

Example b: _____
_____
_____

Rank: _____

16. **I feel like I am going crazy.**

    Explanation: _____

    _____

    _____

    Example a: _____

    _____

    _____

    Example b: _____

    _____

    _____

    Rank: _____

17. **My partner is like me, a victim of others' anger.**

    Explanation: _____

    _____

    _____

    Example a: _____

    _____

    _____

    Example b: _____

    _____

    _____

    Rank: _____

18. **I do not know who I am.**

    Explanation: _____

    _____

    _____

    Example a: _____

    _____

    _____

    Example b: _____

    _____

    _____

    Rank: _____

19. **I cannot imagine trying to live without my partner.**

    Explanation: _____

    _____

    _____

222 Appendix F Workbook About Stockholm Syndrome

Example a: _____

_____

Example b: _____

_____

Rank: _____

20. **If I give my partner enough love, he or she will stop getting so angry at me.**

Explanation: _____

_____

Example a: _____

_____

Example b: _____

_____

Rank: _____

21. **My partner is as much a victim as I am.**

Explanation: _____

_____

Example a: _____

_____

Example b: _____

_____

Rank: _____

22. **I have conflicting feelings about my partner.**

Explanation: _____

_____

Example a: _____

_____

Example b: _____

_____

_____

Rank: _____

23. **It is really hard for me to question whether my relationship with my partner is good for me.**

Explanation: _____

_____

_____

Example a: _____

_____

_____

Example b: _____

_____

_____

Rank: _____

24. **If my relationship were to break up, I would feel so much pain that I would want to kill myself.**

Explanation: _____

_____

_____

Example a: _____

_____

_____

Example b: _____

_____

_____

Rank: _____

25. **If I even suspect somebody is rejecting me in any way, I cannot stand it.**

Explanation: _____

_____

_____

Example a: _____

_____

_____

Example b: _____

_____

_____

Rank: _____

26. **I hate any role that I have that appears to be associated with my partner to criticizing or getting angry at me.**

    Explanation: _____
    _____
    _____

    Example a: _____
    _____
    _____

    Example b: _____
    _____
    _____

    Rank: _____

27. **Because I cause my partner to get angry at me, I am not a good partner.**

    Explanation: _____
    _____
    _____

    Example a: _____
    _____
    _____

    Example b: _____
    _____
    _____

    Rank: _____

28. **The more I talk to people, the more confused I get about whether my relationship with my partner is healthy.**

    Explanation: _____
    _____
    _____

    Example a: _____
    _____
    _____

    Example b: _____
    _____
    _____

    Rank: _____

29. **Without my partner, I would not know who I am.**

    Explanation: _____
    _____
    _____

Example a: _____

_____

Example b: _____

_____

Rank: _____

30. **Any kindness by my partner leads me to hope that things will get better.**

Explanation: _____

_____

Example a: _____

_____

Example b: _____

_____

Rank: _____

31. **I feel good about who I am.**

Explanation: _____

_____

Example a: _____

_____

Example b: _____

_____

Rank: _____

32. **I feel calm and sure of myself.**

Explanation: _____

_____

Example a: _____

_____

Example b: _____

_____

Rank: _____

33. **There are aspects of my relationship with my partner that I see as normal but others see as unhealthy.**

    Explanation: _____

    _____

    _____

    Example a: _____

    _____

    _____

    Example b: _____

    _____

    _____

    Rank: _____

34. **My partner has done things to me that I don't like to think about.**

    Explanation: _____

    _____

    _____

    Example a: _____

    _____

    _____

    Example b: _____

    _____

    _____

    Rank: _____

35. **I feel down and blue.**

    Explanation: _____

    _____

    _____

    Example a: _____

    _____

    _____

    Example b: _____

    _____

    _____

    Rank: _____

36. **I feel like I could not live without my partner.**

    Explanation: _____

    _____

    _____

Example a: _____

_____

_____

Example b: _____

_____

_____

Rank: _____

37. **If others try to intervene on my behalf when my partner criticizes me or gets angry with me, I need to take my partner's side against them.**

Explanation: _____

_____

_____

Example a: _____

_____

_____

Example b: _____

_____

_____

Rank: _____

38. **I find myself defending and making excuses for my partner when I talk about him or her with others.**

Explanation: _____

_____

_____

Example a: _____

_____

_____

Example b: _____

_____

_____

Rank: _____

39. **When others ask me how I feel about something, I do not know.**

Explanation: _____

_____

_____

Example a: _____

_____

_____

Example b: _____

_____

Rank: _____

Rank: _____

40. **I find it difficult to concentrate on tasks.**

Explanation: _____

_____

_____

Example a: _____

_____

_____

Example b: _____

_____

_____

Rank: _____

41. **I switch between seeing my partner as either all good or all bad.**

Explanation: _____

_____

_____

Example a: _____

_____

_____

Example b: _____

_____

_____

Rank: _____

42. **When my partner is less critical of me, I become hopeful.**

Explanation: _____

_____

_____

Example a: _____

_____

_____

Example b: _____

_____

_____

Rank: _____

43. **It is hard for me to make decisions.**

   Explanation: _____

   _____

   _____

   Example a: _____

   _____

   _____

   Example b: _____

   _____

   _____

   Rank: _____

44. **I have different personalities depending on who I am with.**

   Explanation: _____

   _____

   _____

   Example a: _____

   _____

   _____

   Example b: _____

   _____

   _____

   Rank: _____

45. **I cannot make decisions.**

   Explanation: _____

   _____

   _____

   Example a: _____

   _____

   _____

   Example b: _____

   _____

   _____

   Rank: _____

46. **I make jokes to others about the times my partner has been really angry at me.**

   Explanation: _____

   _____

   _____

Example a: _____

_____

_____

Example b: _____

_____

_____

Rank: _____

47. **I work hard to get people to like me.**

Explanation: _____

_____

_____

Example a: _____

_____

_____

Example b: _____

_____

_____

Rank: _____

48. **I get angry at people who point out ways in which my partner is not good to me.**

Explanation: _____

_____

_____

Example a: _____

_____

_____

Example b: _____

_____

_____

Rank: _____

49. **(Write about a situation that was not listed in the items above.)**

Explanation: _____

_____

_____

Example a: _____

_____

_____

Example b: _____

_____

_____

Rank: _____

Practice Exercise No. 2

Name: _____Age: _____ Gender: _____Date: _____

Instructions

Now go back through the statements, and review your explanations and examples for each. Then rank these statements in order of importance to you or in order of which ones you want to improve. That is, write 1 for the most important statement or the situation you most want to improve; write 2 next to the second most important statement or situation you want to improve second, and so on. Write "NA" next to any statements that are not important to you or do not need improvement.

Follow-Up Exercise

Name: _____Age: _____ Gender: _____Date: _____

Purpose

Use this exercise to review whether this workbook was helpful to you.

13. Select the answer that fits how you feel about this workbook.
    a. I did not like using this workbook at all. _____
    b. I did not like this workbook at all, but I am glad I got to use it. _____
    c. I am delighted I got a chance to use this workbook. _____
    d. I am not only delighted about using this workbook, but I wish all people with my experiences had a chance to use it. _____

14. How helpful was it to use this workbook? Check the answer that applies to you.
    a. Not helpful at all _____
    b. Somewhat helpful _____
    c. Helpful _____
    d. Very helpful _____

15. Which exercise did you like best? Write down the exercise number, and explain why you liked it best.

_____
_____
_____
_____
_____

16. Which exercise did you like least? Write down the exercise number, and explain
    why you liked it least.

    _____
    _____
    _____
    _____
    _____

Index

L.M. Hooper et al., *Models of Psychopathology: Generational Processes
and Relational Roles*, DOI 10.1007/978-1-4614-8081-5,
© Springer Science+Business Media New York 2014